Julia Bachelder

D1217551

37c
27-225(1)
-150

$45
Botch

Bricks & Brownstone

Bricks & Brownstone
The New York Row House, 1783 - 1929
An Architectural & Social History

by Charles Lockwood

Introduction by
James Biddle President
The National Trust for Historic Preservation

McGraw-Hill Book Company

New York: St. Louis: San Francisco: London: Sydney: Toronto

For my mother and father

Copyright © 1972 McGraw-Hill, Inc. All rights reserved. Printed in the United States of America. No part of this publication may be reproduced, stored in a retrieval system, or transmitted, in any form or by any means, electronic, mechanical, photocopying, recording, or otherwise, without prior written permission of the publisher.

Library of Congress Catalog Card Number: 72-9000
First Edition
SBN: 07-038310-3

The Editor of this book was Walton Rawls, the Designer was Martin Stephen Moskof, and its production was supervised by Frank Matonti and Steven Miller.

This book was set in Musica by University Graphics, Inc. It was printed by Halliday Lithography Corporation and bound by A. Horowitz & Son.

Introduction

New York is notoriously the largest and least loved of any of our great cities. Why should it be loved as a city? It is never the same city for a dozen years altogether. A man born in New York 40 years ago finds nothing, absolutely nothing, of the New York he knew. If he chance to stumble upon a few old houses not yet leveled, he is fortunate. But the landmarks, the objects which marked the city to him, as a city, are gone.

Harper's Monthly, *June, 1856*

Those sentiments about New York City, or any other American city for that matter, are as cogent today as they were more than 100 years ago. But, people now are doing more than just talking about the loss of landmarks and destruction of old neighborhoods. In New York City, young couples and families are buying and renovating old and often-decrepit row houses throughout Manhattan and downtown Brooklyn's "brownstone crescent." As thousands of row houses have been renovated, many neighborhoods—some inching close to derelict status—have been revived and given a new sense of identity.

This reawakened interest in New York's row houses—often called the "brownstone revival"—has benefited the city and the cause of historic preservation. Many families have chosen to live in the city—with all its delights and difficulties—rather than move to the anonymous suburban sprawl. As old neighborhoods come back to life, their residents have an increased sense of belonging, often lacking in America's big cities. When asked where they live, people often say with pride "Greenwich Village," "Park Slope," or "Chelsea," rather than the amorphous "Manhattan" or "Brooklyn."

With the ongoing "brownstone revival," the quality of housing has improved dramatically in some neighborhoods. When an owner plans to make a brownstone his home, the renovation usually is a better job than that by an absentee owner interested in the building primarily as an investment. In the years after the renovation, the proud owner-occupant of a brownstone also often maintains his property better than the absentee landlord.

In New York City's "brownstone revival," thousands of fine mid- and late-nineteenth-century dwelling houses and several entire neighborhoods have been rescued from further decay and eventual demolition. In the last few years, New York City's Landmarks Preservation Commission has designated such architecturally and historically distinguished areas as Greenwich Village, Brooklyn Heights, Chelsea, and Cobble Hill as "historic districts" so that their handsome nineteenth-century dwelling houses of three and four-story human scale and the sunny, tree-lined streets are a source of pleasure and a lesson of the past for present and future Americans.

It is vital to the health of New York City that the "brownstone revival" has made the city a more pleasant residence for people who can live there by choice. But what about those poor, often minority group families who have no choice in their housing location? Suburban housing is too expensive or it is restricted to them; they have to live in the city, near the traditional job centers.

In New York City, government-sponsored rehabilitation of row houses for low and moderate-income families has occurred in parts of Harlem, Bedford-Stuyvesant in Brooklyn, and the Bronx. In some instances this rehabilitated housing is in or near several handsome areas designated as "historic districts" by the Landmarks Preservation Commission.

But, in too many cases, the traditional urban renewal process is the only answer for decent housing. Streets of run-down but once-attractive row houses and several-story-tall apartment buildings are demolished and replaced by stark high-rise buildings set in barren plazas and fenced-off lawns. The physical needs of the families have been improved—modern plumbing, good kitchens, and sound walls—but the past, a means through which to evaluate the present, is missing from this setting.

Is it possible to offer good housing to poor families and still keep the potentially pleasant old houses and streets? The Pittsburgh History & Landmarks Foundation, a member organization of the National Trust for Historic Preservation, is proving that good housing can be rescued from the past and made available for all. Through its "Preservation for the People" program, quality housing is being provided for both the urban poor and the middle class, and with the values of historic preservation in mind.

In the "Mexican War Streets Area"—so called because the streets were named after battles in that war—for example, sixteen blocks of old dwelling houses are being restored for a variety of socio-economic groups. The neighborhood is regaining its former vitality without losing all its poor residents.

Rehabilitation work is done on several levels, ranging from minimal work to complete renovation and restoration. For poor families, the basic renovation often includes replacing cracked and broken plaster with drywall or new plaster, carpentry, some new plumbing and kitchen appliances, electrical work where needed, and a paint job. The exterior is painted in a historically appropriate manner.

At the other end of the scale, a complete renovation for a higher-income family includes retention and restoration of original exterior and interior architectural details along with modern bathrooms and kitchens and air conditioning.

A major stumbling block in Pittsburgh, as elsewhere, is the high cost of renovation work. Under the Pittsburgh History & Landmarks Foundation program, middle-class families pay the cost of renovation. But how does housing for poor families get paid for? The Foundation has set up a revolving fund from money raised locally to pay for renovation. In the case of inexpensive housing, the Foundation often rents the units to the Pittsburgh Housing Authority at a level that enables it to recoup its investment slowly. The Housing Authority in turn rents the units to poor families whose payments are subsidized by federal rent supplements. The Foundation's leases require the house to be returned in the same condition as it was received.

The rehabilitation of city houses and entire neighborhoods by private citizens or agencies is taking place in many other large American cities—Boston, Providence, Philadelphia, Baltimore, Washington, Richmond, Charleston, Savannah, Chicago, San Francisco, Cincinnati—to name a few. But nowhere have more row houses and neighborhoods been improved than in New York City.

The renovation program of the Pittsburgh History & Landmarks Foundation is unusual because modern accommodations are made available to low and moderate-income families in attractive houses in a historic area. This successful program should serve as a model for similar action throughout the nation. Quality housing in America's cities is needed for all people—young and old, black and white, rich and poor, married and single. The preservation of our nineteenth-century urban housing and neighborhoods can contribute significantly toward improving the urban environment. We are proving that landmarks, "the objects which marked the city—as a city," need not all be lost or useless.

James Biddle
President
National Trust for Historic Preservation

Acknowledgments

In researching and writing this book, I became indebted to many people. Chief among them were Professor Donald D. Egbert, of the Department of Art and Archaeology at Princeton University, Edward Sullivan, Dean of the College, and Professor Robert W. van de Velde, Director of the Undergraduate Program of the Woodrow Wilson School of Public and International Affairs, who jointly arranged for me to become a "University Scholar," and permitted my study of the New York row house on nearly a full-time basis.

For his assistance with this book, I probably owe most to Professor Egbert. A fine teacher, concerned with his students as well as his academic material, Professor Egbert closely directed my research and progress in this project. Devoting long hours to my work, he painstakingly read and criticized my early manuscripts and, thereby, helped me learn to organize scholarly material and write well.

In researching this book, I relied upon the splendid libraries and photograph collections at Avery Library at Columbia University, The Museum of the City of New York, The New-York Historical Society, The New York Public Library, and the Firestone and Marquand libraries at Princeton University. These libraries have permitted me to reproduce numerous photographs, engravings, and architects' drawings from their collections. Their staffs always were courteous and helpful in supplying the books I requested.

Besides library research, I systematically walked off the blocks with remaining nineteenth-century row houses throughout Manhattan and Brooklyn to examine the architectural styles and to become acquainted with these areas. I visited numerous houses to view interior architectural design of the different eras. My thanks go to everyone who graciously showed me their houses and particularly to those people who permitted interior photographs for this book. L. J. Davis, Everett and Evelyn Ortner, Kendall and Francis Shaw, Charles Willard, and particularly Ruth Wittenberg told me of the "intact" houses in their neighborhoods and often arranged with the owners for me to see them.

When I enlarged and rewrote the manuscript in 1970–72, James Biddle, Alan Burnham, Charles Gillispie, Ellen Kramer, Clay Lancaster, Everett Ortner, Peter-Ayers Tarantino, Nathaniel Thayer, Robert Weinberg, and especially Fred Fried offered advice for the text and gave me leads to additional research material. Morrison Heckscher gallantly read the manuscript at two different times and made several valuable suggestions as to its content. John Adams Dix drafted the row house floor plans throughout the book.

Grants from the Eva Gebhard-Gourgaud Foundation and the National Science Foundation defrayed my photography, typing, and travel expenses.

Robert Mayer's splendid photographs of the city's row houses are an indispensable part of this book. By their nature, city row houses are a problem to photograph, and in New York these shots are even more difficult because of cars illegally parked, garbage and dog refuse in nearly all the gutters, and overly inquisitive, if not malevolent, pedestrians. These photographs often portray an orderly and attractive New York which does not exist today—if it ever did.

I am especially indebted to Walton Rawls, my editor, whose aid and commitment to the project went far beyond the call of duty. The physical beauty of the book is the work of its designer, Martin Stephen Moskof.

My thanks to friends Lawrence R. Barker, Marshall G. Devor, Leland B. Grant, Robert B. Mayer, Peter R. Munkenbeck, and Thomas Howard Tarantino for their patience during my single-minded pursuit of this work.

I am also grateful to my mother and father for their continual encouragement of this project and tireless criticism of the manuscript.

Charles Lockwood

Preface

In the last ten years, one of the most positive and exciting trends in the American city has been the rediscovery and renewal of nineteenth-century houses and neighborhoods throughout the nation. No longer are Beacon Hill in Boston, Greenwich Village in New York, and Georgetown in Washington, D.C., the only well-kept areas in America with handsome old row houses on tree-shaded streets. Now, nearly all large cities on the East Coast and in the South have renascent nineteenth-century enclaves— Back Bay and the South End in Boston, College Hill in Providence, Society Hill and the Washington Square area in Philadelphia, Capitol Hill in Washington, D.C., the old town and Ansonborough in Charleston, and downtown Savannah, to name a few.

Nowhere has there been greater row house renovation and neighborhood renewal activity in the past ten years than in New York City. A housing shortage, rapidly increasing rents, and a nostalgic yearning for a simpler past have spurred young couples and families to purchase and renovate decrepit row houses, or "brownstones," in run-down neighborhoods throughout Manhattan and Brooklyn. This "brownstone revival" has led to the transformation of thousands of row houses and entire streets in Manhattan's Chelsea, East Village, Stuyvesant Square area, and the West Side off Central Park, and in Brooklyn's "brownstone crescent" around Brooklyn Heights, the areas of Boerum Hill, Carroll Gardens, Cobble Hill, Fort Greene, and Park Slope. The brownstone revival has preserved architecturally and historically distinguished houses and neighborhoods for the future and strengthened New York by keeping articulate and committed middle-class families in the city who otherwise might have moved to the suburbs. In contrast to the stylish high-rise warrens that line Third Avenue in oppressive monotony or the barren city-subsidized middle-income projects, the brownstone offers solid, spacious, even elegant living quarters on handsome streets of human-scale three- and four-story-tall buildings.

This book is organized around the architectural styles of the New York row houses and the aesthetic, social, and technological forces which shaped these styles and the life of the family in the house. Between the end of the American Revolution and the early 1830s, the city's dwelling houses employed the Federal style, which continued the long-standing classical tradition of architectural simplicity. These houses relied upon the contrast of building materials and pleasing proportions of façade parts for architectural impact. From the early 1830s to the early 1850s, dwelling houses in New York relied upon the Greek Revival style, which continued the architectural simplicity of the earlier Federal style and yet forecast the Romantic movement in architecture by its nostalgic associations with ancient Greece.

The Gothic Revival style, though more appropriate to country houses and churches than row houses in the bustling mid-nineteenth-century city, enjoyed a brief vogue in New York in the 1840s and 1850s and, importantly, introduced the Romantic architectural ideals of dark colors and bold ornament to the city's houses. From the late 1840s to the mid-1870s, the Italianate style row house epitomized Romantic architectural ideals and the prosperous city in shadowy brownstone facades and lush naturalistic ornament carved in stone around doors and windows. In the unparalleled wealth of the post-Civil War years, a rage for the Paris of Louis Napoleon's Second Empire swept the nation, and Italianate style row houses often were built with fashionable mansard or French roofs.

When the post-Civil War bubble of prosperity burst in the Panic of 1873, row house construction in New York practically ceased and did not resume on a large scale until the late 1870s. By then architectural taste had changed, and the development and construction of row house areas had been transformed by transportation advances and the appearance of large-scale builders. This book, therefore, devotes just one chapter to the city's row houses from the Panic of 1873 to the demise of the row house as a single-family dwelling after World War I. Besides, to tell the story of the city's late-nineteenth- and early-twentieth-century row houses in the same detail as the period of 1780 to 1875 would take another book of this length.

By the mid-1870s, the elaborately carved ornament and sweeping streetscapes of the Italianate style had lost favor to the ideal of individuality for each row house. Under the Neo-Grec, Queen Anne, and Romanesque styles of the late 1870s and 1880s, row houses sprouted bay windows, oriels, and gabled rooflines, employed building materials of varying colors and textures and, in a wave of eclecticism, mixed the several styles on one building. By the 1890s, New Yorkers had tired of architectural eclecticism and looked to the urbane Renaissance and Colonial Revival styles for the following decades.

Although the architectural styles and mechanical equipment of a New York row house reflected the aesthetic, social, and technological forces sweeping the nation, the New York row house also took on several characteristics which befitted America's richest and most cosmopolitan city. Throughout the nineteenth century, the row houses in New York excelled those of other cities in size and splendor. In the prosperous 1820s, row houses in the elegant Washington Square area often boasted marble or granite fronts and, by the 1850s, the haughty "brownstone-fronts" of Fifth Avenue dazzled New Yorkers with elaborately carved stone ornament, plate-glass windows, and black walnut front doors with silver hardware. In New York row houses of all periods, the parlors, with their marble mantels, lofty ceilings, and mahogany doors, always surpassed the street front in grandeur.

The splendor of the New York row house stemmed from the wealth accruing to merchants and businessmen and the presence of a large prosperous middle class. In a city of well-to-do and many newly rich families, the social life was more competitive than in other cities, and often the home epitomized the family's patrician roots, refinement, and social position—real or imagined. In recent years, renovation-minded New Yorkers have reclaimed some of this vanished splendor from beneath layers of cheap paint and behind rooming-house partitions.

Throughout much of the nineteenth century, builders constructed nearly all New York row houses on speculation and, lest they lose any customers, employed a fairly standard floor plan and architectural treatment for the façade and interior year after year. For ordinary houses an architect was considered an extravagance, and when constructing a row of houses the builder either copied some dwellings already built or purchased a standard set of plans from a draftsman. Only with the architectural eclecticism of the 1880s and the fashion that each house be different in appearance from those nearby did architects begin to design New York dwellings.

Before the 1880s, the New York row house was slow to reflect national architectural trends. Builders sometimes employed a style years after it had lost fashion, simply because they hesitated to abandon a style in which they had become skilled and to which their cautious house buyers were accustomed.

The New York row house also incorporated several architectural features peculiar to the city. The first-floor parlors rose anywhere from three to twelve feet above the street on a high basement and, therefore, a flight of steps known as a "stoop" was necessary to reach the front door. In the nineteenth century, row houses in other American cities sometimes had a flight of steps to the front doorway, but nowhere was the stoop as universal a feature or on so grand a scale as in New York. The stoop served a practical as well as ornamental function on the New York row house. In New York, few streets had service alleys behind the houses, so a doorway beneath the stoop served as a service entrance to the kitchen through the basement hallway.

New York row houses employed brownstone trim and façades with a passion unmatched elsewhere in the nation. In New York, the brownstone front was so popular for row houses for so many years that, even now, any row house in New York, even an early-nineteenth-century Federal style red-brick dwelling or a white limestone-front dwelling of the 1890s, is still popularly termed a "brownstone."

The architectural treatment and plan of the New York row house, however, was a problem for the city's builders because of its dimensions and the high cost of building lots in the city throughout the nineteenth century. The design opportunities on a twenty-five-foot-wide row house front are more limited than those for a four-sided freestanding house. For the early- and mid-nineteenth century, row house design was little more than the embellishment of doorways and windows in the currently fashionable style.

The high cost of building lots not only hindered row house design but eventually doomed the single family house in Manhattan. From the 1840s onward, always rising land costs caused the city's row houses to shrink in width. In the early nineteenth century, the row house of a well-to-do family around the Battery or on Bond Street was twenty-seven, twenty-nine, or more feet wide, but, by the 1860s, the fine brownstones near Madison Square or in Murray Hill were at most twenty-five feet wide. For middle-class families, row houses shrank from a pleasant twenty-two or twenty-five feet in width to an awkward eighteen, sixteen, or even twelve feet. The architectural embellishment of a twenty-foot-wide row house, needless to say, was minimal and its interior layout usually cramped.

By the early twentieth century, the continually increasing cost of land had driven the single-family row house in Manhattan beyond reach of all but the richest families. As apartment living became fashionable and the subway system opened, eight- to ten-story-tall apartment buildings rather than four-story-tall townhouses were built on the city's vacant lots. Along Fifth Avenue, Riverside Drive, Central Park West, and wide sidestreets such as East and West 72nd or 79th streets, even the millionaires left their lavish but costly-to-maintain mansions for opulent high-rise apartment buildings.

After World War I, row houses in fashionable areas were remodeled into small, high-rent apartments. The high stoop was removed and a new street-level doorway given a pseudo-Georgian treatment, the carved stone ornament shaved from the front, and the "old-fashioned" marble mantels, mahogany doors, and ornamental ceiling plasterwork removed from the interior. In less affluent areas, the brownstones became rooming houses. But, few rooming-house owners spent money to modernize their old-fashioned houses, and the marble mantels and handsome paneling, though disguised by layers of cheap paint, usually have survived to the present day.

Although as early as the 1920s New Yorkers reclaimed handsome row houses along tree-lined streets of Greenwich Village or along the East River in the East Fifties, it is only within the last ten years that thousands of decrepit brownstones throughout the city have been renovated, and New Yorkers once again recognize the style and comfort of the city's row houses.

Throughout the nineteenth century, New Yorkers were notoriously fickle in their architectural fashions. Whenever a new architectural style appeared on the city's dwellings, architects and newspapers roundly criticized the then-passing style, which originally had been greeted with enthusiasm. In the late 1860s, for instance, one architect, obviously tired of the once-acclaimed Italianate style, observed that "when he has seen one house he has seen them all. The same everlasting high stoops and gloomy brownstone fronts, the same number of holes punched in precisely the same places . . . the same huge cornices bristling with overpowering consoles and projections, and often looking, in their cumbersome and exaggerated proportions, like whole regiments of petrified buffaloes leaping headlong from the roof."

Besides telling the architectural and social history of the New York row house, each chapter of this book describes the nineteenth-century appearance of outstanding Manhattan and Brooklyn neighborhoods of that era. Manhattan is a narrow island, and, in the decades of frantic population increase in the nineteenth century, row house construction quickly marched northward up the island along major avenues and transportation lines. In Brooklyn, city growth was not focused in one direction but generally reached south and west from the Fulton Ferry and Brooklyn Heights. Then, as today, the houses of each area employed architectural styles which reflected the era of the neighborhood's growth. In 1871, one guidebook to the city declared that, along Fifth Avenue, "houses, which were considered to be 'just the thing' ten years ago, are out of date today. Observe the style of houses about 14th Street, for instance; then 25th to 30th streets; and, again, those which are now being erected ten or twenty streets farther up."

Although few New York row houses retain any semblance of their original appearance, and entire neighborhoods have vanished with hardly a trace, one can still find occasional untouched houses and such enclaves as Greenwich Village or Gramercy Park which recall nineteenth-century life in a brownstone and a less hurried city. At one time, Federal style dwellings, many of them frame, covered Manhattan from the Battery to the area around Washington Square. An advertisement in 1845 for a VALUABLE LEASEHOLD PROPERTY on Park Place, now in the shadow of the World Trade Center, recalls the charm of downtown streets once lined with pleasant red-brick three- and four-story-tall dwellings.

> For sale, the House and Lot on College Place, northwest corner of Robinson st. House 25 feet by 60 deep—lot 25 feet by 130. The house is three stories with attic, high basement and counter cellar 7 feet in the clear and perfectly dry, paved, &c. From the Southern exposure of the house, it is cool and pleasant in summer and warm in winter. . . . The view in front, particularly from the second and upper stories, over [the one-time Columbia] College Green up Park Place and across the Park, is exceedingly beautiful, particularly in summer. . . . For further particulars, inquire on the premises.

The city neared Washington Square in the 1830s, and, by the time the brownstone era dawned in New York in the late 1840s, the city had swept past 14th Street. In the years after the Civil War, row house construction neared the foot of Central Park and, in some places, entered the East Sixties and Seventies.

Throughout the nineteenth century, row house construction marched ever-northward on Manhattan, and once-tranquil residential areas downtown fell before the relentless tide of demolition for stores, lofts, and tenements. In the 1820s, James Fenimore Cooper sadly reported that few Dutch houses remained in lower Manhattan. As early as the 1840s, Philip Hone declared: "Overturn, overturn,

overturn! is the maxim of New York. The very bones of our ancestors are not permitted to lie quiet a quarter of a century, and one generation of men seems studious to remove all relics of those which precede them."

This history of the New York row house shows that much of the city's distinguished past and delightful city areas have been destroyed. In 1867 Trinity Church and the owners of the fine Federal style row houses around St. John's Park sold the handsome private park to Commodore Vanderbilt for a railroad terminal for $1,000,000 and expected that their property values would rise as the area became commercial. To the greedy owners' chagrin, the area soon filled with saloons and cheap boarding houses, not stores and lofts. Today, not a vestige of the elegant dwellings and secluded park remains, and only the entrance roadways to the Holland Tunnel mark this once-charming spot.

In those same prosperous post-Civil War years, stores appeared on elegant 14th Street and on Fifth Avenue, and wealthy residents abandoned the proud brownstone-fronts, then ten to twenty years old. Today, Fifth Avenue and its adjacent sidestreets in the Madison Square area are lined with decrepit lofts and office buildings.

More insidious than outright demolition of a row house is the unsympathetic alteration of the façade and interior or the removal of distinguishing architectural details. In the 1920s and 1930s, and even today, hundreds of brownstones lost their stoops and ornamental façade detail in spurious remodelings as "town houses." This book will clear up the confusion about row house architectural styles which has given rise to the unfortunate "Colonial," "Victorian," and even "Colonial-Victorian" brownstone, and it offers the information and illustrations necessary to restore a row house to its correct original appearance. And, as people learn the history of the city's dwellings, perhaps they will respect better the original architectural styles and realize the importance of the row house to the city's charm and scale.

Although New Yorkers cherish the city's row houses and brownstone neighborhoods, high-rise residential construction or commercial redevelopment threatens such historically distinguished areas as Brooklyn Heights, Greenwich Village, and Murray Hill. In recent years, citizen involvement in historic preservation in New York and enactment of the Landmarks Preservation Law are encouraging signs that at last we may be learning from the losses of our city's past. For, by guarding New York's remaining nineteenth-century row houses and neighborhoods, we save an important part of our past as a lesson for the future and maintain interesting neighborhoods of human scale for pleasant living today.

Table of Contents

List of Illustrations

(Photos not otherwise attributed are by Robert Mayer)

Stuyvesant-Fish House (1803–1804), No. 21 Stuyvesant Street. This handsome house has the doorway, Flemish-bond brick front, and pitched roof with dormer windows so characteristic of the Federal style.

Chapter One
Federal Style

New York in 1783.

When the British Army evacuated New York in 1783, at the end of the Revolutionary War, the city bore little resemblance to the thriving social and commercial metropolis captured seven years earlier after the victory over the American forces at the Battle of Long Island. Few American cities suffered as much actual destruction as had New York during the seven-year-long British occupation. Together, two fires had destroyed over one-third of all buildings in the small city, then clustered near the Battery, and charred rubble and fallen timbers remained in vacant lots for several years after the end of the war. Wharves had fallen into disrepair because of the virtual halt of trade during the war.

A drastic drop in population during the British occupation dramatically reflected New York's decline. A prosperous city with 25,000 inhabitants in 1775, New York's population had dropped to 12,000 persons by 1783. Of the remaining residents, many were living in "Canvas Town," a miserable collection of shanties and huts, which started, according to a contemporary report, when "the ruins on the southeast side of the town were converted into dwelling places by using the chimneys and parts of walls which were firm, and adding pieces of spars with old canvas from the ships."

Nonetheless, New York recovered rapidly. By 1790, its population rose to 33,000, and, between 1790 and 1800, the city was the capital of the United States. Its wealth multiplied as merchants rebuilt the city's shipping facilities and looked to trade in the Caribbean, Europe, and the Orient. At the same time, the city experienced a modest building boom which replaced those dwellings destroyed in the fires and began to house a rapidly growing population. The number of dwellings in the city increased from an estimated 3,000 in 1783 to nearly 5,000 in 1790 and, only four years later, had nearly doubled to 9,000. In 1794 alone, 850 wooden and brick houses were completed in the city.

By 1800 New York was the second most populous city in the nation, surpassed only by Philadelphia. Boston, once the nation's largest city, had slipped to third place. Meanwhile, New York had grown northward a mile from the Battery to the vicinity of the present City Hall, albeit with many vacant lots and gardens still sprinkled among the dwellings. A jumble of narrow, irregular streets served the growing city. Broadway, which by then extended as far north as the present-day Astor Place, was New York's best-known street, an unusual seventy feet wide and, in some places, bordered with poplars. In the words of the "English gentleman" whose imaginary travels in America in the mid-1820s provided James Fenimore Cooper with the framework for an account of early-nineteenth-century America, and particularly of New York and its row houses, in *Notions of the Americans: Picked Up by a Travelling Bachelor* (1828): Broadway "is the fashionable mall of the city, and certainly, for gaiety, the beauty and grace of the beings who throng it . . . may safely challenge competition with most if not any of the promenades of the old world."

Despite Cooper's brave words for Broadway, early-nineteenth-century New York was a small and backward community when compared to the magnificent city of only several decades later. Even the city's most elegant dwellings lacked such conveniences as the running water, furnaces, toilets, and cooking ranges that were to be taken for granted in the 1850s. Pigs foraged for garbage in the muddy, rutted, unlit streets. The Bowery was a country road lined with old Dutch farmhouses and linked the farms of the Bronx and Westchester County with the city. Canal Street was still a canal, an unfinished project of the Dutch, designed to shorten the distance for ships between the Hudson River and Long Island. New Yorkers picked blackberries on present-day Bleecker Street, and fishermen hauled their nets ashore from the Hudson River at a beach at the foot of Greenwich Street.

New York's Unforeseen Boom and Growth.

In the early years of the nineteenth century, few New Yorkers foresaw the phenomenal growth about to overtake their prosperous, but still markedly rural, city. In 1806 a Lutheran church, in financial difficulties, refused a gift of six acres of land at Broadway and Canal Street as not worth the expense of fencing. Only three decades later, that intersection was to be the center of the city's most fashionable shopping district. A year later, in 1807, the public laughed at the Randall plan which proposed an unbroken grid of streets from today's Houston Street to 155th Street. A chagrined city government stated that,

> It may be a subject of merriment that the commissioners have provided space for a greater population than is collected at any spot this side of China. . . . It is not improbable that considerable numbers may be collected at Harlem before the high hills to the south of it shall be built upon as a city, and it is improbable that for centuries to come the grounds north of Harlem Flat will be covered with homes.

The city fathers already had shown a remarkable lack of foresight in the construction of the new City Hall, which opened in 1811, designed by McComb and Mangin. Although willing to spend $500,000 with the aim of making it the most beautiful public building in the nation by providing a white Massachusetts marble facing for its east, south, and west sides, they decided to save $15,000 by facing the north side in common brownstone. The city, they argued, lay to the south of the new City Hall, and a marble facing would have been a needless expense since "it would be out of sight to all the world!"

This comfortable small-town attitude of the city's residents did not last long into the nineteenth century. By the 1820s, New Yorkers boasted about the splendid destiny of their city, especially after the 1820 census ranked New York as the nation's most populous city. In 1829 one newspaper proudly contrasted New York with America's other leading cities, Boston and Philadelphia:

> We do not measure our steps as they do in Philadelphia. We do not study fluxions and eat cod for salmon as they do in Boston. . . . There is more life and spirit and variety in New-York in one day, than in all other cities put together in a fortnight. New-York is Athens revived. . . . Everybody wants to know what's the news? So did they of Ancient Athens. . . . How would the people of Baltimore, or the readers of Philadelphia, or the *classiques* of Boston get along in the world, if they had not a New-York—a great, active, bustling, ever curious New-York to furnish them with topics and news; to show them the way of living and moving, and to tell them what is fashionable in politics or pantaloons—in commerce or in coats and corsets?

Looking into the city's future, another newspaper in 1836 foresaw,

> What enormous and magnificent edifices will . . . be erected! What splendid hotels! What charming private residences! What majestick [*sic*] city halls, courts, colleges, libraries, academies. . . . What fine rows of buildings! What streets and squares! What parks, theatres, opera houses, arcades, and promenades! . . . In short, situated as our city is—commanding, as it does, the trade of the western continent—with all the wealth of the world rushing into its bosom by means of railroads, canals, steamers and packet ships—will not this become one of the most wealthy, populous, and splendid cities of the globe?

The Reasons for this Great Growth.

The enormous growth of the city's share of American foreign and domestic trade fueled the city's prosperity and, thereby, a rapidly increasing population and building boom. Between 1800 and 1830, the value of foreign goods passing through New York increased over 400 percent. The city's share of the nation's foreign trade rose from 9 percent in 1800 to 37 percent in 1830 and reached a staggering 62 percent by 1860. So rapid was New York's commercial ascendency that the famous Bostonian Dr. Oliver Wendell Holmes, father of the noted Supreme Court Justice, somewhat resentfully described New York as "that tongue that is licking up the cream of commerce and finance of a continent."

A splendid natural harbor, New York's geographic position, the hard work of the city's merchants, and some luck accounted for New York's dominance of American domestic and foreign commerce. The city's commercial growth began after the War of 1812. During the war, when trade between Europe and the United States had come to a virtual standstill, American industry, still in its infancy, had been unable to meet the domestic demand for manufactured goods. By the end of the war, in

(top) Broadway and City Hall, in 1819. Although New Yorkers and visitors to the city praised Broadway as one of the finest streets in the world in the early nineteenth century, the street still had a half-built-up appearance in the City Hall vicinity.

(bottom) Broadway, View North from Bowling Green, about 1826. Lower Broadway, and the area around the Battery, was New York's most fashionable neighborhood in the late eighteenth and early nineteenth century. Fortunate residents enjoyed splendid Battery Park and the view overlooking New York Bay, but the then-secluded area was only a five or ten minute walk from the East River and Hudson River docks and countinghouses.

1815, there was a large and ready market for manufactured goods from Europe. Meanwhile, the concurrent Napoleonic wars prevented British manufacturers from selling to their usual European markets, and huge inventories had accumulated in their warehouses. At the end of these wars with Napoleon and the United States, British manufacturers dispatched veritable fleets of ships laden with manufactured goods to the United States and, significantly, mostly to New York.

The city immediately recovered from the commercial doldrums of the past decade. The federal customs revenue generated in New York jumped from $500,000 in 1814 to $14,000,000 in 1815. In one three-day period alone, in 1815, sixty-five British vessels docked at New York. Looking back at one boom year, 1816, one New Yorker recalled that "this year will be ever memorable with commercial men in this city, for the prodigious importation of merchandise, of every description, from Europe, which gave an impulse to business that was felt by all classes." The growth of trade facilities and the expertise gained by New York merchants in these few years after the War of 1812 in turn attracted additional foreign trade in following years. At the same time, the city's merchants took other steps to strengthen New York's supremacy in foreign and domestic trade in the United States. The city's merchants developed an auction system to market the British goods to local wholesalers. New York also was the first American city to offer shippers and passengers alike a regularly scheduled transatlantic packet to Europe. In 1817 the Black Ball line operated four ships in transatlantic service and sailed to Liverpool on the first of every month. By the next year, several additional ship lines sailed for Liverpool and, altogether, offered a departure every week. With this expertise in trade and the European connections, America's Southern planters sent their valuable cotton crop to New York, where it was transshipped to British or New England textile mills.

But, the Appalachian Mountain range blocked trade between the rapidly growing Mid-West and the East Coast. The several mountain passes only offered a limited land route for settlers moving West. In early-nineteenth-century America, nearly all roads were narrow and rutted, muddy when it rained, and virtually impassable in winter. Twenty miles a day was good progress, when shipping goods by wagon. Even though the turnpikes of the period did provide a few adequate roads and reasonably fast travel, the tolls were so high that commerce generally followed the slow but smooth inland waterways.

With the completion of the Erie Canal in 1825, the trouble-free water link between the Great Lakes and Hudson River made New York the terminus for the shipment of crops and goods from the Mid-West and of manufactured goods to the Mid-West. Whereas it took $120 and three weeks to ship a ton of wheat, itself worth $40, from Buffalo to New York City by land, on the Erie Canal the shipping cost dropped to $6 a ton for grain and the time to eight days. At the Erie Canal's dedication ceremony, one New Yorker wisely foresaw that "there will be no limits to your lucrative extensions of trade and commerce. The Valley of the Mississippi will soon pour its treasures in this great emporium, through the channels now formed and forming."

Building Boom in the 1820s and 1830s.

The flourishing domestic and foreign trade brought prosperity and enormous population growth to New York. The city's population increased from 124,000 in 1820 to 203,000 in 1830, and reached 313,000 in 1840, and 516,000 in 1850. To accommodate this growing population, the city raced northward on Manhattan in a continual building boom, only interrupted by occasional depressions or wartime economic uncertainty.

After the end of the War of 1812 and a modest recession in 1817–1818, construction started in earnest about 1820. New Yorkers were fascinated by their city's awesome growth. One gentleman's journal noted that in 1824 "more than 1600 new houses were erected, nearly all of them of brick or stone." In 1830 Philip Hone, mayor of the city in 1825–1826 and a well-to-do merchant whose 2,000,000-word journal gives a fascinating view of New York in the 1830s and 1840s, observed that "our country at large, and particularly this city, is at this time prosperous beyond all former example . . . real estate, up and down town, equally high; houses in great demand, at advanced rents." So great was this building boom of the 1820s and 1830s that Stoke's monumental *Iconography of Manhattan Island* recalled that,

> In 1825 more than three thousand dwellings were in course of construction, and there was said to be no vacant house in the city; indeed, it was quite common for families to move into half-finished houses, so great was the demand for dwellings.

New Yorkers soon realized that the only unchanging aspect of their bustling city was change itself. In 1839 Philip Hone declared in his journal that "the pulling down of houses and stores in the lower parts [of Broadway] is awful. Brickbats, rafters, and slates are showering down in every direction. There is no safety on the sidewalks." Hone concluded that "the spirit of pulling down and building up is abroad. The whole of New York is rebuilt about once in ten years."

New York's ceaseless northward growth and rebuilding of existing areas soon obliterated all traces of its Dutch-settled New Amsterdam past. As early as 1788, one magazine stated that "there are remaining a few houses built after the old Dutch manner. . . ." In *The Travelling Bachelor* (1828), Cooper observed that "a few old Dutch dwellings yet remain, and can easily be distinguished by their little bricks, their gables to the street, and those steps on their battlement walls . . . invented, in order to ascend to regulate the iron weathercocks at every variation of the fickle winds." In a startling sign of the city's growth, Cooper estimated that "there are not five hundred buildings in New-York, that can date further back than the peace of '83 [1783]."

The Federal Style: The Row House Front.

The architectural style for row houses built in this prosperous period was the "Federal," the name given to the style prevailing from the Revolutionary War to the 1830s. Based primarily on the work of the Adam brothers, in Great Britain, the Federal style was an architectural link between the pre-Revolutionary tradition, derived from the English Georgian style, and the heyday of Classical revivals in the 1830s, 1840s, and 1850s. In its simplicity, the Federal style row house followed the Classical tradition in architecture of the eighteenth century, an influence also pervasive in that period's literary classicism and in the scientific work of such men as Descartes and Newton. The Classical tradition in architecture sought principles worthwhile in all times and circumstances. British architects in this tradition looked to the ruins of Greece and Rome, not to idealize or to copy the specific era, but to find universal principles and forms that were appealing beyond shifts in architectural fashion.

This pervasive British influence in American architecture in the late eighteenth and early nineteenth century confirmed that the Revolutionary War had been a political, not a cultural, revolution, and visitors from Great Britain to the United States then noted the similarity of British and American architectural styles. Cooper's traveling bachelor observed that "the Americans have not yet adopted a style of architecture of their own. Their houses are essentially English," and one English visitor about 1820 remarked that "the houses in the Broadway are lofty and well built. They are constructed in the English style and differ little from those of London at the west end of town; except that they are universally built of *red* brick."

In the early nineteenth century, New York row houses were distinguished by modesty in scale and simple architectural ornament—particularly compared to similar dwellings of later decades. This handsome simplicity of the Federal style showed that the Classical ideals of architectural restraint were influential then, that the high cost of hand labor made elaborate architectural forms and details too costly except for the finest houses, and that social customs in New York did not yet demand a pretentious dwelling. Not until the late 1820s did New Yorkers tire of the long-lived Federal style, and, out of the great wealth then flowing to the city's merchants, the elaborate Late Federal style appeared on the city's largest row houses. The narrow front of a row house also discouraged a pretentious architectural treatment. "The exterior necessarily presents a narrow, ill-arranged façade, that puts architectural beauty a good deal at defiance," wrote James Fenimore Cooper. "The most that

Nos. 155, 157, and 159 Willow Street (*ca.* 1829), Brooklyn Heights. These three Federal style dwelling houses have escaped the modernizations and demolitions that have destroyed so many nineteenth-century buildings in New York. These houses' simply ornamented façades and the well-kept gardens on tree-lined and relatively traffic-free Willow Street recall the long-vanished dignity of early-nineteenth-century New York's houses and streets.

can be done with such a front is to abstain from inappropriate ornament, and to aim at such an effect as shall convey a proper idea of the more substantial comforts, and of the neatness that predominate within."

The front of Federal style row houses usually was red brick, ordinarily laid in Flemish bond, which showed alternately the long side and the end of the brick. The doorway and window trim of brownstone, granite, or marble was modestly detailed and barely broke the planar smoothness of the façade so important to Classical unity. During the early-nineteenth-century hegemony of the Federal style, the brick fronts of New York row houses usually were painted red or occasionally gray or cream and then false mortar lines added between the bricks in white. Some houses were even built of a drab-colored brick intended to receive paint. Although this fashion disappeared in the 1830s with the onslaught of new architectural ideals and appears strange, if not ugly, today, Cooper praised this practice which "scarcely alters their original appearance, except by imparting a neatness and freshness that are exceedingly pleasant."

"Excepting in a few low quarters," visitors to early-nineteenth-century New York recalled its "cheerful" and "neat" row houses. "The inhabitants of New York inherit the taste of their Dutch ancestors for fresh paint; every house of any pretension is annually coated with scarlet or grey, the divisions of the bricks are picked out with white," observed one Englishwoman.

The row house rose above a high basement of brick, blocks of brownstone with a plain surface and sharply beveled joints, or rusticated blocks of brownstone or marble. In the early nineteenth century, the same dark red sandstone, or brownstone, that epitomized luxury and architectural sophistication in the 1850s and 1860s was an inexpensive local substitute for marble or limestone of pretentious buildings. The brownstone basement, door, and window trim presented a pleasing contrast of color and texture on the red-brick house front, and in her *Domestic Manners of the Americans* (1831) Frances Trollope wrote that the city's builders "are now using a great deal of a beautiful stone called Jersey freestone; it is of a warm rich brown, and extremely ornamental to the city wherever it has been employed."

Throughout the early nineteenth century and particularly after the opening of extensive marble and granite quarries near New York in the 1820s, fine row houses employed the costly and classically more appropriate marble for street-front trim rather than the local brownstone. "Since the discovery of the vast quarries of white marble in Westchester County, the effect is everywhere manifest," declared one newspaper in 1827. "The brown sand stone of New Jersey is quite neglected in domestic architecture, compared with its former exclusive use," observed one New Yorker a year later. The light color marble or granite "now introduced into buildings . . . have conduced much to improve

the aspect of the city." Some marble or granite-front row houses were built in the late 1820s and early 1830s and immediately excited comment in the city. In 1833 one newspaper praised marble-front dwellings as "another improvement" in the city and "the employment of a nobler and more durable material in building" than brick. Observing that nearly all the city's row houses had brick fronts, the newspaper bemoaned the "numbers of private houses upon which no cost has been spared, except the cost of erecting them of a material which defies the tooth of time."

The emergence of marble-front row houses and the elaborate Late Federal style of large dwellings in the 1820s revealed the tiring for the simplicity of the long-lived Federal style and the city's unparalleled prosperity. Reflecting this rising taste, one newspaper wrote in 1827 that,

> Elegant pillars, pilasters, pediments, caps, steps, sills, etc., many of them presenting the most ingenious specimens of architecture and carved work, are among the striking embellishments which adorn numbers of newly erected houses. While these things impart an aspect of peculiar richness and beauty, they . . . are as creditable to the taste of our citizens, as they are to the skill and ingenuity of our artists.

While significant to the architectural development of the New York row house, these lavish marble fronts and elaborate ornament appeared only on a handful of the city's most costly dwellings.

On most Federal style dwellings, the front doorway provided one of the few enriching touches on the street façade. Because the first floor—also known as the parlor floor—was above the street over a high basement, a low flight of brownstone or marble steps known as a "stoop" led to the front door. The original Dutch settlers of New Amsterdam, as New York was then called, brought the concept of the stoop, as well as its name (from the Dutch *stoep*), from the Netherlands where the continual threat of flooding made the elevation of the principal floor above ground a practical necessity. Because New York faced little threat of flooding, people often saw the stoop as merely an ornamental feature and, indeed, the elevation of the first floor several feet above the street did satisfy a yearning for architectural grandeur.

Not all New Yorkers admired the city's nearly universal stoops. The influential architect Alexander Jackson Davis often criticized the stoop and in the late 1840s designed row houses with just two or three modest steps between the front doorway and the street level. While admitting that New Yorkers "cherish the clumsy inconvenient entrances," Cooper described stoops as "hideous excrescences . . . found disfiguring the architecture, cumbering the side-walks, and endangering the human neck. . . ."

The stoop did serve a practical as well as decorative function. Because Manhattan and Brooklyn blocks rarely had service alleys behind the houses, as in fine streets in Philadelphia or Baltimore, the doorway under the stoop provided a much-needed separate entrance to the kitchen by way of the basement hallway. In the early nineteenth century, well-to-do New Yorkers already had discovered the pleasures of "stoop sitting" on warm evenings. During evening parties in hot summer months, "it is customary to sit out of doors on the steps that ornament the entrances of the houses," wrote an Englishman in the 1820s. "On these occasions, friends assemble in the most agreeable and unceremonious manner. All sorts of cooling beverages and excellent confectionary are handed round, and the greatest good humour and gaiety prevail."

Besides providing the important service entrance, the stoops, declared Cooper, "compensate, in a slight degree, for the pain of ascent . . . by their admirable neatness, and the perfect order of their iron rails and glittering brass ornaments." The safety considerations that required handrailings for the stoop and a fence separating the sidewalk from the dug-out areaway made for exceptionally handsome hand-wrought iron work on the city's early-nineteenth-century row houses.

In the 1820s and 1830s, the front fences for the areaway had pineapple, pine cone, or acorn finials on top of the vertical iron shafts or on the top and bottom railings between the shafts. The stoop railing's newel post usually was a four-sided "hollow cage" which either rose directly from the sidewalk or sat on a modest stone pedestal, often a section of a column. The hollow-cage newel posts often employed picturesque "Gothick" arches on their sides, and in a further display of early-nineteenth-century artisans' skills were topped by a small pineapple or by a large, hollow urn, itself terminating in a pineapple, the symbol of hospitality. Built-in boot scrapers usually were a part of the stoop railing or newel post and indicated that most of the city's early-nineteenth-century dwellings originally were built on unpaved streets. Although very few hollow-cage newel posts or hollow urns have survived to the present day, handsome wrought-iron stoop railings and areaway fences occasionally remain on Federal dwellings otherwise lacking in prominent architectural features.

The elegant front doorway, usually the most elaborate feature of the restrained row house front, reflected the good taste and fine workmanship of the early nineteenth century. The usual Federal style doorway had a delicately leaded rectangular toplight and, often, leaded sidelights. The single wooden door had six or eight deeply set panels, often edged with a delicate egg-and-dart pattern or beading, and brass or silver doorknob and knocker. The fanlight doorway, commonly associated with the Federal style, was used in New York only in the 1820s and early 1830s, generally in the Late Federal form. Doorway size and ornamentation depends upon the size of the dwelling and its date of construction. The high cost of hand labor, even then, reserved the highly decorated doorway for the houses of the rich. Elaborate doorways also became stylistically more acceptable in the late 1820s and early 1830s, partly as a reaction to the simplicity of the long-lived Federal style and partly because

(top left) Boot Scraper, No. 59 Morton Street (1828), Greenwich Village. Few streets in early-nineteenth-century New York were paved, and in wet weather or winter they turned into a muddy morass.

(top right) Doorway, No. 22 Charlton Street *(ca.* 1825). In the 1820s, the doorways of modest row houses had rectangular toplights for ornament rather than the elaborate fanlight and sidelight arrangement commonly associated with Federal style houses.

(bottom) Hollow Urn Newel Post, No. 56 West Tenth Street (1831–1832), Greenwich Village. Wrought-iron hollow urns graced the stoop railings of many fine New York row houses in the 1820s and 1830s, but unfortunately most have disappeared.

of the wealth accumulating in the city which encouraged more elaborate houses.

On most row houses, windows were modest in scale, small-paned and double-hung, usually six-over-six. Unlike the row houses of the mid-nineteenth century in which windows diminished in size on the upper, less important floors, the first- and second-floor windows of the Federal house were nearly the same size. Shutters or window blinds, usually painted green, added a cheerful note to the front and, when shut, offered some relief from winter winds or summer sun.

The occasional Late Federal house of the late 1820s and early 1830s introduced parlor windows that dropped to the floor, a typical feature on a Greek Revival row house. Here, windows either were double-hung, i.e., six-over-six, or triple-hung, i.e., six-over-six-over-six. These long windows added a note of grandeur to the rich façade and brought more light and air into the large parlors of these houses. To shield the parlor from the view of passersby, the architect-builder added an iron guardrail to the lower two or three feet of the window or a several-foot-high balcony running between the two windows. Largely gone today, these iron guardrailings or balconies exhibited Late Federal or Greek Revival design of great beauty.

Brownstone or marble lintels over the windows and door were a decorative touch and usually reflected the degree of façade embellishment set by the doorway and its enframement. Often the flat lintel over a door followed the design of the window lintels. On the many houses where the basement and first floor have been converted into a storefront, the stone lintels of the second-floor windows often are the only obvious clue that the building is a much-altered early-nineteenth-century row house.

The Federal row house usually was smaller in scale than the comparable houses of succeeding decades. Most houses built before 1830, and modest houses well into the 1830s, followed the same general design: two full stories over a high basement topped by a pitched roof with two dormers. On the pitched-roof house, the cornice at the roofline provided a casing for the gutter whose drainpipe ran down the street front. To minimize the visual intrusion of these drainpipes, a single pipe sometimes emptied the gutters of the two houses on either side. An important visual element, the cornice clearly marked the top of the house front and, thereby, defined the façade's proportions by its width and height. The cornice also added a note of richness to the restrained façade. The twelve-to-eighteen-inch-high fascia board, which stretched from one side of the façade to the other, usually was a plain and flat surface except for occasional fluting. In most houses, an egg-and-dart or dentil molding appeared just below the fascia board.

Above the cornice, the two dormer windows, aligned over the solid piers of the wall, pierced the pitched roof and made the attic a lighted and well-ventilated area. Characteristic of the Federal style, the dormers took a variety of handsomely simple forms and architectural ornament. On a single row *(top)* Dormer Windows, No. 52 West Tenth Street (1830–1831), Greenwich Village. Notice the incised lintels above the second floor and dormer windows.

(bottom left) Doorway, No. 59 Morton Street (1828), Greenwich Village. This widely admired doorway epitomizes the elegance and good taste of the Federal style with its leaded fanlight and sidelight windows, columns at each side of the door, and stone arched lintel above the elaborate fanlight window.

(bottom right) Doorway, Late Federal Style, Old Merchant's House (1831–1832). In the late 1820s and early 1830s, large New York row houses had Late Federal doorways with richly ornamented fanlight and sidelight windows, Ionic columns, and arched stone moldings.

house or several houses in a row, the pitched roof and two dormers lent a picturesque distinction to the streetscape quite lacking in the streets entirely lined with flat-roofed houses of succeeding styles.

Few pitched roofs now remain on the city's surviving Federal style row houses. With the city's constantly rising land values, many house owners replaced the pitched-roof attic with a full third floor and new cornice. A later-style cornice or third-floor lintel on an otherwise Federal style row house will indicate the addition of a third floor and, to the architecturally knowledgeable, the approximate date of this addition. Some alterations, however, were more careful than others, and the new cornice and window lintels copy the original forms.

The Federal Style: Row House Plan and Interior Design.

By the 1820s, a plan for the layout of the New York row house had evolved which was to last into the 1890s with only occasional modifications. In the early nineteenth century, the typical row house was twenty to twenty-five feet wide and, for the sake of adequate lighting and ventilation, only two rooms deep. With the usual thirty-five to forty foot depth, row houses had a deep back yard or garden.

The original uses of the rooms in the city's early-nineteenth-century row houses are well documented except for the front room of the basement. Tradition, travel accounts of several Englishmen in America, and common sense place the dining room in the front room of the basement floor, convenient to the kitchen in the adjacent back room. Only for formal dinner parties, a rare occasion in early-nineteenth-century New York, did the servants set up a table in the handsome back parlor and bring the food up the stairs from the kitchen below. Not only was it difficult to serve meals in the back parlor from the basement kitchen in an era with a "servant problem" but also, a formal dining room in the back parlor with heavy table and breakfronts would have prevented the family from opening the sliding doors between the parlors and using the full expanse of the front and back parlors for the usual receptions and dancing parties.

One Englishman, Joseph J. Gurney, declared that the dining room was in the basement front room and the first floor was totally given over to two parlors.

The private houses . . . are generally of neat red brick-work, four stories high, besides the basement. This last [floor] in New York generally contains the dining-room; so that we descend to dinner. . . . The drawing room . . . usually occupies the whole of the first story, being divided in two by large folding doors. These apartments are often very spacious. . . .

The back parlor of Philip Hone's elegant row house at No. 235 Broadway, opposite City Hall Park, likely was a reception room rather than a formal dining room. After a party at the Philip Hone

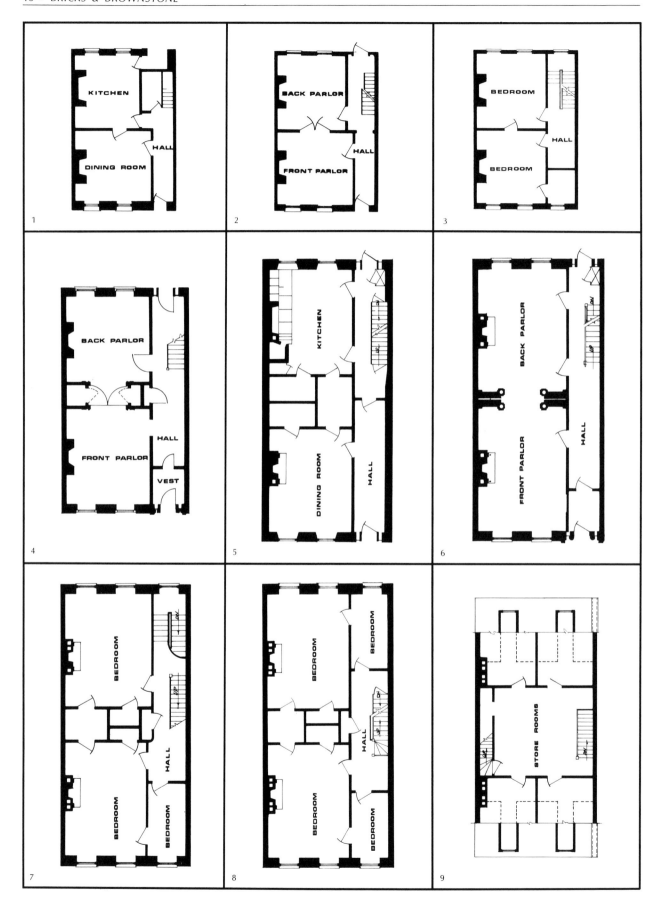

Plans 1–3. Small house, 1820s, without
hinged parlor doors. Basement, first,
and second floors.
Plan 4. Large house, 1820s, with hinged
parlor doors. First floor.
Plans 5–9. Large house, 1830s, with
sliding parlor doors. Old Merchant's
House. Basement, first, second, third,
and attic floors.

residence, Mrs. Basil Hall observed that "there were two large rooms open, communicating by folding doors and handsomely furnished and lighted. Quadrilles were danced in both rooms."

On the other hand, other early-nineteenth-century travelers in America stated that the back parlor was a formal dining room and the front room of the basement a nursery or an office. Mrs. Frances Trollope remarked that "in nearly all the houses the dining and drawing-rooms are on the same floor, with ample folding doors between them," and, according to Mrs. Felton, "the dining and drawing rooms are situated on the lower [first] floor, and so arranged, as by throwing open a large pair of folding doors, to form one splendid apartment." Furthermore, the French visitor Jacques Gerard Milbert called the front room of the basement "la nursery" and "le logement des enfants," and the well-informed Cooper declared that "the basement contains a nursery and the usual offices."

Despite the contradictory evidence of these sources, the front basement room's convenience to the kitchen and the small pantrylike rooms between the front room and the kitchen indeed suggest that it was an informal dining room in the 1820s and 1830s. Besides, the handsome mantels and wood paneling in the front basement room of some early-nineteenth-century row houses were architectural features too elaborate for rooms of such an ordinary function as a nursery or office.

In the 1820s and 1830s, the first-floor back parlor probably was a formal dining room only for occasional dinner parties, and, significantly, it was in these festive circumstances that such distinguished British visitors as Frances Trollope and Mrs. Felton visited the city's row houses. Only with the ready availability of servants from waves of European immigrants after the 1840s and the widespread appearance of the dumbwaiter in large row houses in the 1850s and 1860s did the back parlor actually become the usual formal dining room. Only then did the front basement room become an informal dining room for breakfast and supper and occasionally an office or nursery.

In the ordinary row house, the basement ceiling originally was six-and-a-half to seven feet high. In the eighteenth century, it must be recalled, people were generally shorter than today, and the family's limited use of the basement, mainly for two or three meals each day, made seven feet an acceptable ceiling height. But, for the servants in the open-hearth kitchen the heat in summer must have been intense. Very few row houses today retain this original seven-foot-tall basement floor ceiling. Over the years, not only has the average man's height increased but there is also an incentive to increase rentable space and make a single-family row house into a multiple dwelling. With the basement ceiling unalterable, the room's height is increased by lowering the floor several feet through excavation.

Unlike later houses, the modest Federal row houses lacked a furnace and rarely had a cellar for storage. Often, the wide plank floor of the family dining room and kitchen sat on a cheap subflooring

(top left) Newel Post, Old Merchant's House. This elaborately carved newel post is a showy touch in the first floor hallway of the 1830s home of a prosperous merchant.

(top right) Hallway, Old Merchant's House. In the early nineteenth century, stairways rose from the first floor to the second floor at the back of the house and were lit and ventilated by a window between the two floors.

(bottom left) Front Parlor, Charlton Street. Notice the Federal white and black marble mantel, handsome carved window moldings, and ceiling cornice.

(bottom right) Back Parlor, West Tenth Street, Greenwich Village. Notice the hinged parlor doors and paneled back parlor, used as a dining room.

which rested on the bare earth. The Federal row house nevertheless had considerable storage space. Many houses of the period have vaults, about ten feet wide and twenty feet long, extending underneath the street in front of the house to store food and, in wet weather, dry firewood as well. Placed several feet below the level of the basement, these vaults had comfortable, eight- to ten-feet-high ceilings and were constructed of stone and brick rubble held together by mortar. One usually entered the vault through a door under the stoop and walked down a steep flight of wood or stone steps.

By the mid-nineteenth century, the gardens or back yards were dug out so as to be on the same level as the basement. In the early nineteenth century, this practice was unknown, and a sunken areaway with steps led from the garden to the back door of the basement. In many houses of the Federal period, the kitchen had a small, several-foot-high food-storage vault sunk into the garden between the kitchen's two windows and directly accessible, like a cupboard, from the kitchen. The relatively low and constant temperature of these vaults was, of course, a great help in food preservation.

On the first floor, the front door usually led directly into a long and narrow hallway along the side of the house or, in some large row houses of the period, a large vestibule and a second doorway. This "little vestibule, which may be some twelve feet long, by eight in width," wrote Cooper, was,

> entirely unfurnished, and appears only constructed to shelter visiters [*sic*] while the servant is approaching to admit them through the inner door. The general excellence of the climate, and, perhaps, the customs of the country, have, as yet, prevented the Americans from providing a proper place for the reception of the servants of their guests: they rarely wait, unless during the short calls, and then it is always in the street.

This vestibule led into a side hallway with the stairway to the second-floor bedrooms placed at the end rather than the center as in later decades, to receive daylight from a rear window placed between the first and second floors. The hallway usually was carpeted and had several chairs and a table with a lamp.

The front and back parlors, nearly square and usually nearly identical in shape, opened off this long side hallway. In the early nineteenth century, visitors to New York always admired the elegance of the parlors which displayed the richest architectural ornament, finest materials, and best furniture of the family house. In the 1820s Cooper described the parlors in the elegant row house of a New Yorker "in the first society of the country, and of what is here called an easy fortune," on then-fashionable Broadway:

> Each room is lighted by two windows; is sufficiently high; has stuccoed ceiling, and cornices in

(top left) No. 24 Middagh Street (ca. 1824), Brooklyn Heights. This charming Federal style house, with a richly detailed front doorway, is one of the finest remaining early-nineteenth-century frame houses in New York.

(top right) Parlor Doors, Charlton Street. The hinged doors between the front and back parlors often were the most elaborate feature in the Federal row house. Here, pilasters at each side and richly carved rectangular center block and square end blocks frame the doorway.

(bottom) Mantel, Old Merchant's House. This white marble mantel has the early-nineteenth-century coal grate and fireplace tools.

white; hangings of light, airy French paper; curtains in silk and in muslin; mantel-pieces of carved figures in white marble (Italian in manufacture, I should think;) Brussels carpets; large mirrors; chairs, sofas, and tables, in mahogany; chandeliers; beautiful, neat, and highly wrought grates in the fireplaces of home work; candelabras, lustres, &c. &c., much as one sees them all over Europe.

Even the often-critical Mrs. Trollope remarked that "the dwelling-houses of the higher classes are extremely handsome, and very richly furnished."

In the early nineteenth century, New Yorkers and visitors admired the row houses of the city's middle-class families. "On entering the house of a respectable mechanic, in any of the large cities of the United States," wrote one Englishman, "one cannot but be astonished at the apparent neatness and comfort of the apartments, the large airy parlors, the nice carpets and mahogany furniture." Cooper's thorough description of the "second-rate genteel" row houses in New York is particularly charming:

There is a species of second-rate, genteel houses, that abound in New-York, into which I have looked when passing, with the utmost pleasure. They have, as usual, a story that is half sunk in the earth, receiving light from an area, and two floors above. The tenants of these buildings are chiefly merchants, or professional men, in moderate circumstances, who pay rents of from 300 to 500 dollars a year. You know that no American, who is at all comfortable in life, will share his dwelling with another. Each has his own roof, and his own little yard. These buildings are finished, and exceedingly well finished too, to the attics; containing, on the average, six rooms, besides offices, and servants' apartments. The furniture of these houses is often elegant, and always neat. Mahogany abounds here, and is commonly used for all the principal articles, and very frequently for doors, railings of stairs, &c. &c.

In an early-nineteenth-century row house, the rooms usually had pleasing proportions and an overall human scale. The relatively low cost of building lots in the early nineteenth century made possible a twenty-five-foot-wide lot even for middle-class row houses. Even with the space devoted to the stair hallway from the front to the rear of the house, the rooms were fairly square in shape, rather than the impressive but awkward parlors of narrow width and great length in row houses of later decades when high land costs permitted a twenty-five-foot-wide lot only for the finest houses. Nine- and ten-foot-tall ceilings on the parlor floors enhanced the feeling of homeyness and restraint evoked by square rooms and modest forms.

Within the modestly scaled parlors, such elements of interior design as mantels, doorways, or ceilings were characterized by restrained forms and enriched with occasional ornamental detail. Except in the largest houses, the early-nineteenth-century dwellings lacked the grand scale, bold (top) Mantel, Basement, Front Room, Charlton Street. The mantels in the basement dining room or second and third floor bedrooms usually employed simpler designs and materials than those in the parlors.

(bottom left) Parlor Doors, Charlton Street. When fully opened, hinged parlor doors formed a paneled wall which concealed the closets and pantries between the front and back rooms.

(bottom right) Door, Basement, Front Room, Charlton Street. This door in a basement dining room characteristically is simpler than the parlor doors on the floor above.

forms, and elaborate embellishment of the aesthetically and socially more pretentious styles that followed.

On the first floor, rectangular double doors separated the front parlor and the back parlor and, in many cases, the front and back bedrooms on the second floor as well. In most Federal row houses, the double parlor doors were hinged. Although double doors, which slid into the wall on metal tracks, did appear in large row houses of the mid-1820s and in the Greek Revival parlors of Late Federal dwellings then, they did not displace the hinged parlor doors in modest row houses until the mid-1830s. In the 1820s, the enframement of the mahogany- or rosewood-veneer parlor doors consisted of pilasters, at each side, supporting a horizontal lintel with carved square end blocks and, in the center, usually, a large rectangular carved block. On the first floor parlor, boldly carved acanthus or oak leaves enriched these end and center blocks. These double parlor doors and their enframement with richly carved pilasters and center blocks evidence the simplicity of form, relieved by occasional ornamental details, so valued in the Federal style dwellings.

A small antechamber separated the front parlor and back parlor, and some houses boasted two sets of doors for the two rooms. Fully opened into the hallway, the two sets of double doors—or even the single pair of doors—formed handsome paneled walls. The fully opened doors concealed china closets or a small butler's pantry in the hallway. On the second floor, one side of this hallway, between the front and back bedrooms, often originally was a clothes press, while the other concealed washbasins and chamber pots. These sets of hinged double doors and the connecting hallways clearly defined the separateness of the front and back rooms. With the introduction of sliding doors in the 1820s these hallways—or "pantries" as they were then called—disappeared on the parlor floor, and the space of two parlors flowed directly into each other.

In the early nineteenth century, a wood-burning fireplace was the usual source of heat. Handsome marble or wood mantels graced most rooms in the Federal row house. Reflecting the overall architectural modesty of the period the parlor mantels usually had a plain rectangular shelf supported by plain or fluted columns, flat side jambs, and a horizontal jamb, above the fireplace opening, usually ornamented by a deeply set panel in the center. The favorite materials were wood, white marble, a mixture of white and black marble pieces, or, forecasting the taste of the Greek Revival style, black marble veined with gold.

Mantels were "highly ornamental, when tastefully constructed" but often "the magnitude of a chimney-piece does not always correspond with that of the room in which it is situated," architect Asher Benjamin declared. "Columns are often employed in their decoration" and "in large apartments may sometimes be employed to advantage," but this impressive mantel style was "in small plain

rooms, to be avoided." In their large scale and rich ornament, such mantels, with columns supporting the shelf, were inappropriate to a small and otherwise simply detailed room.

Following this sensible advice and, at the same time, keeping an eye on construction costs, row house builders in New York installed handsome mantels of a simpler design in the second-floor bedrooms than in the first-floor parlors. These mantels usually omitted the ornamental and costly columns which supported the shelf and instead relied upon their pleasing proportions and the paneled horizontal jamb above the fireplace opening for decorative effect.

In the early nineteenth century, firewood was sold from wagons that stopped at the street corners, and the servant who sawed the firewood into suitable logs and kept the fires burning usually was given the privilege of selling the ashes. Even then, long-burning anthracite coal, in an iron grate, began to replace wood as a source of heat in the city's large dwellings, a development evidenced by the reduced size of the fireplace opening and the appearance of ornamental iron screens in an occasional dwelling of the late 1820s and early 1830s.

The parlor walls were painted plaster, with a single foot-high molding or baseboard at the floor, enhancing the overall feeling of simplicity. Occasionally a room recalled the earlier Georgian tradition and was wood-paneled from floor to ceiling in small deeply set panels. Where the walls met the ceiling, the cornice usually was two moldings, separated by several inches to make a coved form.

By the 1820s, the appearance of elaborate interior embellishments in large row houses signaled the emergence of the tiring for restrained Federal style forms and forecast the Greek Revival style. In 1829 the noted New York architect Minard Lafever declared that "carved mouldings have of late, become very fashionable in this city, and are indeed very beautiful, and thereby have excited the carvers to prodigious extravagances, both in the quality of work and position of the ornaments." Another evidence of the increasing splendor of row house parlors was the widespread appearance of a ceiling "centerpiece" or "centerflower," a plaster or stucco medallion consisting of foliate forms thrusting outward to a circular molding and placed in the center of the ceiling. "Centre Flowers may be classed among the finest order or Ornaments in interior furnishing, and is indeed as beautiful and produces as lively an effect as any other Ornament in Architecture," wrote Minard Lafever.

The stairway to the upper floors, it has been pointed out, was at the back of the long side hallway and was lit by a rear window between the first and second floors. The stairway rose to the second floor in graceful elliptical turns, a form emphasized by the simple handrail. Very often the round post took a simple baluster form and railing spindles lacked any turning. A semicircular niche, erroneously termed a "coffin niche," usually graced the curving wall at the top and bottom of each flight. These cylindrical niches reputedly allowed a coffin to be carried from the second-floor parents' bedroom to the parlor without marring the walls but actually were an ornamental feature which enhanced the elliptical form of the stairway and usually held a statue or lamp. "The plans of niches with cylindrical backs should be semicircular . . . as deep as may be necessary for the statues they are to contain," wrote Asher Benjamin in 1830.

The position of the stairway, in the back of the hallway, pointed out the pleasant plan of the early-nineteenth-century New York row house. When rapidly rising land costs in later decades forced a narrow width in row houses, the hall stairway moved to the center of the house so that the back parlor could occupy the full width of the house. After the 1830s, most New Yorkers never again enjoyed the light, air, and handsome proportions of the nearly square double parlors in the Federal row house.

In nearly all nineteenth-century row houses, it must be remembered, the architect-builder lavished the most effort and expense on the first-floor parlors where the family received its guests or gave dinner parties. The basement, which housed the kitchen and family dining room, did not exhibit much in the way of ornamental detail or expensive materials, nor did the top floor where bedrooms for the children and live-in servants were located under the pitched roof.

Less spartan, but still far plainer than the rooms on the parlor floor, were the second-floor bedrooms. The second-floor double-door enframement continued the forms of the first floor but omitted the costly hand-carved foliate forms in the end and center blocks. Second-floor ceilings usually lacked the ornate centerpiece of the parlor-floor ceiling, and mantels seldom displayed the delicate fluting or classical foliate detail.

Frame Row Houses in New York—and City Building Codes.

Fire was a constant threat to all eighteenth- and nineteenth-century cities. New York's frantic early-nineteenth-century building boom partly was to replace business buildings and dwelling houses destroyed by the periodic large-scale conflagrations. "Scarcely a night passes without our citizens being awakened by the cry of 'Fire!'" remarked Philip Hone in 1829. Fires were so frequent in New York that visitors regarded them as one of the city's tourist sights. "'When the fire breaks out tonight,' Carl said to me one day, 'we'll go out and take a look at it,'" observed a Swedish visitor in the 1840s. "It was like deciding to go to the theater to see a play that had been announced and that could be counted on with certainty to come off. And sure enough, we did not have long to wait for the spectacle."

To lessen the chance of disastrous fires, the city periodically passed ordinances which encouraged citizen participation in fire fighting, required regular chimney cleaning and repairs, and forbade the storage of such combustible materials as hay, straw, or gunpowder within built-up areas. In the late eighteenth century, the state and city also enacted building codes to aid in fire prevention. State laws of 1791 and 1796 declared that, thereafter, all buildings taller than two stories and a basement, south of Broome Street, be built of brick or stone with a tile or slate roof. Wooden structures already standing within this "fire district" might remain unchanged; but, if these wooden structures became deteriorated, they had to be demolished or rebuilt under the new building regulations. In succeeding years, the city forbade the construction of wooden structures of any height within the fire district and periodically extended the fire district to the north to include new areas of row house development.

These building codes soon affected the appearance of New York. The city's "houses were formerly built of wood, with shingle roofs," wrote one New Yorker around 1820, "but these are fast disappearing, and substantial brick houses, with slated roofs, rising in their places. . . . This interference on the part of the Legislature has introduced much neatness and regularity to the general aspect of the dwelling-houses." So effective were the building codes or fire-district regulations, combined with the continual rebuilding of the city's downtown areas, that in the mid-1840s one Englishwoman remarked that "wooden buildings are scarcely to be seen in the city of New York."

Today late-eighteenth- and early-nineteenth-century frame buildings, often concealed beneath a mid-nineteenth-century brick front or a recent layer of shingles, survive among the skewed streets of the West Village and in the northern edge of Brooklyn Heights. One of the finest wooden row houses in the city is at No. 24 Middagh Street, the former Eugene Boisselet house, at the corner of Willow Street, in Brooklyn Heights. Built in 1824, this basement-and-two-story-tall clapboard house is one of the oldest dwellings in Brooklyn Heights. The front doorway, with its delicately leaded toplight and sidelights and elegantly carved ornaments, is a particularly rich note in the façade. Two dormer windows pierce the modest gambrel roof, enhanced by small lunette windows on the Willow Street side. The original carriage house survives at the back of the garden and is connected to the house by a wooden garden wall.

Row House Construction in the Early Nineteenth Century.

In the early nineteenth century, ordinary carpenters and masons and large-scale professional row house builders with a crew of workmen, each of whom performed his own specialty, whether bricklaying, cellar digging, or plastering, designed and built nearly all the city's houses. Very few houses were built for a particular family and its specifications. The professional builder usually erected rows of at least three or four houses on speculation and, as time went on, was responsible for a greater and greater portion of the city's row houses. In the early nineteenth century, ordinary masons and carpenters built dwelling houses singly or in groups of two or three—as seen in the pleasant variety of doorways, stoop iron work, and cornices on remarkably well-preserved Charlton Street in Greenwich Village.

From the number of houses actually owned by the builder at the construction site, a house or even several houses apparently could be built without large amounts of capital. Even so, most row houses of the period, particularly the large dwellings, were built on speculation for wealthy investors.

An Englishman in New York after the War of 1812 described certain aspects of row house construction at the time:

> Building appears brisk in the city. It is generally performed by contract. A person intending to have a house erected contracts with a professed builder; the builder, with a bricklayer; and he, with all other necessary to the completion of the design. In some cases, a builder is a sort of head workman, for the purpose of overseeing the others; receiving for his agency seven-pence per day from the wages of each man; the men being employed and paid by him. There are occasional instances in which there is no contract, everything paid for according to measure and value.

This last sentence distinguished between "construction by contract," in which incentive existed to finish a house as quickly as possible and start another one, and "day's work," in which workmen were paid by the day and were expected, therefore, to do the highest quality work.

The speculative builder started construction in the summer of one year and completed the house in the next March or early April so that it was rented or sold before May 1, the general moving day throughout the city at that time. Only the large, elaborately ornamented row houses or freestanding mansions took more than one year to build.

One reason for the important role of the mason and carpenter in row house construction in the early nineteenth century was the simplicity of the house. Until the widespread introduction of plumbing and heating in the 1840s, almost the builder's entire effort was to erect well-built and handsome structures. With the appearance of complicated and expensive mechanical equipment to install in the 1840s and 1850s, the small builder lacked construction expertise and capital to build fine houses and slowly disappeared from the city's housing construction scene.

Builder's Guides and the New York Row House.

"The old New York streets were neither dark nor unlovely," wrote Montgomery Schuyler in 1899. "They were gay and positively attractive, by reason of the architectural tradition that had grown up among the mechanics. The houses were more than decent; they were 'elegant.' That adjective cannot be applied to the contemporary small houses of Philadelphia or of Boston."

(top left) No. 7 State Street (1794–1806), James Watson House. This elegant Federal mansion, attributed to John McComb, Jr., is the only survivor of the fine houses that once clustered around the Battery and lower Broadway. It now is the Shrine of Blessed Mother Seton.

(top right) Business Card of Alexander Jackson Davis, one of America's leading mid-nineteenth-century architects.

(bottom left) No. 4 Minetta Street, in 1935. Diminutive row houses on the narrow twisting streets of Greenwich Village long have captivated New Yorkers.

(bottom right) Plans for a Row House Front (*ca.* 1820), by Calvin Pollard, a New York architect.

The Federal style row house gained its dignity from the quiet contrast of red brick, brownstone door and window details, a white-painted wood door and cornice, and pleasant façade proportions, in which the height of the house is not much greater than its width. The small New York house, wrote Schuyler, also "owed its elegance to the ornament which was applied to it, very modestly and very sparingly, but none the less effectively."

Throughout the nineteenth century, architects rarely designed New York row houses. At that time, the professional architect—hired by a client to design a house, handle all legal details, and supervise construction—scarcely existed in this country. In New York the builder hired an architect to design the fronts and interior embellishment only in the most fashionable locations or for large projects. Among the earliest architect-designed row houses in New York were those along State Street, facing the Battery, attributed to John McComb, Jr., of which the James Watson house, No. 7 State Street, is the lone survivor. Other leading architects who occasionally designed New York's early-nineteenth-century row houses were Josiah Brady, Samuel Dunbar, Minard Lafever, Calvin Pollard, Martin E. Thompson, and the firm of Town and Davis.

Rather than hire an architect, most builders purchased standard row house front and interior plans in the then-fashionable style from amateur architects or ordinary draftsmen. In his *Autobiography,* architect James Gallier described the usual position of the architect in row house design in early-nineteenth-century New York:

> I found that the majority of people could with difficulty be made to understand what was meant by a professional architect; the builders, that is, the carpenters and bricklayers, all called them-selves architects, and were at that time the persons to whom owners of property applied when they required plans for building; the builder hired some poor draftsman, of whom there were some half a dozen in New York at that time, to make the plans, paying him a mere trifle for his services.

Although "The drawings so made were . . . but of little value," wrote Gallier,

> some proprietors built without having any regular plan. When they wanted a house built they looked about for one already finished, which they thought suitable for their purpose; and then bargained with a builder to erect for them such another, or one with such alterations upon the model as they might point out.

Except for the design of a large public or commercial building or an extravagant mansion, the employment of an architect was considered a needless luxury. In the public mind, the profession of architect hardly existed, because there was little or no difference between a builder and an architect or between an architect and a draftsman.

Nos. 512–514 Broome Street (ca. 1820), in 1935. Today the area from Canal to Houston streets—now called "SOHO"—is known for its artists' lofts and splendid cast-iron commercial buildings of the 1860s and 1870s. But, in the early nineteenth century, three and four-story-tall dwelling houses lined these same now densely built-up and often-cluttered streets. These ragged buildings recalled the area's residential past in their pitched roofs and dormer windows. Like so many overlooked one-time Federal dwelling houses, these buildings have disappeared without a trace.

The "builder's guides" or "pattern books" were the source for the handsome up-to-date architectural style in the city's Federal and Greek Revival row houses. Written by professional architects, the builder's guides described sound construction methods and illustrated doors, mantels, and cornices in the then-popular styles which a builder could reproduce with local materials and labor. The builder's guides also inspired many of the row house plans sold to builders by architectural draftsmen.

Builder's guides originated in the seventeenth and eighteenth centuries. In colonial America, builders relied on the English pattern books of Batty Langley, Abraham Swan, William Pain, Peter Nicholson, George Andrew Cook, and Isaac Ware, among others. These guides were popularizations of books by the architectural leaders of the Renaissance tradition: Vignola, Andrea Palladio, James Gibbs, and Sir William Chambers.

Asher Benjamin's *The Country Builder's Assistant* (1797) was the first builder's guide by an American author. In 1810, architect Owen Biddle remarked: "I have experienced much inconvenience, for want of suitable books on the subject. All that have yet appeared, have been written by foreign authors, who have adapted their examples and observations almost entirely to the style of building in their respective countries, which in many instances differs very materially from ours."

By the late 1820s, builder's guides by American authors began to appear in great numbers. These American builder's guides borrowed freely from British and other American pattern books. "I have not, from prejudice, omitted anything useful contained in the books already published on this subject," wrote Owen Biddle in his builder's guide. "The proportion of the four Orders I have taken from Pain's work, with but little variations; and, for some of the Geometrical Problems, I am indebted to Peter Nicholson, whose works are held in deserved estimation."

For a builder in an always fashion-conscious New York, an important portion of the builders' guides was the line drawings of then-stylish doorways or mantels. Here the architect showed his talent for design and spread the latest architectural styles to builders in the city and country. Although some builders exactly copied designs in the builder's guides, they usually adapted them to their own taste and their workmen's skills and local building materials. "How very soon these [builders] got tired of copying the lessons in architectural books," wrote one magazine in the 1860s, "and began to develop 'patterns'—for so only can they be called—of their own."

The authors of builder's guides knew about the on-site adaptation of their designs. Discussing his design for a parlor door, Minard Lafever remarked that "in some instances, a drawing may appear exceedingly well; but when executed, will appear very deficient in all its parts" and "therefore, I do not wish my patrons to understand that I have introduced this Elevation for a perfect model, but for

(top) Frame Row Houses, Lower East Side, in 1911, Jackson and Front streets, northwest corner. In the early nineteenth century, modest but respectable houses of working class and middle class families lined the streets of the Lower East Side. Jackson Street runs into the East River near Corlears Hook, and today vast public housing projects and river-front parks dominate the area.

(bottom) Steamship Row, Bowling Green, in 1896. Though altered into offices for steamship lines, these houses on the south side of Bowling Green reveal their earlier residential elegance in arched doorways and fanlight windows.

a guide by which they may be enabled to execute according to any variation agreeable to their own fancy." In a footnote to this paragraph, Lafever does remind the reader that "I say not a perfect model, but if well executed, would appear exceedingly well."

Because of their control of construction and design, except for the inspiration from builder's guides, the builders of the city's early-nineteenth-century row houses might be more accurately termed "architect-builders." The professional architect, of course, published the builder's guides and, therefore, developed and spread the contemporary architectural styles used by the builder.

Several general themes in the architectural history of the New York row house reflected the role of the architect-builder in their design and construction. New York row houses usually were slow to reflect national architectural ideals. Some architect-builders clung to a style for years after it had gone out of fashion, because they were slow to give up a style in which they had become skilled and to which their middle-class clients were accustomed. Stylistic change and innovation also occurred more slowly in less expensive Manhattan houses and in all Brooklyn row houses. The result was a lengthy and gradual transition between styles, with a new style in its first years usually incorporating many elements of the one it replaced.

The design of the New York row house reflected the union of several contradictory forces. Beginning with the 1820s, New York was a rich, ambitious, cosmopolitan, and fashion-conscious city, all of which tended to stimulate an elaborate, consistent architecture for row houses, often with rich decorative details. "The consequences of its rapid growth, and the extraordinary medley of which its population is composed, serve to give something of a peculiar character to New-York," wrote Cooper in the 1820s. "It is the only city in the Union that has not the air of a provincial town."

City houses also were expected to be more ornate, formal, and fashionable than suburban or country houses. In the 1840s Andrew Jackson Downing, a prominent landscape gardener and some-time-architect in the romantic Gothic Revival style, recommended that the country house,

> should always be furnished with more chasteness and simplicity than a townhouse; because, it is in the country, if anywhere, that we should find essential ease and convenience always preferred to that love of effect and desire to dazzle, which is begotten, for the most part, by the rivalry of mere wealth in town life.

Downing advised leaving "the complex intricacy and richness of ornamental details to the more elaborate and showy life of those who live in fine townhouses."

Two already noted contradictory forces, however, hindered these tendencies toward fashion and ornateness in New York dwellings. The architect-builder, usually speculating with his own money,

resisted any departure from a proved and profitable design. And, the cost of convenient land in Manhattan and Brooklyn limited architectural extravagance; the architectural effect possible on the front of a twenty-foot- or twenty-five-foot-wide house was obviously much less than for the four-sided freestanding house.

The Battery Area.

The James Watson house, at No. 7 State Street facing the Battery, probably is the city's finest remaining late-eighteenth-century row house. Attributed to John McComb, Jr., an architect of the City Hall, the James Watson house was built in two sections: an eastern half, completed *ca.* 1794, and the western half, completed in 1806, with a curved three-story colonnade, which offers an elegant architectural solution to an oddly shaped, curving corner lot. The house façade itself is typical of the period: a red-brick façade laid in Flemish bond, and windows enhanced by splayed lintels with double keystones. The lintels, window sills, and string course above the first floor originally were common brownstone but were replaced with white pressed-stone in a 1965 façade restoration. The once-splendid interior has been lost in the building's recent remodeling as a church and museum.

Once part of an elegant row of houses along State Street, the James Watson house is the last tangible reminder that the Battery and lower Broadway areas were the city's finest residential districts in the late eighteenth and early nineteenth centuries. In the 1750s, the city's rich residents lived around Hanover Square and Franklin Square. The Battery's residential fashion emerged when the Earl of Cassilis built a splendid mansion at No. 1 Broadway, later known as Kennedy Mansion, opposite Bowling Green and its equestrian statue of King George III. For the first time in history, the city's most fashionable residential district moved south in Manhattan rather than north.

In the late eighteenth and early nineteenth centuries, the Battery was one of the city's few parks and, on pleasant afternoons and evenings, the shaded winding paths were the favorite promenade of fashionable New Yorkers. From the waterside path, and particularly from the upper floors of the patrician State Street dwellings, New Yorkers enjoyed the view of the verdant hills of Brooklyn and New Jersey and, on New York Bay, the sight of "little, fairy skiffs," "magnificent steamers," and "noble merchantmen" of the bustling harbor. Besides this incomparable setting, the quiet Battery and lower Broadway area was only a five- or ten-minute walk from New York's thriving water front and emerging Wall Street community. In 1827 the real estate advertisement for the "Substantial House" at No. 38 Broadway declared that "tis seldom a house is offered for sale in so central and desirable a situation," and the same year an advertisement for a twenty-room mansion overlooking "the *Battery, Castle Garden,* the North river, the Bay" stated that "its situation is not excelled by any in this city."

This handsome area, unfortunately, did not survive for long into the nineteenth century. Although visitors to New York in the 1820s admired the "lofty" and "modern built" houses near the Battery, Cooper declared in 1828 that "commerce is gradually taking possession of the whole of the lower extremity of the island, though the Bay, the battery, and the charming Broadway, still cause many of the affluent to depart with reluctance."

By the 1830s and 1840s, shops, offices, and warehouses had invaded the Battery area. At the foot of Broadway, the Bowling Green became an omnibus stand, and along the sidewalks, reported one newspaper, "you can scarcely get along for dust, piles of brick, bales, boxes, and vehicles of business." Soon the once-fine dwellings became saloons, oyster cellars, and boardinghouses for sailors and workmen at the nearby Hudson and East River docks. In the 1850s, the old fort Castle Clinton became the landing place for millions of immigrants from Europe, and the Battery and nearby streets swarmed with impoverished and confused foreigners.

In the 1850s, a visitor to New York, one William Bobo, who described himself as "a South Carolinian, who Had Nothing Else to Do," observed that,

> Around this place was considered a few years back the most desirable to live at in the city, and all the wealth and aristocracy had their residences here if possible. Now, I believe, there is but one family who pretends to move in the upper story of society remaining.

That aristocratic stretch of State Street, facing the Battery, was among the last streets in the area taken over by business and subsequently demolished for commercial buildings. In the 1890s, one New Yorker recalled that,

> As recently as twenty years ago the generous windows were draped with lace curtains, and the occupants were determined to oppose the encroachments of business life. But now these same houses are converted into offices for steamship lines, commission merchants, money exchanges, and homes for immigrants.

Today only the splendid James Watson house remains to tell of the Battery area's proud past.

The March Uptown.

In the city's never-ending march northward up Manhattan from the Battery, block after block of fine row houses were built to accommodate the city's increasing population. By 1830, the city growth had passed Houston Street and extended into the Village and the Astor Place area. In the past 100 years,

Beach Street, Opposite St. John's Park, about 1866. In the 1820s, 1830s, and 1840s, palatial row houses of the wealthy and fashionable lined Hudson Square or St. John's Park, a private park. A commercial tide, however, engulfed the once-tranquil neighborhood in the 1860s. After the Civil War, Trinity Church and the house owners around St. John's Park assured the area's destruction by selling the private park to Commodore Vanderbilt, who erected the massive Hudson Terminal on the site. Today, the entrance to the Holland Tunnel marks the location of St. John's Park, the chapel, and fine early-nineteenth-century row houses. Even Commodore Vanderbilt's terminal has vanished from this now-desolate and traffic-filled area.

commercial buildings and tenements of different eras have since replaced nearly all these dwellings between the Battery and Greenwich Village. As early as 1899, Montgomery Schuyler remarked that "a quarter of a century ago these [Federal style] houses were to be seen by whole blocks. Now the march of improvement has pretty well obliterated them." New York's continuous growth and redevelopment have destroyed all the city's Federal style dwellings—except for the Charlton-King-Vandam streets area, some blocks of the West Village, and a few streets in Brooklyn Heights.

The rest of Manhattan south of Houston Street—the Lower East Side, Little Italy, the Cast-Iron District, the Lower West Side, or the Wall Street area—have changed to such an extent over the years that it is difficult to imagine the original appearance of these areas. In the 1830s, one Englishwoman admired the handsome streets along the East River, between the present-day Manhattan Bridge and Williamsburg Bridge: "East Broadway is a spacious and elegant street on the east side of town, and parallel with it are Henry, Madison, and Monroe-streets, all handsomely built up with private residences, in the neighborhood of the East River." By the 1890s, this area, wrote one New Yorker, was "reputed as harboring the lowest people in our city's population. . . . The buildings are exclusively tenements and old private houses adapted to the occupancy of many families. The people . . . swarm out of the houses all over the steps, the sidewalk, and the roadway." Today, except for a few forgotten row houses, tenements and public housing projects now fill this once-pleasant area.

Throughout these residential and commercial areas south of Houston Street, an occasional Federal row house remains as a remarkable survivor of the past in an ever-changing city and as a reminder of the area's original appearance. Unlike the well-maintained dwellings of Greenwich Village or Brooklyn Heights, these tenuous survivors are repainted, refaced, and usually have been altered into stores. Because of these disfiguring remodelings and the unlikely locations, few New Yorkers know of these rich physical remnants of their city's past. In a walk through Little Italy or the Cast-Iron District, a pitched roof with or without dormers, a modest dentiled cornice, Federal style lintels, or a Flemish-bond brick front will catch the experienced eye. But, all too often, one finds a vacant lot where a building has been demolished recently, with only the walls of the adjoining structure showing the telltale traces of the pitched-roofed house which once stood there.

St. John's Park or Hudson Square.

Few New Yorkers now realize that one of the city's most fashionable residential districts in the 1820s, 1830s, and 1840s was located near the present-day entrance to the Holland Tunnel, just south of Canal Street. Not a trace remains of St. John's Park or the fine row houses and St. John's Chapel around its sides. In 1807, the Trinity Church parish built the handsome St. John's Chapel on Varick Street at the

No. 36 Beach Street (*ca.* 1820), opposite St. John's Park, about 1910. Years of delapidation cannot hide the onetime grandeur of this Federal row house. The richly detailed fanlight doorway, basement windows, carved window lintels, and dormer windows all bespeak a patrician past for the house and the street. But, decay has triumphed—a fire escape marring the front, broken window shutters, motley window curtains, and the cruel sign "ROOMS" nailed to the front door. Like all the row houses in the St. John's Park area, No. 36 Beach Street has disappeared without a trace.

outskirts of the city. Many people saw the chapel as a folly; it was too fine and costly a structure for its unlikely surroundings at that time, overgrown fields and cow pastures. Several years later Trinity Church laid out St. John's Park, or Hudson Square, bounded by Varick, Beach, Hudson, and Laight streets, and the surrounding streets attracted prominent and wealthy families, many of them fleeing the increasingly commercial lower Broadway and Battery areas. In the tradition of London's West End, the owners of the elegant row houses around the park actually owned the park, and only they had keys to open the park gates. Gramercy Park, laid out in 1831, was the only other private park in the city.

The St. John's Park area was an extraordinarily beautiful and retired setting—"a spot of Eden loveliness and exclusiveness." St. John's Park was "the fairest interior portion of this city," wrote one New Yorker in the 1820s.

> The regularity of the elegant mansions surrounding it, together with the choice trees and shrubbery, and the costly and much admired metropolitan church of St. John's, with its lofty and beautiful spire, places this square at once as the most desirable residence, and most judiciously embellished spot contained in the city.

The elegant park was planted with catalpa trees, cottonwood, horse-chestnuts, and silver birches; gravel paths wound among the trees, shrubs, and many flower beds. Mrs. Trollope remarked that "the square is very beautiful, excellently well planted with a great variety of trees . . . and it will give some idea of the care bestowed on its decoration, to know that the gravel for the walks was conveyed by barges from Boston, not as ballast, but as freight." From the open doors of St. John's Chapel, one could look through the tree-shaded park and down Hubert Street to the sail-flecked sparkling Hudson River.

This *rus in urbs* setting was to survive for only a few decades. Wealthy and socially prominent families began to leave St. John's Park in the 1850s, and nearby streets began to deteriorate. The fine houses facing the park continued to be well-maintained and occupied, for the most part, by families into the 1860s. But, the commercial encroachments which drove away the socially prominent families so as to be "above Bleecker" [Street] soon brought the area's complete destruction.

In October, 1866, Commodore Vanderbilt announced the purchase of St. John's Park for $1,000,000 and began to erect his massive Hudson Terminal. In this transaction, Trinity Church parish, which owned St. John's Chapel, received $400,000 for its share of the park, and each of the forty houseowners on the park received about $13,000. According to newspaper articles at the time of the sale, the houseowners on the park expected to profit as well from the rising real estate values as the area became commercial. However, once the huge Hudson Terminal rose on the site of the park, the

ERICKSON HOUSE
36 Beach St., N.Y.
UNDERHILL, Photographer, N.Y.
B-19858

(top) St. John's Chapel and Park, in 1829. New Yorkers rightly hailed St. John's Park as a "spot of Eden loveliness and exclusiveness."

(bottom) Mr. & Mrs. Ernest Fiedler, No. 38 Bond Street, in 1850. The marble mantel adorned with Grecian caryatids and the Ionic columns between the front and back parlors recall the restrained architectural taste of the 1820s and 1830s when this Bond Street mansion was built. The furniture and dress of the family, however, foretell the extravagant dwelling houses and competitive social scene in New York during the 1850s and 1860s. Despite the splendor of this family scene, fickle fashion already was abandoning Bond Street by 1850.

houses in the area had become cheap boarding houses. In the following years, factories and warehouses were built in the area, and one by one the once-fine Federal row houses were torn down. St. John's Chapel and several adjacent houses survived as recently as 1917, when they were demolished by the city in its widening of Varick Street.

The Bond Street Area.

In the 1830s and 1840s, the city's most fashionable and best-known residential district was the Bond Street area, the streets north of Houston Street and adjacent Broadway. Then, elegant brick and marble-front row houses and mansions, the homes of some of New York's leading families, lined the area's serene tree-lined streets. "The elegance and beauty of this section cannot be surpassed in the country," exclaimed one New York newspaper in 1835.

The growth of the Bond Street area started in the first years of the nineteenth century. In 1805 the city opened Broadway to Prince Street, in 1806 to Great Jones Street, and in 1807 to Astor Place. At the same time, Bleecker, Bond, and Great Jones streets were cut through from Broadway to the Bowery. In 1809 the city paved Broadway and built sidewalks as far north as Astor Place.

The area's growth, however, was stalled over a decade because of the restricted trade in the years before the War of 1812, the collapse of trade and economic uncertainty during the War, and a mild depression of 1818–1819. Row house construction in the Bond Street area, therefore, began around 1820 and lasted into the 1840s. "In Houston, Bond, Bleecker, Fourth, and many other streets, large blocks of spacious and elegant houses are erecting or just completed," one newspaper observed in 1831, "and preparations for as many more are actively going forward."

The Bond Street area dwellings epitomized the city's unparalleled wealth and the good taste of the era's residential architecture. The row house in this section surpassed in size and splendor all dwellings of earlier decades. An 1829 real estate advertisement for an "elegant house and lot" on Bond Street declared that "in point of eligibility of situation, convenience of arrangement and costliness of finish, this splendid establishment is not surpassed by any in the city." And, from an architectural viewpoint, these costly row houses adopted, and often initiated, the latest fashions. In the Bond Street area, the lavish Late Federal style and marble or granite row house front were employed most extensively and the succeeding Greek Revival style first was introduced into the city.

Bond Street, a single 1,000-foot-long block, was the best-known street in the area. In 1820 Jonas Minturn built the first fine row house on Bond Street, No. 22, in a plain Federal style but with a startling white-marble front. By 1835 about sixty lavish row houses lined the block, ranging in style from Federal and Late Federal to Greek Revival.

(top left) Charlton Street (1820s). The north side of Charlton Street between Varick Street and Sixth Avenue has the longest unbroken stretch of row houses in New York from the 1820s and 1830s.

(top right) No. 153 Bleecker Street (*ca.* 1830), at Thompson Street, northeast corner, about 1870. With its columned doorway porch, tall windows with shutters, and parlor window balcony and stoop railings, this house and others on the blockfront projected an air of wealth and leisure. Perhaps the carriage in the foreground belonged to the family in this corner house.

(bottom) Depau Row (1829–1830), south side of Bleecker Street, between Thompson and Sullivan streets, in 1896. Depau Row was one of the city's first uniform blockfronts or terraces.

In the 1820s, two trees had been planted in front of each house on Bond Street, and, by the 1850s, their foliage was so dense in summer that only the stoops of the houses and gaslights could be seen easily from carriages in the street.

One block to the south, Bleecker Street was not so well known as Bond Street in the decades before the Civil War, but it was more significant to the architectural history of the city's row houses. In 1826 Isaac G. Pearson purchased the building lots on both sides of Bleecker Street, between Mercer and Greene streets, for $400 to $600 a lot. Renaming the block Le Roy Place, in honor of the prominent New Yorker Jacob Le Roy, Pearson built two fine rows of elegant houses on each side of the street. Built in a simple Federal style, the Le Roy Place houses had showy granite fronts and sold for a then-staggering $11,000 to $12,000 each. An 1827 real estate advertisement for the then-just-completed Le Roy Place houses gave a rare description of their plan and appointments.

> FOR SALE OR TO LET, The elegant block of 3 story granite Houses, in Bleecker st. near Broadway. The lots are 25 by 100, and 25 by 125, and the Houses are 25 x 50 feet each; they are built in the most substantial and best manner, and are to be finished with plate glass, iron balconies, and piazzas to parlour windows, with marble chimney pieces in each story, mahogany sliding doors in the 1st, and folding doors in the 2d stories; 1st and 2d floors deafened and laid with narrow plank, pantries, wardrobes, drawers and shelves in each story; the garrets will be divided into bed rooms, entirely finished with hard walls, and the house will be completed with blinds, grates, bells, and every possible convenience by the first of May next. There are spacious vaults front and rear, with large cisterns and wells of excellent water in the yards; court yards in front to be enclosed with iron railings.

Le Roy Place was vitally important to the history of the New York row house as the first planned monumental blockfront in the city. Isaac G. Pearson purposefully built the houses with a unified, impressive blockfront. An excerpt from the just-quoted 1827 real estate advertisement reads:

> The block extends from Mercer to Greene sts., and it is intended to erect a block of Houses on the opposite side of Bleecker st. in a corresponding style, so placed as to make a distance of 80 feet between the two fronts, and one of the handsomest places for an elegant and genteel residence in the city.

The houses were set back a uniform ten feet from the front lot line—leaving each house with a small front yard and giving the street a feeling of greater width and a more dignified scale than available in the usual crosstown street. In an 1831 print of one side of Le Roy Place, drawn by the architect Alexander Jackson Davis, the row houses are identical, except for two houses in the center which are taller than the others and step out a few feet from the blockfront. On all the houses, a continuous areaway fence, balconies for the tall second-story windows, and a classically inspired balustrade at

(top) Le Roy Place (late 1820s), north and south sides of Bleecker Street, between Mercer and Greene streets, in 1831. Le Roy Place was the first planned monumental blockfront or terrace in New York.

(bottom) Bond Street, In 1857, View from Broadway to the Bowery. In the 1830s and 1840s, the Bond Street area probably was the city's most desirable neighborhood. Elegant row houses and mansions, sometimes with showy marble or granite fronts, lined the serene tree-lined streets and cost a then-staggering $20,000 to $30,000. Today Bond Street is a run-down light manufacturing area. Only a handful of decrepit houses survive among the lofts, warehouses, and parking lots of the bustling streets.

the roofline enforce the visual unity and monumentality of this blockfront. On the other side of the street, the houses formed a uniform but nonetheless impressive blockfront.

Several blocks away, on the south side of Bleecker Street, between Sullivan and Thompson streets, Depau Row (1829–1830) was another early monumental streetscape in New York. Built by Francis Depau, a merchant, and attributed to architect Samuel Dunbar, the restrained Depau Row houses formed a uniform blockfront united at the second floor with a continuous verandah. An 1833 real estate advertisement for "that valuable house and lot, known as No. 146 Bleecker street," in Depau Row stated:

> The building is 25 feet, front and rear, and 54 feet deep. The lot is 125 feet deep. The house was erected in 1830, in the most elegant, and substantial manner, and is three stories high, of brick and a slated roof. There is a building in the rear containing a tea room and a library, and a well and cistern in the yard. The house is every way calculated for a large and fashionable private family.

New Yorkers in the 1830s admired the planned regularity of the Le Roy Place and Depau Row blockfronts. The fine houses of Le Roy Place, observed a guidebook to New York in the 1830s, "afford a new evidence of the surprising improvements visible in the city" and "have a uniform color, and present an imposing appearance." By then, New Yorkers had begun to tire of the usual street built up haphazardly, "wherein each [house] is of different height and composed of different materials."

New Yorkers also began to admire the width and rectangular layout of streets in the Bond Street area as an improvement over the jumble of streets in much of Manhattan south of Houston Street. "The streets in the lower and older portion of the city are very narrow and crooked, and what is more immediately inexcusable, are kept in very bad order," wrote a British traveler around 1820. "The more modern streets are greatly superior in every respect; they are in general wide and straight, and the footwalks comparatively free from projections and encumbrances." The irregular streets of the West Village, which today form a pleasant contrast with the ubiquitous grid, were old-fashioned to early-nineteenth-century New Yorkers.

Bond and Bleecker streets were just two of the elegant streets in the Bond Street area. Fine row houses lined Great Jones Street, the next street to the north, although several carriage houses for houses on adjacent Bond Street somewhat marred the street's fashion. Originally Jones Street, it was renamed Great Jones Street in the 1830s, apparently a more impressive name to the residents. After the diarist Philip Hone regretfully, but profitably, sold his house, No. 235 Broadway, opposite City Hall Park, he lived at No. 1 Great Jones Street, a marble-front mansion at the southeast corner of Broadway, from 1838 until his death in 1851. Other fashionable residential streets in the Bond Street area were East Fourth Street, Lafayette Place, St. Marks Place, and Broadway itself.

No. 69 Downing Street (*ca.* 1830), near Varick Street, Greenwich Village, in 1915. Surrounded by tenements and a vacant lot, this narrow row house evokes a charming sense of pastness in its shuttered windows and decaying stone stoop.

The Bond Street area's years of residential fashion sadly were fleeting. By the late 1840s, elegant shops and hotels began to replace the fine dwellings along Broadway in the Bond Street area and marked the beginning of the area's decline as a residential neighborhood. "The mania for converting Broadway into a street of shops is greater than ever," wrote Philip Hone in 1850. "There is scarcely a block in the whole extent of this fine street of which some part is not in a state of transmutation." Fleeing this unwanted commercial intrusion, the rich and socially elect families abandoned their by-then-old-fashioned dwellings in the Bond Street area for the showy "brownstone-fronts" of Fifth Avenue and Madison Square. "Broadway has not much to boast of in its houses, and the dearness of land, and the noise and bustle of the great thoroughfare having driven all the wealth and fashion which centered there, into Fifth and Second Avenues, and the neighboring cross streets," observed one magazine in 1847. "It must depend for its embellishments upon the club-houses, theatres, and hotels, which, in a few years, will line it from one end to the other."

By the 1850s, one magazine observed that "Bond and Bleeker [*sic*] streets, that were then the *ultima thule* of aristocracy, are now but plebian streets." Bond Street then was renowned for its many dentists' offices. "The number of teeth that are pulled out or 'filled' in Bond Street, in one day, would afford a curious statistic," observed another magazine several years later. Nevertheless, "there still reside in it some of our best families. The houses are large . . . now held at princely prices."

After the Civil War, the Bond Street area lost all semblance of its patrician past. The elegant dwellings became "restaurants or private boarding-houses, barrooms or groceries, peculiar physicians' offices or midwives' headquarters." Other houses became sweatshops, lofts, or warehouses. "No street in the Metropolis has changed more than Bleecker," wrote one New Yorker in the late 1860s. "The grand mansions stand conspicuously in the thoroughfare, with a semblance of departed greatness, and an acknowledgement of surrendered splendor. The high stoops before which private carriages stopped, and emptied loads of feminine fragrance, the broad halls and airy drawing-rooms that were trodden by dainty feet, and filled with soft voices and voluptuous music, are profaned today by more common uses."

In the 1880s, the city extended Lafayette Place, originally several blocks long, from Great Jones Street south to the City Hall area—thus cutting a rude swath through the middle of Bond and Bleecker streets. Noisy wagons and, later, trucks rumbled through the once-serene streets of the Bond Street area. Soon after World War I, the last private dwellings on Bond Street succumbed to commercial usage.

When one knows of the Bond Street area's splendid past, a visit to the neighborhood today presents one with a shock. Le Roy Place now is the site of the huge Washington Square Village, and only a bedraggled handful of row houses survive on Bleecker, Bond, Great Jones, and East Fourth

No. 8 Grove Street (1829), Greenwich Village. Charming row houses like these on Grove Street must have inspired James Fenimore Cooper's often-quoted praise of New York's "second-rate genteel houses." In a New York of high-rise office and apartment buildings, traffic-clogged avenues, and screeching subways, the remaining nineteenth-century buildings maintain a needed variety of scale and recall our past for present and future generations.

streets. On Bond Street, for instance, only No. 26, with its elaborate fanlight doorway and dormer windows intact, recalls the street's past dignity. A few pathetic houses still stand at the Broadway and Bowery ends of the block—the basement and first floors converted into a store front or truck-loading platform. Other one-time dwellings wear the tawdry remodeled fronts of the 1920s and 1930s and retain only the width, height, and floor levels of a Federal style row house. On the north side of Bond Street, parking lots occupy the sites of recently demolished original row houses, whose pitched-roof profiles survive on the walls of adjacent eight-story-tall loft buildings. The few remaining Federal row houses on this and neighboring streets probably will meet the same fate.

By day, Bond Street and adjacent streets bustle with the activity of a warehouse and light manufacturing loft district. Noisy trucks line the curbs and clog the streets. Workers from garment lofts and machine shops hurry along the stained and cracked sidewalks—often dodging piles of refuse or trucks loading and unloading merchandise. Derelicts doze in doorways or weave along the sidewalks asking prosperous-looking pedestrians for a quarter.

In the midst of this decay and disorder, the Seabury Tredwell house at No. 29 East Fourth Street alone retains some of its original grandeur. Built in 1832, in a row of similar speculative dwellings, it was owned by the Tredwell family for just over one hundred years. The street front exhibits the rich Late Federal style once so prevalent in the area. The house retains its original Greek Revival interior, more up-to-date than the façade, as often was the case, and contains much of the family's original furniture. Saved by a foundation in the 1930s, at the death of the last Tredwell daughter, the house is now open to the public as the "Old Merchant's House."

The Charlton-King-Vandam Streets Area.

In pleasant contrast to the butchered Bond Street area, a fine concentration of Federal row houses survives on Charlton, King, and Vandam streets, just south of Houston Street. The north side of Charlton Street offers the longest unbroken streetscape of row houses from the 1820s and 1830s in New York. Here, better than any block in the city, one sees the unconscious visual unity of the early-nineteenth-century streetscape. Then such modest houses usually were built in one's and two's by different architect-builders, without any conscious attempt to correspond to neighboring houses or form a monumental streetscape. The doorways and stoop iron work of the houses differ in design, the windows and doors are on differing levels, and the varying cornice line emphasizes the different heights of the houses. Despite the differences in the individual houses, the streetscape gains a unity and dignity from the warm red-brick fronts, the modest brownstone or white-marble doorway and window details, and the three-story-tall human scale of these houses.

No. 4 St. Marks Place (1831–1832). Only the ornamental stone molding remains on this Late Federal fanlight doorway. The stone steps leading to the front door have been worn down by thousands of feet in the past 140 years. In 1969 the city's Landmarks Preservation Commission designated the building a landmark to protect it from further alterations or demolition. The "DO NOT USE THESE STAIRS FOR SITTING, ETC." disappeared when the stoop was painted blue in 1972.

Today, the Charlton-King-Vandam streets area reflects remarkable unity as a neighborhood and a separateness from the surrounding blocks—a quality traced to the history of these three streets. These three blocks are the remnants of a larger, but nevertheless distinct, area, originally bounded by Greenwich Street, then the Hudson River, King Street, Macdougal Street, and Vandam Street. In the late eighteenth and early nineteenth century, the Richmond Hill mansion sat on a four-hundred-foot-high hill, with gardens, meadows, and woods, overlooking the Hudson River. Undoubtedly it was one of the finest country estates in eighteenth-century New York. Richmond Hill served as George Washington's temporary headquarters in the summer of 1776 and, for some years, was the residence of Vice President John Adams.

In the mid-1790s, Aaron Burr, then Vice President to John Adams, purchased Richmond Hill, and his entertainments there were among the most lavish in the city at that time. By then, the northward growth of the city already approached the Houston Street area, and a road parallel to present-day Greenwich Street led directly to the still-small New York City to the south. In 1797 Aaron Burr filed a still-extant map that plotted today's Charlton, King, and Vandam streets and divided the six-acre estate into the twenty-five-foot by one-hundred-foot building lots then standard in the city. After his notorious duel with Alexander Hamilton in the same year, Aaron Burr left New York in disgrace, and John Jacob Astor held the estate for him. In 1817 Astor purchased the estate from Burr and proceeded to develop the property. The Richmond Hill mansion was moved to the southeast corner of Varick and Charlton streets, and its lofty hill was leveled. Building lots were laid out and sold to local architect-builders. Nearly all the surviving row houses in the area were erected in the early- and mid-1820s by these builders on speculation rather than for their family residences. The original residents of Charlton, King, and Vandam streets were prosperous builders, lawyers, and merchants—the latter group usually dealing in foodstuffs at the wharves on the Hudson River, then just west of Greenwich Street. The Richmond Hill mansion became a theater in 1831, later a circus, a menagerie, a tavern, and was demolished in 1849.

In the late nineteenth and early twentieth centuries, large industrial buildings invaded nearby streets of row houses, but these three blocks of Charlton, King, and Vandam streets between Varick Street and Sixth Avenue always retained a well-kept residential character. "Vandam Street . . . is an old-fashioned residence street," wrote one New Yorker in the 1890s, "and the well-kept three-story houses, with their polished door plates and brass knockers, are occupied by their owners, most of whom were born in them. It is a typical street of old Greenwich Village. There is scarcely any traffic, and the street is quiet and orderly." At the turn of the century, Montgomery Schuyler recalled Cooper's praise of the city's "second-rate genteel houses" in the 1820s and declared that "the nearest approach that remains to . . . the second-rate genteel houses of 1825 . . . are two rows, one in Vandam street and one in

Charlton, between Macdougal and Varick, in blocks which not so very long ago were lined with like houses from end to end and gave an impression of decorum and refinement for which one would search any more modern quarter entirely in vain." In dramatic contrast to the thundering traffic of lower Sixth Avenue and factory-lined Varick Street, these serene, fashionable blocks are a pleasing oasis of a simpler and quieter past in the midst of the modern city.

Greenwich Village.

Greenwich Village contains nearly all the city's surviving Federal style row houses, except for the Charlton-King-Vandam streets area to the south and Brooklyn Heights. In the mid-eighteenth century today's Greenwich Village became an area of fashionable country estates, known as "Greenwich," following the purchase of a large tract of land by the socially prominent Captain Peter Warren. By the 1780s and 1790s, some merchants and bankers who built summer houses in the area, by then sufficiently settled to be called "Greenwich Village," began living there the year around to escape the rapidly increasing commotion and crowding of Lower Manhattan.

Greenwich Village's city growth began with the yellow-fever epidemic of 1822, a recurring event in nineteenth-century New York. "The malignant or yellow fever generally commences in the confined parts of the town, near the waterside, in the month of August or September," wrote one British visitor after the 1805 epidemic.

> As soon as this dreadful scourge makes its appearance in New York, the inhabitants shut up their shops, and fly from their houses into the country. Those who cannot go far, on account of business, remove to Greenwich, a small village situated on the border of the Hudson river, about two or three miles from town. Here the merchants and others have their offices, and carry on their concerns with little danger from the fever, which does not seem to be contagious beyond a certain distance. The banks and other public offices also remove their business to this place; and markets are regularly established for the supply of the inhabitants.

Unlike earlier years, New Yorkers panicked in the 1822 epidemic. For the first time in memory, the yellow fever broke out on the presumably healthy Hudson River side of town, near Rector Street, rather than in the run-down, crowded streets along the East River. The city government declared the area below City Hall an "infected district" and evicted all persons from their houses there who had not fled the city already. Greenwich Village filled with refugees overnight. "Hundreds of wooden homes were reared up in a twinkling and even Sunday put no stop to the sound of the hammer or the saw," wrote one astonished Englishman. Although there was some talk of abandoning New York altogether and building another city at Greenwich Village, nearly all the sojourning businesses and families returned to Lower Manhattan in October with the first frost and the end of the epidemic.

Greenwich Village never was the same after the 1822 epidemic and the flood of refugees. Temporary wooden dwellings, put up that summer, now housed laborers and immigrants. In any event, the Village's countrified setting would have been short-lived. By the early 1820s, the city's growth had reached Houston Street, and Greenwich Village was next to undergo development, particularly today's West Village which was accessible to Lower Manhattan by a road to the Battery.

In the citywide building boom of the 1820s and 1830s, row house construction quickly marched north of Houston Street along lower Sixth Avenue and Hudson Street and started to fill in the winding West Village blocks. Local architect-builders erected modest Federal row houses, singly or in small groups, for craftsmen, sailmakers, and shopkeepers whose place of business was a convenient few blocks west at the Hudson River or east along Sixth Avenue. "Greenwich is now no longer a country village," wrote one newspaper in 1825. "Such has been the growth of our city that the building of one block more will completely connect the two places; and in three years time, at the rate buildings have been erected the last season, Greenwich will be known only as a part of the city, and the suburbs will be beyond it." During the continuing growth of the 1840s and 1850s, some substantial row houses and several impressive streetscapes in the then-fashionable Greek Revival and Italianate styles were built within its crooked byways. Although tenements invaded the area in the late nineteenth century, and the construction of the Seventh Avenue IRT subway forced the cutting of Seventh Avenue South through the old street network, hundreds of well-kept early and mid-nineteenth-century row houses still survive in Greenwich Village.

The Decline of the Federal Style.

The decline of the Federal style's popularity was gradual. Around 1830 builders adopted the Late Federal style for costly row houses—although modest row houses continued to appear in a Federal style into the 1830s. In Late Federal dwellings—such as the Old Merchant's House on East Fourth Street—large Ionic colonettes, which flank the front door and support the fanlight window, herald the emergence of the Greek Revival style. By the early 1830s, fine row houses were built in what already was regarded as the more sophisticated Greek Revival style.

Federal style row houses once covered most of Manhattan below Washington Square, but the city's awesome growth and rebuilding has spared only a handful of these houses. The lovingly maintained Federal houses in Greenwich Village or the pathetic survivors of Bond Street give only a hint of the beauty and order of entire blocks built in this modest and yet elegant style. They are well worth seeking out as gracious reminders of a more orderly, self-confident era of architectural simplicity and good taste.

Nos. 21–23 Washington Square North (1835–1836), Greenwich Village. The Greek Revival style mansions on the north side of Washington Square are some of the finest nineteenth-century row houses remaining in New York. These buildings epitomize the elegance of the Greek Revival style—in their freestanding columned doorway porches, smooth red brick fronts, and fine iron work exhibiting the anthemion and Greek key.

Chapter Two

Greek Revival Style

Emergence of the Greek Revival Style in New York.

In 1832 a now-unknown architect-builder completed a row of several houses on East Fourth Street, just west of the Bowery, of which the Seabury Tredwell house, or Old Merchant's House, is the only survivor. Despite its grand scale and elaborate ornamentation typical of the Late Federal style, the Seabury Tredwell house was part of the declining Federal tradition. By the early 1830s, a new era in the architectural history of the city's row houses already had dawned.

Around the corner on Lafayette Place, Seth Geer had begun the spectacular "Colonnade Row," nine houses in the Greek Revival style, faced with white marble and united by a monumental two-story colonnade running the length of the row. A few blocks to the west on Washington Square, three architect-builders worked on thirteen palatial row houses along the north side of the newly opened park. Although these thirteen red-brick houses, known as "The Row," lacked the avowedly Classical white-marble façades and colonnade of the Colonnade Row, they clearly expressed the newly fashionable Greek Revival style in the fluted Doric columns of the doorway porches and in the Greek motifs on the iron front fences. The Colonnade Row on Lafayette Place and The Row along Washington Square North were among the very earliest examples of the Greek Revival style in New York City and set a high standard of taste and opulence in city row houses perhaps unequaled anywhere in nineteenth-century America.

With these splendid inspirations, New York architects and architect-builders abandoned the Federal and Late Federal styles for the fashionable Greek Revival. In these years of rapid population growth, unparalleled prosperity, and, hence, much construction in the city, row houses, expensive and inexpensive alike, adopted the handsome Greek Revival forms and ornament, and public buildings and even churches displayed Greek temple porticoes. The triumph of the Greek Revival style was so complete in New York that one English resident declared in 1834:

> The Greek mania here is at its height, as you infer from the fact that everything is a Greek temple from the privies in the back court, through the various grades of prison, theatre, church, custom-house, and state-house.

This sudden and nationwide "mania" completely dominated American architecture from the late 1820s to the late 1840s. It swept from the East Coast into the Mid-West as far as Iowa and Wisconsin, and was especially well received in the deep South. So strong was the sway of ancient Greece and Classical antiquity that by the end of the rage the United States had gained not only countless Greek Revival structures all over the nation but also fifteen Romes, twelve Carthages and twenty-seven Troys!

An Age of Revivals.

The Greek Revival style introduced an age of revivals to American architecture which lasted for several decades. Although the Greek Revival row house was similar in appearance to the Federal, its design expressed a far different aesthetic intent. Rather than relying on the pleasing proportion, handsome materials, and modest ornament of the Classical tradition, as did the Federal style, the Greek Revival, and indeed all revival styles, self-consciously recalled a distant time or place and its architecture. A revival style tried to evoke an "association" that stimulated the emotions. For Andrew Jackson Downing, noted landscape gardener and sometime architect, revival styles provided,

> another source of pleasure to most minds, which springs not from beauty of form or expression in these styles but from personal or historical *associations* connected with them; and which, by a process half-addressed to the feelings and half to the intellect, makes them in the highest degree interesting.

By replacing "beauty of form or expression" as an architectural standard with "personal or historical *associations*," the revival style rejected the Classical tradition's idea that forms were beautiful only in themselves and, instead, accepted the Romantic movement's concept that forms were beautiful for the emotions they evoked.

Although Greek Revival buildings rarely employed the "picturesque" asymmetrical massing and rich ornament of the Romantic movement in architecture, the association with an ancient Greece, so tantalizingly distant in time and place, made it as much a part of the Romantic tradition as the picturesquely massed and ornamented Gothic Revival country house or church. In 1835 Philip Hone described the moonlit appearance of a Greek Revival style hotel he owned in Rockaway, Long Island, in Romantic terms.

> The view was unspeakably grand. The broad red moon, setting over the tops of the mountains of Neversink, threw a solemn light over the unruffled face of the ocean, and the lofty columns of the noble piazza, breaking the silver streams of light into dark and gloomy shadows, gave the edifice the appearance of some relic of classical antiquity.

The age of revivals dominated American architecture well into the Civil War era, and the architect's imagination knew no bounds in the search for stirring associations and picturesque forms. In the 1860s the respected architect Alexander Jackson Davis offered to execute designs for country houses in these styles:

the American Log Cabin, Farm Villa, English Cottage, Collegiate Gothic, Manor House, French Suburban, Swiss Chalet, Swiss Mansion, Lombard Italian, Tuscan from Pliny's Villa at Ostia, Ancient Etruscan, Suburban Greek, Oriental, Moorish, Round and Castellated.

Nevertheless, in New York, the Greek Revival style dominated row house architecture in the 1830s and 1840s for practical, as well as emotional, reasons.

Background to the Greek Revival Style.

The Greek Revival style was the culmination of an interest in Classical antiquities which emerged in the middle of the eighteenth century. Archaeological discoveries in Italy provided the impetus. Excavations at Pompeii and Herculaneum, begun in 1735 and 1755, gave eighteenth-century Europe its first view of life in Classical antiquity and focused attention on ancient Rome and, through Rome, on ancient Greece.

Archaeologists, many of them also architects, published the results of their discoveries. In Great Britain, for instance, The Society of the Dilettanti sponsored the publication of Stuart and Revett's *Antiquities of Athens,* Richard Chandler's *Ionian Antiquities,* Robert Wood's *Ruins of Palmyra* and *Ruins of Balbec,* and Robert Adams' *Ruins of the Palace of the Emperor Diocletian at Spalatro.* Especially influential to the Greek Revival was James "Athenian" Stuart's and Nicholas Revett's four-volume *Antiquities of Athens,* published between 1762 and 1816, a detailed study of ancient ruins in Greece with numerous illustrations and restorations. From this and similar books, British and American architects frequently borrowed details for their designs and builder's guides. Minard Lafever wrote of the *Antiquities of Athens* that "perhaps there are none superior to it," and Alexander Jackson Davis declared that "this is a work of great value indeed, and quite indispensable to the architect."

International interest in ancient Greece increased in the early nineteenth century after Lord Elgin, British ambassador to Turk-held Greece, received permission in 1801 to take "a few blocks of marble with inscriptions and figures" from the Acropolis. With several hundred men and part of the British fleet in the Mediterranean, Lord Elgin removed almost all of the sculptured metopes, the frieze, and the tympanum from the Parthenon and also part of the front porch and a caryatid from the Erectheum. His loot, the "Elgin Marbles," excited a widespread interest in ancient Greece among educated men throughout Europe and the United States.

The Greek War for Independence from the Turks (1821–1824) evoked international sympathy for the Greek patriots and kindled even greater interest in the civilization of ancient Greece, especially in America, itself only recently freed from foreign domination. The death of the Romantic poet Byron in that war in 1823 also focused worldwide attention on the struggle.

Emergence of the Greek Revival Style in the United States.

Since the early eighteenth century, American architects had worked with classical designs of Renaissance and, then, of direct Roman inspiration. In 1785 Thomas Jefferson, with the aid of the French architect-archaeologist Charles-Louis Clerisseau had designed the Virginia State Capitol, closely modeled on the Maison Carrée, a first century A.D. Roman temple at Nîmes. Then ambassador to France, Jefferson wrote that the Maison Carrée "is allowed without contradiction to be the most perfect and precious remain of antiquity in existence." The Virginia State Capitol was the first monumental building in the United States to be modeled on an entire temple. William Thornton's 1791 design for the United States Capitol at Washington, D.C., also revealed an ancient Roman inspiration in the shallow dome of the Rotunda modeled after the dome of the Pantheon at Rome and in the Roman hemicycle form of the Senate and House of Representatives chambers.

Even in the eighteenth century many Americans were familiar with the architecture of ancient Greece, for as early as 1770 the Carpenter's Company of Philadelphia owned a copy of Stuart and Revett's *Antiquities of Athens,* a book also in Thomas Jefferson's library. At that time scholars throughout the world considered ancient Greek architecture and culture an offshoot of the Roman. Accordingly, architects neglected Greek motifs until the German archaeologist Winckelmann proved beyond doubt that, in fact, Greek culture and architecture had profoundly influenced that of ancient Rome. For this and other reasons, American attitudes in the 1820s had become highly favorable toward the Greek Revival.

Architects and government leaders had begun to look for a style with more "American" and more democratic connotations than the Federal style, too specifically British in its origins. American nationalism was on the rise and increasingly dictated a casting off of all remnants from our colonial past. American nationalism was stimulated by the successful defense of American independence in the War of 1812 and by the surge in nationalism in the Western world following the French Revolution and Napoleon's final defeat at Waterloo.

By the 1820s, the once-fashionable Roman influence in architecture had lost favor with many Americans. Napoleon had used the Roman triumphal arches, fasces, and eagles in his Empire style. A style associated with the despot Napoleon and imperial Rome was unsuitable for the new American republic and its democratic ideals. The Roman mode appeared even less appropriate with the opening of the frontier and the beginning of the Populist movement, which would flower into Jacksonian democracy. The Greek Revival style, on the other hand, recalled the democratic city states of ancient Greece and, in its simple forms and spare ornament, was a style that could be appreciated by all Americans. "The two great truths of the world," wrote Nicholas Biddle of

Andalusia and Bank of the United States fame, "are the Bible and Grecian architecture."

The Second Bank of the United States (1819–1924) in Philadelphia was the first building where the entire front of a Greek temple was copied completely and therefore is regarded as the first fully developed American example of the Greek Revival style. Designed by William Strickland, this large, marble-faced bank had Doric porticoes, inspired by the Parthenon at Athens, and marked the first great triumph of the Greek Revival style over the Federal style and Roman influence of the early nineteenth century. Visitors to Philadelphia described the Bank as "chaste," "noble," "majestic," and often considered it the most beautiful building in the United States at that time.

The Greek Revival Style in New York.

During the 1820s, Greek Revival motifs occasionally appeared on churches or commercial buildings in New York—notably Martin E. Thompson's Phoenix Bank (1825) on Wall Street, his Church of the Ascension (1827–1829) on Canal Street, Josiah R. Brady's Second Unitarian Church (1826) at Mercer and Prince streets, and Ithiel Town's Bowery Theater (1825).

Greek Revival touches also appeared on occasional New York row houses in the late 1820s. An 1829 elevation drawing by Martin Thompson shows a Greek Revival doorway porch of Doric columns and an entablature on an otherwise Federal style row house. An 1827 real estate advertisement for a 3 story House, being one of the range of 12 houses now erecting . . . [on] *Fourth-street, opposite to Washington square"* stated that "the fronts and rears of the whole range are to be finished in the same style as the front of the Bowery Theatre." These fine dwelling houses on the south side of Washington Square had Greek Revival doorways with flat pilasters and entablatures with laurel wreaths and the distinctly Federal style pitched roof with dormer windows.

New York was slower to adopt the Greek Revival style on a large scale than other big cities, mainly due to the conservative influence of such architects in the Classical tradition as John McComb. The city's architect-builders also were slow to abandon the Federal style to which their workmen and their cautious house-buying customers had become accustomed.

Several years before Greek Revival style row houses were constructed in New York in the early 1830s, designs in that style, mainly ornamental and detail work, did appear in American builder's guides. The sixth edition of Asher Benjamin's *American Builder's* Companion (1827) pictured several Greek ornamental details. Figure No. 5 of Minard Lafever's *The Young Builder's General Instructor* (1829) was a "Grecian" front doorway, which consisted of fluted Greek Doric columns on each side of the door which, together with pilasters at each side, support a flat entablature. This handsome "Grecian doorway" was a popular form on the city's costly row houses.

Nos. 20–26 Willow Street (*ca.* 1846), Brooklyn Heights. These row houses in the secluded northern section of Brooklyn Heights show the austerity of the row house façade so highly valued in the Greek Revival years. Window lintels and sills barely break the planar brick front. The protruding doorway enframement and stoop railings, by contrast, point out the simplicity and planar smoothness of the street front.

Alexander Jackson Davis claimed in his daybook that he introduced the Greek Revival style to New York dwellings in a row of houses on Bleecker Street. Whether or not this is so, Davis' work in the 1820s and 1830s played a large part in the style's acceptance. The monumental Colonnade Row on Lafayette Place, begun in 1832 and often attributed to Davis, dramatically showed the elegance of the Greek Revival style for row houses, as did the thirteen red-brick row houses begun in 1831 on Washington Square North, east of Fifth Avenue, whose architect is not definitely known.

The Greek Revival Style: The Row House Front.

At first glance, the Greek Revival row house front appeared to be nearly identical to that of the Federal style. Like the Federal dwelling, the Greek Revival row house had the warm red-brick façade, set off by brownstone or white-marble trim, and relied on the contrasts of these materials and on the pleasing proportions of the street front and its parts for architectural effect. Unlike the vernacular Federal style, the Greek Revival was a thoroughly self-conscious and much-thought-about style. Once architects and architect-builders deliberately evoked associations of ancient Greece in New York row houses, they also built the impressive house and streetscape suitable to the increasingly powerful city and its well-to-do residents.

Only a close examination of the street front revealed the several differences between a Federal and Greek Revival style row house. The Greek Revival row house sought a greater dignity and monumentality than the Federal row house. Higher ceilings made for a taller, hence more impressive, house, and a full third floor replaced the pitched roof and dormer window arrangement of earlier years. "A style less tawdry and more in consonance with the rules of good taste has been introduced," reported one newspaper in 1833. "These ugly projections from the roofs, called dormant [*sic*] windows, which in many streets disfigure almost every private building, have been generally banished from the new edifices." The flat roofline also was thought to make for a more impressive house and streetscape than the dormer window treatment. "To judge of our principal street, Broadway, you would think that the first object with every person about to build, had been to measure with his eye the houses adjacent and take care to order his to be several inches higher or lower than his neighbor's," observed one newspaper in 1828. "But in those [houses] now erecting, or lately erected, this old, ugly, and absurd custom is avoided."

A unity of the street front characterized the Greek Revival row house beyond the flat roofline and emerging concern for a unified streetscape appearance. To enhance the large, smooth expanses of the row house front, lampblack was mixed with the mortar to minimize the joints between bricks. The rectangular window lintels and sills were simple in form and spare in ornament and were almost

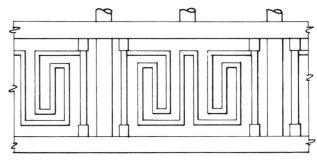

(top left) Anthemion. This stylized honeysuckle motif appears on iron work and interior ornament of Greek Revival style houses.

(top right) Greek Key or Fret, another decorative motif.

(bottom left) Doorway, No. 410 West 20th Street (1839–1840), Chelsea. The usual Greek Revival doorway—a single-paneled door, plain rectangular sidelights and toplight, and flat pilaster and horizontal entablature enframement in brownstone.

(bottom right) Doorway, No. 4 Washington Square North (1832–1833). The freestanding doorway porch, with fluted columns supporting a heavy horizontal entablature, appeared only on the finest houses.

flush with the façade. Only the projection of the door enframement and stoop broke the planar unity of the row house front, and the severity of the door enframement and the rich ornament of the stoop iron work enhanced the monumentality of the street front by pointing out its smoothness.

The Greek Revival row house evidenced a simplicity of forms and ornament which, architectural theory then declared, alone could be grasped easily by the mind. The difference between the elaborate Late Federal doorway, marked by a many-paneled door and leaded fanlight and side windows, and the plain, rectangular transom and single-panel door of the Greek Revival doorway epitomized the emergence of the pervasive ideal of architectural simplicity. Under these ideals, New York's once-admired City Hall with its rich Classical ornament was scorned. City Hall, according to one newspaper in the 1830s, was "deformed with a mass of gingerbread," and a visitor to the city in the 1840s, declared that its "architecture . . . is thought by many to be faulty. . . . The prevailing defect is the absence of simplicity and grandeur." On the other hand, a magazine in Philadelphia admired that city's Second Bank of the United States because the viewer "is forcibly struck with the grand appearance of the front and the unity and *entireness of view* under which it is presented to him. The platform with its gradation of steps, the massive yet well-proportioned columns, the long line of entablature, and surmounting pediment, are embraced by the eye at the first glance."

In New York row houses, the Greek Revival style, it has been noted, first appeared in the late 1820s in the front doorways of otherwise Federal style dwellings as delicate Ionic colonettes which separated the door from the sidelights and supported the architrave and a lacy toplight. When the Greek Revival style first appeared on large row houses around 1830, a handsome doorway porch consisted of freestanding and generally fluted Doric or Ionic columns supporting a heavy horizontal entablature. The Doric order was preferred to the Ionic because of its massive scale and simple forms, and from a picturesque standpoint, Minard Lafever admired the Doric order for "the bewitching variety of light and shade."

The high cost of cutting fluted columns and building a freestanding porch limited this doorway treatment to only the finest row houses. In most row houses, the doorway treatment consisted of rectangular pilasters set flat against the façade and supporting a horizontal entablature scaled to the pilasters. Sometimes, a triangular pediment replaced the conventional horizontal entablature and an "anthemion," a honeysuckle motif, or a "palmette," a stylized palm frond, projected from the peak of the pediment as an "acroterion." On some houses of the 1840s, the outside edge of the doorway pilaster sloped outward as it neared the base—hinting the ancient Egyptian "battered wall" effect— and protruding "Greek ears" usually marked the top corners of the enframement. The rectangular pilaster was a far simpler form for the builders' workmen to execute than the ideal freestanding and *(top left)* Iron Work Advertisement, 1846. This advertisement shows the various factory-made house parts available to builders in the 1840s. By the late 1840s, the Italianate influence and its rounded forms already were replacing the Greek Revival style in row house iron work.

(top right) Cast-Iron Wreaths around small attic windows on West 20th Street. An attractive ornament rarely encountered today.

(bottom) Cast-Iron Verandah, No. 3 Gramercy Park West (*ca.* 1850). This verandah or porch, attributed to architect Alexander Jackson Davis, employs the entire repertoire of Greek Revival ornament with dazzling richness.

fluted column and because of its construction economy, as well as the beauty of this form, saw far greater use than the freestanding doorway porch, which inspired it.

On some dwellings, the doorway enframement simply was four wood boards nailed together, but usually it was of the local brownstone or a light-color limestone, granite, or marble. In the 1820s, a costly pale gray stone was preferred to brownstone for doorway porches and window trim. Because of its softness and the proximity of quarries to New York, brownstone was an inexpensive building material in the city, and, for reasons of economy, modest Greek Revival row houses employed brownstone rather than the "correct," but costly, marble.

Architectural fashion changed by the early 1840s. Under the ascendant Romantic movement, "picturesque" dark colors were fashionable, and brownstone replaced light-colored marble for doorway and window enframements on most dwellings in the 1840s. "The flights of steps at the front doors, of a reddish brown sandstone . . . have a remarkably handsome appearance. Sometimes they are to be seen, at every successive door, along an extensive street," wrote one admiring English traveler in the 1840s.

In the Greek Revival row house, a recessed doorway enhanced the monumentality of the street front by introducing a dramatic recessed dark volume to the otherwise flat and modestly ornamented front. The recessed doorway also offered a sheltered space for visitors between the outdoors and the interior of the house. The doorway reflected a simplicity of form so valued by architectural ideals of the era and was intended to complement the broad expanses of the street front. The richly detailed leaded fanlight and sidelights, characteristic of the Federal doorway, disappeared with the advent of the Greek Revival row house. The transom, which replaced the fanlight doorway, and the sidelights were plain panes of glass separated by wood muntin bars. In another simplification of form, the door was a single vertical panel, two vertical panels, or three horizontal panels, usually edged with an egg-and-dart molding, rather than the six- and eight-panel doors of the Federal style row houses.

Despite an impressive street front unity and simplicity of forms, the Greek Revival row house relied on handsome ornament for much of its aesthetic impact. The most popular motifs were the "fret," or Greek key; the acanthus leaf; and the "anthemion," the stylized honeysuckle. The decorative repertoire also included the "meander," an endless fret design; the "guilloche," a border of two or more bands interlaced in a repeating pattern; floral forms in double relief, usually a rosette with a slender, several-inch foliate form extending above and below; the lyre; an upright obelisk; and sharp-pointed geometric cones.

Because it was easier to shape iron into elaborate forms than to carve them in stone, most ornament appeared in iron work, usually in the stoop railings and areaway fences. Some iron work

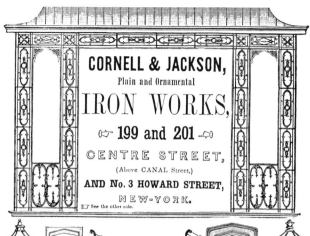

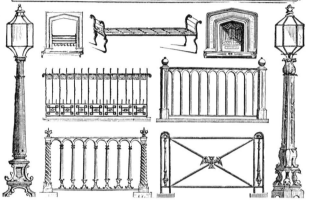

(top) No. 110 Second Avenue (1839). The last nineteenth-century residence on once-elegant lower Second Avenue. Notice the fine parlor window balcony.

(bottom left) Iron Work, detail from parlor window balcony, No. 21 Washington Square North (1835–1836). A handsome combination of the anthemion and the Greek key on a wheel, the classical symbol of eternity.

(bottom right) Iron Work, detail from parlor window balcony, No. 73 Washington Place (1847), Greenwich Village.

was hand-wrought, but machine-made casting became available in the 1830s and soon replaced the costly hand-wrought iron on all but the finest houses. In *Practice of Architecture* (1833), Asher Benjamin devoted a page to "a series of designs for Fences, Window Guards, &c." in handsome Federal and Greek Revival styles and, at this early date, declared that "in this construction a view was had to their being made of cast iron." By the 1840s, advertisements for factory-made stoop railings and front fences appeared in the New York and Brooklyn directories. The iron work illustrated in these advertisements survives on many houses throughout the city today.

Some of the most beautiful Greek Revival style iron work was on the parlor-window balcony, a feature introduced on New York row houses around 1830. The palatial Late Federal row houses often were built five or ten feet deeper than similar houses only a few years earlier to gain the large parlors suitable for entertaining, and parlor windows dropped to the floor to light and ventilate the large rooms. To shield the parlor from the sight of passersby on the street, the builder added a simple iron railing or "window guard" to the lower portion of each parlor window or a single several-foot-high balcony, protruding several feet from the façade and running between the two windows. With a larger area than the stoop railing or single window guardrailing, the two-window-wide balcony offered splendid opportunities for iron-work decoration, and most New York row houses had parlor windows that dropped to the floor and were shielded by the low iron balcony into the 1850s. Though most are gone because of decay and wartime scrap-iron drives, the few remaining parlor-window guards and balconies in Manhattan and Brooklyn show the iron work and Greek Revival decorative motifs in perhaps their most elaborate and imaginative forms.

The cornice enriched the plain street front and also defined the top of the row house, as the rusticated basement indicated the lower limit. The simplest cornice treatment was a flat horizontal board, known as a "fascia," across the full width of the house just below the roofline. Above the fascia board the builder usually added dentiled molding, an ornamental row of small toothlike blocks. The dentiled cornice often had another decorative molding such as the egg-and-dart, an eggshaped ornament alternating with a dartlike form, or the leaf-and-tongue, often combined with the bead-and-reel.

In the Federal style dwelling, dormer windows lit and ventilated the attic beneath the pitched roof. Despite appearances to the contrary, the Greek Revival row house had a slightly pitched or backward sloping roof and there was an attic, lit by small windows which unobtrusively pierce the fascia board of the cornice. These small windows, usually a single pane or two horizontal panes, usually do not survive on Greek Revival row houses in New York. To make the attic another fully usable and rentable floor, they have been enlarged over the years into small double-hung or casement

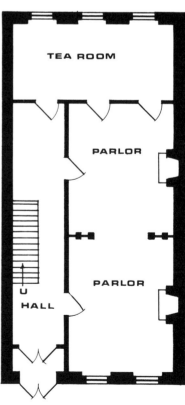

(top) Back Porches or Tearooms, Nos. 20–26 Willow Street (1846), Brooklyn Heights. A view of the "tearooms" that often appeared on New York row houses in the 1840s and 1850s.

(bottom left) Mantel, parlor, Columbia Heights, Brooklyn Heights. The black marble veined with gold so fashionable for Greek Revival mantels.

(bottom right) Plan, first floor, the double parlor and back porch or tearoom arrangement popular for New York row houses in the 1840s and 1850s.

windows, thus cutting into the ornamental cornice molding above and below the fascia board, or completely replaced by a full story added to the house. Cast-iron laurel wreaths sometimes encircled these small attic windows, and even ornamented a cornice without attic windows or the horizontal entablature of a doorway porch.

Ornamental iron work in New York row houses attained its fullest development in the ten- to twelve-foot-tall porches or verandahs across the width of the row house front. Slim vertical roof supports and several-foot-high railings employed Greek Revival style ornament with a freedom and richness rarely seen in the city's row houses at that time. Apparently at variance with the era's ideal of architectural severity, the lacy cast-iron of the verandah offered a pleasing contrast with the plain brick row house front and suggests that, by the 1840s, New Yorkers were tiring of the longstanding architectural restraint in the city's houses. These elaborate cast-iron verandahs also pointed out the degree to which machine technology served, and indeed shaped, row house architecture of the period.

These cast-iron verandahs appeared throughout New York State, Pennsylvania, and Ohio in the 1840s and 1850s but saw the most imaginative and widespread use in such Southern cities as Charleston, Savannah, Mobile, and particularly New Orleans. In New York, cast-iron verandahs also appeared on the Italianate style row houses of the 1850s.

The cast-iron verandah often was employed in New York on row houses in a *rus in urbs* setting. In an era which idealized the rugged countryside and nature, the verandahs denoted the countryside, even in the city, and were deemed particularly appropriate to row houses facing a park or with handsomely planted ten- to twenty-foot-deep front yards. Probably the finest remaining row house verandahs survive on Nos. 3–4 Gramercy Park West. Attributed to Alexander Jackson Davis, these verandahs employ a full repertoire of Greek Revival motifs with a dazzling richness.

Another sign of the rising Romantic appreciation for "natural" countryside was the "garden block" or "garden row." At the loss of back yard space, the houses in "garden rows" were set back twenty to thirty feet from the street. Occasionally, rows of earlier houses, such as Le Roy Place on Bleecker Street (1826–1827) or The Row on Washington Square North (1831–1833), were set back ten feet from the front lot line, but the architectural intent in these severely classical blockfronts was to enhance the monumentality of the row by making for a wider street. On the other hand, the deep front gardens of the 1840s and 1850s were intended to bring a feeling of picturesque countryside into the city and were part of the Romantic movement which replaced the Classical tradition in architecture.

Among the finest garden rows in the city was Rhinelander Gardens at Nos. 102–116 West Eleventh Street, just west of Sixth Avenue, in Greenwich Village. Built sometime after 1854 and attributed to (top) Parlors, Old Merchant's House. View from the formal dining room into the front parlor. With its unaltered rooms and original Tredwell family furniture, the Old Merchant's House offers a rare glimpse of the well-to-do New York family's house and lifestyle in the early nineteenth century.

(bottom left) Parlor Doors, Remsen Street, Brooklyn Heights.

(bottom right) Parlor Doors, Old Merchant's House. Notice the original wall-to-wall carpet and rich ceiling plasterwork.

James Renwick, Jr., the eight houses tragically were demolished in 1955 for the construction of P.S. 41. These notable basement-and-three-story-tall houses had deep gardens facing the street and elaborate cast-iron porches of Gothic Revival style design running the length of the row on all three stories of each house.

The Greek Revival Style: Row House Plan and Interior Design.

The New York row house of the 1830s and 1840s, except for several small changes for added comfort and grandeur, had the same floor plan that evolved in the 1820s—in the basement, a dining room in the front, kitchen in the back; on the first floor, front and back parlors, the back parlor occasionally used as a formal dining room; and, on the upper floors, bedrooms and servants' rooms. In one early change, the height of the basement ceiling increased from seven and seven-and-one-half feet to eight or nine feet. The front dining room was more spacious, the kitchen was cooler in summer than formerly, and a high basement raised the parlor floor farther from the street for a more impressive house. In the first-floor parlors, ceilings rose to eleven or twelve feet and, in the large houses, reached a spectacular fourteen feet. In the late 1820s, sliding parlor doors, which rolled out of sight into the walls on metal tracks, appeared in the lavish Greek Revival style parlors of otherwise Late Federal row houses and, within a few years, had replaced folding doors in the parlors of all but the simplest dwellings. Minard Lafever's *The Modern Builder's Guide* (1833) carried a design for sliding parlor doors, enframed by handsome flat pilasters and entablature, which appeared in many Greek Revival row houses in New York. The sliding parlor doors and high ceilings introduced a feeling of unusual spaciousness and a free flow of space between the front and back parlors.

In some fine row houses, a pair of Ionic or Corinthian columns, supporting a horizontal entablature, replaced the flat pilaster and entablature enframement for parlor doors. The Seabury Tredwell house at No. 29 East Fourth Street has this "screen of columns" as enframement for the sliding parlor doors. In other Greek Revival row houses, a double pair of columns replaced the sliding door and wall between the front and back parlors.

In the early nineteenth century, the stairway to the second floor occupied the back of the side hallway and was lit by a window at the landing between the first and second floors. In the 1830s, the stairway often was moved to the center of the hallway and lit by a skylight in the roof several floors above. When only identical front and back parlors occupied the first floor, this space at the back of the hallway might have been a butler's pantry to the back parlor, when used as a formal dining room, a small servant's stairway behind the centrally located main stairway, or a bathroom.

In the 1840s and 1850s, New York row houses sometimes had several-story-tall open galleries

(top) Lafayette Place, About 1866, View North from Great Jones Street. A verdant and tranquil Lafayette Place was the setting for the spectacular white marble Colonnade Row. Today, Lafayette·Place is a major north to south traffic artery, and trucks and cars race relentlessly past the area's shabby garages and loft buildings.

(bottom left) Front Parlor, West Eleventh Street. This relatively simple parlor in an 1840s row house is an interesting contrast with the resplendent double parlors of the Old Merchant's House.

(bottom right) Bedroom, second floor, Old Merchant's House, with original family furniture.

across the back of the house. On the first floor, French doors led from the splendid back parlor to the open porch, or a windowed porch known as the "tearoom." Because of the several windows overlooking the back yard, the tearoom did not appreciably diminish the light or ventilation in the back parlor. When these porches reached the second floor, they were open porches separated from adjacent porches by a brick wall. Many galleries or tearooms did not survive or, at best, sag and lean, because builders did not always build them upon as firm a foundation as the house proper.

The interior design of the Greek Revival row house continued the simple forms relieved by occasional rich ornament as seen on the street fronts. The wainscoting and wood paneling of the Federal style were gone; walls were of plaster painted a light color and relieved by simple baseboards, a plaster cornice at the ceiling, and perhaps a simple, unmolded chair rail around the room at waist height. The floors were of light-color wood planks, often one foot wide and one inch thick.

The doors usually were the most elaborate feature of the parlors. Each parlor door, usually mahogany or rosewood, had one large, deeply set panel or two long and narrow panels, impressive for the simple form and rich wood finish. The simplicity of the doors themselves point out the elaborate enframement. The pilasters which support the horizontal entablature had acanthus leaf capitals and, in many cases, an inset panel running the full length with applied Greek Revival detail, such as the anthemion. The horizontal entablature also displayed Greek Revival motifs, such as the anthemion and Greek key or several rows of egg-and-dart or dentiled molding. When the parlors employed a "screen" of Ionic or Corinthian columns, with or without the sliding parlor doors, the double parlors took on a richness and flamboyance hardly expected behind the severe street front.

Mantels were massive, severe, and in design resemble the usual doorway enframement of the flat pilaster and horizontal entablature. Only in the finest dwellings did columns or caryatids, rather than flat pilasters, support the mantel shelf. Applied or carved Greek Revival details occasionally ornamented the mantel's smooth surfaces, and the preferred material was marble, especially black marble veined with yellow or gold. In rooms other than the parlors, and in the parlors of small houses, the mantel was a white-gray marble, a slate oiled to appear as black marble, or ordinary painted wood. In the early Greek Revival row houses of the early- and mid-1830s, the mantels in rooms other than the parlors likely were the just-passing Federal style.

In the parlor, the ceiling decoration usually was a cornice of simple molding or two moldings enclosing a rounded cove and an ornate and heavy sculptured centerpiece in the center. The centerpieces varied from a simple circular molding to stylized foliate forms reaching out from a central rosette to an outer edge which varied from a plain molding to an elaborate arrangement of circular and polygonal forms within each other.

Eng.^d by J.F.Morin N.Y

(top left) Doorway, parlor, Old Merchant's House. A striking display of a fine mahogany door, plaster ceiling ornament, Ionic columns for parlor doorway enframement, and a fine carpet.

(top right) Ceiling Centerpiece or Rosette, Old Merchant's House. This centerpiece with its acanthus leaves and lush ornament reveals the richness which occasionally appeared on New York's generally restrained early-nineteenth-century row houses.

(bottom) Doors, from Minard Lafever's The Beauties of Modern Architecture, 1835. Notice the "battered" or outward sloping sides of the Egyptian influence which was popular on New York row houses in the 1840s and 1850s.

By the 1830s, ceiling cornices and centerpieces generally were larger and more boldly detailed than in earlier decades—partly to satisfy an emerging fashion for impressive dwellings and to complement the new scale of the high ceilings and larger rooms. "In adjusting the proportions of these cornices, the size and height of the rooms should be taken into consideration," wrote Asher Benjamin. With the higher ceilings and the greater distance between the viewer and the ceiling, ceiling plasterwork might be less precise in workmanship, as well as larger, than in earlier years. "When ornaments are liable to close inspection, every part should be well expressed and neatly furnished," warned Asher Benjamin, "but when their situation is such that they can be seen only at a distance, the nice finish may be omitted, but their details must be strongly expressed."

The handsome ceiling plasterwork of a Greek Revival row house often was machine-made, rather than handmade, and of papier maché or stucco, rather than plaster. Just as factory-made cast-iron replaced hand-wrought iron for stoop railings and areaway fences in the 1830s, steam-powered machinery mass-produced interior architectural ornament and doors and wood moldings. Quite often, factory designers copied their patterns from popular builder's guides, and, therefore, when some street front and interior details duplicate a plate in an Asher Benjamin or Minard Lafever pattern book these were not necessarily copied during construction by a carpenter or a plasterer but could have been the work of a local factory which selected the particular design for mass production.

Even the era's finest architects and ordinary builders took the short cut of mass-produced interior ornament in New York dwellings. Alexander Jackson Davis noted in his Price Book for May 20, 1842, a purchase of machine-made ornament from John Gallier, at 592 Broadway, as "ornaments of Gallier in composition—honeysuckle, scroll, rosettes, wreath," and Martin E. Thompson's account book similarly records the purchase of "carved work" and "ornament" for several houses he designed.

In the increasingly rich and socially competitive New York of the 1840s, architects and builders often were tempted to build showy parlors with considerable inexpensive machine-made ornament. Most Greek Revival style row houses nevertheless reflected the classical architectural simplicity of past decades. But, by the late 1840s, the advancing mid-nineteenth-century technology joined forces with Romantic architectural ideals and a fashion-conscious citizenry to sweep aside the last vestiges of classical simplicity and restraint in the New York row house.

New York's Prosperity and Growth in the 1830s and 1840s.

The 1830s and 1840s largely were a period of unparalleled prosperity and growth in New York. Manhattan's population increased from 203,000 in 1830 to 313,000 in 1840 and reached 516,000 in 1850. The growth of Brooklyn, then a separate city, was equally staggering: from 21,000 in 1830, to

48,000 in 1840, to 139,000 in 1850! The city's bustling crowds and traffic-clogged streets awed residents and visitors to the city alike. In the mid-1820s, the city's "thrice told multitude" filled a western stranger with "amazement" that "240,000 [*sic*] people" could be living "in one place!"

In the 1830s and 1840s, New York strengthened its supremacy in foreign and domestic trade; the city's share of the nation's foreign trade rose from 37 percent in 1830 to 63 percent in 1860. As railroads began to replace rivers and canals in the 1840s for shipment of crops and goods within the United States, New York built a railroad network that linked the city to all parts of the nation—thereby maintaining the city's leading role in domestic trade. In the decades before the Civil War, New York attracted banking and insurance companies that were to make it the financial center of the nation and, in time, the world.

The city's spectacular population growth and prosperity led to an unprecedented building boom in New York. Row house construction swept relentlessly northward on narrow Manhattan Island to accommodate the city's increasing population and those families fleeing the once-secluded downtown residential districts recently invaded by commercial activity. "The old downtown burgomasters, who have fixed to one spot all their lives," wrote Philip Hone in 1836, "will be seen during the next summer in flocks, marching reluctantly north to pitch their tents in places which, in their time, were orchards, cornfields, or morasses a pretty smart distance from town."

In these years of prosperity and building boom, a feverish speculation in land and building lots seized New York—a mania matched in cities and villages throughout the United States. Much of Manhattan was laid out in row house building lots, and, according to one Frenchman, enough had been sold by 1835 to accommodate houses for two million people. A dizzy rise in all prices accompanied the nationwide speculative fever. "Everything in New York is at an exorbitant price," Philip Hone declared in 1836. "Rents have risen 50 per cent for the next year."

This bubble of false prosperity burst with the Panic of 1837, a several-year-long nationwide depression. In New York, hundreds of businesses failed, and thousands of workingmen lost their jobs. And in the Bond Street area, Philip Hone saw "the sales of rich furniture, the property of men who a year ago thought themselves rich, and such expenditures justifiable, but are now bankrupt."

Real estate values and construction activity suffered in those troubled years. "Real estate is unsalable at any price; rents have fallen and are not punctually paid, and taxes have increased most ruinously," lamented Philip Hone in 1837. The same year, he noted that building lots on the then-rural Upper West Side which brought $480 less than a year earlier had just sold for $50 each. Prosperity returned to the nation and New York by the early 1840s, and the city's building boom and growth resumed its former hectic pace. "The city is spreading north . . . out of all reason and measure," wrote lawyer George Templeton

Strong in his mid-nineteenth-century diaries. The activity of architect-builders, who built row houses on speculation for sale to well-to-do businessmen, always suffered badly in a depression. Row house construction figures in New York from 1834 to 1849 clearly reflect the periods of boom and bust.

Year	Number Completed	Year	Number Completed
1834	877	1842	912
1835	1,259	1843	1,273
1836	1,826	1844	1,210
1837	840	1845	1,980
1838	741	1846	1,919
1839	674	1847	1,823
1840	850	1848	1,191
1841	971	1849	1,618

Builder's Guides and the Greek Revival Style in New York Row Houses.

Although architects introduced the Greek Revival style to New York in such projects as the Phoenix Bank, Second Unitarian Church, and the spectacular Colonnade Row, the style's popularity on the New York row house was not assured until it was accepted by the city's builders. The row house was the product of the architect-builder and his workmen solving architectural and construction problems. The handsome architectural forms and details of the street front and parlor were inspired by or copied from contemporary builder's guides. An outpouring of these guides in the late 1820s and 1830s filled with Greek Revival style designs suitable for city houses helped to assure the style's acceptance.

The most influential and prolific author of the era was Asher Benjamin of Northfield, Massachusetts, whose *Country Builder's Assistant* (1797) was the first builder's guide by an American author. Under such titles as *The American Builder's Companion* (1806), *The Practical House Carpenter* (1830), and *Practice of Architecture* (1833), Asher Benjamin spread the Federal style and later the Greek Revival style among builders of city and country houses throughout the nation. So popular were Benjamin's books that buildings and architectural details as far west as Illinois and Wisconsin are attributed to plates in his builder's guides.

The other leading author of builder's guides was Minard Lafever of Brooklyn. His first book, *The Young Builder's General Instructor* (1829), carried Federal style designs which were clumsy in proportion and details and evidently modifications of contemporary New York row houses. In 1833 Lafever halted sales of *The Young Builder's General Instructor,* because "though others seemed perfectly satisfied with the book, I myself was not." Lafever subsequently published *The Modern Builder's Guide* (1833) and *The Beauties of Modern Architecture* (1835) whose Greek Revival style designs are nearly all original and are extraordinarily handsome in proportion and ornament.

In Greenwich Village and Brooklyn Heights, row house street fronts and interiors have details identical or nearly identical to designs in Lafever's builder's guides. Whether handmade by craftsmen at the site or machine-made in a factory, these Lafever-inspired details reflect the importance of the builder's guides in row house ornament. The Seabury Tredwell house owes much of its handsome details to Lafever designs. So strongly do details of the front and the parlor echo designs in Lafever's guides that it once was thought that Lafever himself designed the house as part of a long row stretching to Lafayette Place. The arched Late Federal doorway, set off with keystones and rustication blocks, is similar to Plate 42 in *The Young Builder's General Instructor,* the Ionic columns and entablature for the sliding double parlor doors resemble Plate 60 of *The Modern Builder's Guide,* and the plaster cornices of the parlor ceilings copy Plate 64 of *The Young Builder's General Instructor.* An occasional confusion of forms in the lavish parlors indicates that an architect-builder probably designed the house from Lafever prototypes.

The builder's guides largely were responsible for the successful adaptation of ancient masonry forms in such books as Stuart and Revett's *Antiquities of Athens* to nineteenth-century American materials and construction technology. Architects modified the proportions of ancient columns to the scale of domestic architecture. "The style of building in this country differs very considerably from that of Great Britain, and other countries," wrote Asher Benjamin in the preface to the first edition of *The American Builder's Companion.* "We do not conceive it essentially necessary to adhere exactly to any particular order, provided the proportion and harmony of the parts be carefully preserved. . . . We have ventured to make some alterations in the proportions of the different orders."

For easier construction, the builder often simplified the already modified designs. In New York row houses, it will be recalled, architect-builders usually substituted simple rectangular pilasters and entablature flush with the façade for the difficult doorway porch with freestanding columns. The American architects' modifications of Stuart and Revett's drawings for their own builder's guides, together with the builder's own changes at the construction site, resulted in a style which, if not classically correct, was structurally and economically practical for the period.

The Colonnade Row and Lafayette Place.

Some of the first, and certainly the most spectacular, Greek Revival style dwellings in New York were the nine marble-front houses of the "Colonnade Row" (1832–1833). Built by Seth Geer and attributed to Alexander Jackson Davis, the Colonnade Row was named La Grange Terrace in honor of the country house of the Marquis de Lafayette and stood on the then-secluded several-block-long Lafayette Place. Acclaimed in the early 1830s as the "most imposing and magnificent" houses in the city, the dazzling Colonnade Row helped to popularize the newly fashionable Greek Revival style among the city's builders and populace.

The Colonnade Row also pointed out the striking potential of the monumental blockfront and streetscape. In the tradition of the terraces and crescents in London and Bath and New York's recent Le Roy Place and Depau Row on Bleecker Street, the nine houses of the Colonnade Row were subordinated to the monumental two-story-tall colonnade running the full length of the row. A heavy bronze cornice reinforced the visual unity of the row and, at the same time, concealed a very unclassical pitched roof. A boldly rusticated basement and first floor visually balanced the two-story colonnade and the heavy cornice. Here, the single row house gives up its individuality for the dignity of the row and streetscape. In the following years, the city's architects and builders began to consider the individual row house in relation to streetscape unity rather than leave the appearance of the blockfront to chance, as in the years of the Federal style. By the 1850s, the monumental streetscape was a stated goal in fine New York streets.

Within the uniform blockfront of the Colonnade Row, the detailing of the individual houses was remarkably sophisticated in concept and extravagant in execution. Greek Doric columns framed front doorways, which were modestly recessed into the rusticated first floor and similar in appearance to the first-floor windows. Elegant cast-iron torches, which remain today only at No. 434 Lafayette Street, stood at each side of the modest several-step-high stoop. Laurel wreaths decorated the lintels, rectangular doorway, and second-floor parlor window, and the capitals of the elaborate fluted Corinthian columns were deeply and freely cut. A drawing titled "Approaching what Lafayette Terrace ought to be," by Alexander Jackson Davis, showed the houses with roof gardens and vine-covered overhead trellises, which never were built.

The construction of the Colonnade Row pointed up the city's continual uptown growth as New York's population increased and commercial activity entered once-secluded residential areas. In 1836, Philip Hone regretfully sold his home, No. 235 Broadway, opposite the City Hall Park, and moved to No. 1 Great Jones Street, several blocks from the Colonnade Row, because "all" the downtown "dwelling houses are to be converted into stores," and "we are tempted with prices so exorbitantly high that none can resist." One-hundred-foot-wide Lafayette Place had been cut through from Astor Place to Great Jones Street only as late as 1826, and while the Colonnade Row was under construction people came "into the fields" to marvel at the houses rising in nearly solitary splendor. Before that

(top) Colonnade Row (1832–1833), Lafayette Place, plan of 1831. The nine white marble mansions of Colonnade Row were some of the most extravagant —and beautiful—row houses erected in nineteenth-century New York or America. At their completion in 1833, the houses sold for a then-unheard-of $25,000 to $30,000.

(bottom left) Colonnade Row, in 1972. A sad sign of our city's and our society's disregard for its past. Today, only four of the original nine houses survive in the Colonnade Row. Surprisingly, several of the houses have some original mantels and ceilings remaining.

(bottom right) Important Auction Sale. 40 Building Lots, 1829. East Sixth and East Seventh streets, between Bowery and Second Avenue.

time, few houses had been built beyond the Bond and Bleecker streets area several blocks to the south. In 1911 Montgomery Schuyler recalled the Colonnade Row at the time of its construction:

> Even from the mellow gray of the relics of the mansions one can understand how electrifying must have been their effect upon New York when their "new-cut ashlar took the light" of 1836 [*sic*] in its glittering freshness of white marble. . . . There were not wanting critics to call the Terrace "Geer's Folly," and to predict that there were not millionaires enough in New York to live up to these splendors especially since "the splendors" were "so far away" . . . almost two miles to the Battery. It is satisfying to know that the enterprising builder confounded his critics and was rewarded for bestowing one of its chief ornaments upon the city by disposing of all the houses at a handsome profit.

During the 1830s and 1840s, Lafayette Place rivaled Bond and Bleecker streets as the city's most fashionable address. The houses of the Colonnade Row "are universally allowed to be unequalled for grandour [*sic*] and effect," declared one magazine in the mid-1830s. "One of the houses was sold not long since for 26,500 dollars, a sum greatly below its value." The Colonnade Row was the residence for some of the city's most notable citizens: at No. 33 Lafayette Place, Irving Van Wart, whose relative Washington Irving often spent entire winters at the house; No. 37, John Jacob Astor; No. 39, Franklin H. Delano, a grandfather of Franklin Delano Roosevelt; and No. 43, now surviving as No. 428 Lafayette Street, the Honorable David Gardner, whose daughter Julia married President John Tyler in 1844. Fine row houses, mansions on tree-shaded grounds, and churches lined the rest of Lafayette Place.

The glory of the Colonnade Row and Lafayette Place was sadly short-lived. Nearby Broadway's transformation from an elegant residential to a fashionable commercial street in the late 1840s and 1850s introduced unwanted nonresidential uses into the neighborhood. The first portion of the Astor Library was built across the street from the Colonnade Row in 1849–1853. In the Colonnade Row itself, Israel Underhill opened Nos. 43 and 45 Lafayette Place as an elegant boardinghouse. In 1859 massive Cooper Union was completed at the Bowery and Astor Place, just to the north of the Colonnade Row. Nevertheless, unlike nearby Bond and Bleecker streets, Lafayette Place was somewhat isolated from the rising commercial activity on Broadway and the Bowery and remained one of the city's finest streets into the 1850s.

With the 1860s Lafayette Place lost any semblance of past residential fashion. William B. Astor moved to a brownstone mansion on Fifth Avenue, and his splendid mansion on Lafayette Place, across the street from the Colonnade Row, became a restaurant. The renowned Walter Langdon mansion was torn down for a loft building, and congregations moved away and sold their churches, one of which eventually became a boxing arena. In the Colonnade Row, Nos. 33–41 Lafayette Place, the five southernmost houses of the row, became part of the Colonnade Hotel, whose entrance faced Broadway.

(top) The Row (1831–1833), Nos. 1–13 Washington Square North, in 1894. The thirteen similar Greek Revival row houses on Washington Square North, east of Fifth Avenue, have been known as The Row since the nineteenth century. Several houses have retained their parlors in nearly original condition.

(bottom) Nos. 14–26 Washington Square North (late 1820s to early 1850s), in 1922. Though lacking the monumental vista of The Row, the dwelling houses along Washington Square North, west of Fifth Avenue, once displayed the Federal, Greek Revival, and Italianate brownstone-front styles. The four nearest houses were demolished in 1950 for the high-rise No. 2 Fifth Avenue apartment building.

During the 1880s, Lafayette Place was widened and extended below Great Jones Street to the City Hall area. The once-patrician row houses along Lafayette Place and adjacent streets became cheap boarding houses and tenements or were torn down for sweatshop lofts and massive warehouses. Heavy wagons and trucks rumbled over the same streets, once tree-lined and disturbed only by the fine carriages of the city's richest families.

In 1901, the construction of the still-standing Wanamaker warehouse destroyed the five southernmost houses of the Colonnade Row, but so soundly had these dwellings been built that dynamite had to be used for the demolition. The four surviving Colonnade Row houses surprisingly retain their original façades and much interior detail. Shabby echoes of their past grandeur, they are the last remaining dwellings on Lafayette Place.

Washington Square and The Row.

New York's beloved Washington Square originally was marshland fed by Minetta Brook and, after 1795, was a paupers' burial ground and the site of the city gallows. In 1826 the city purchased several additional acres of land and converted the area into the "Washington Military Parade-Ground" and a public park. In the next decade, palatial row houses rose along the north, west, and south sides. In 1837, New York University completed its first building, in a Gothic Revival mode, on the east side of the park. "Washington Square is another great and most effective ornament to our city," wrote one New Yorker around 1830. "There have already been erected around it, many handsome private dwellings, and the vicinity has likewise become a most fashionable residence, although somewhat remote at present from the centre of business." Society's fabled march up Fifth Avenue may have begun when well-to-do families, unable to find building lots on Washington Square, built their houses around the corner on lower Fifth Avenue.

Today, Washington Square retains a large measure of its original dignity. Despite some changes over the years, the Greek Revival row house mansions along the north side of Washington Square are among the city's finest remaining nineteenth-century dwellings and, with their restrained red-brick fronts, white-marble porches, and planted front yards, recall a seemingly more pleasant and gracious New York of the nineteenth century.

Nos. 1–13 Washington Square North (1831–1833), east of Fifth Avenue, were among the finest and earliest Greek Revival row houses in the city. An 1833 real estate advertisement for a just-completed No. 2 Washington Square North declared that this "ELEGANT PRIVATE RESIDENCE . . . is believed to be inferior to no house in the United States, either in workmanship or convenience." Although the red-brick street fronts, rising from a rusticated white-marble basement, epitomize the

severity valued by the Greek Revival style, the houses have several rich and highly original ornamental features. The square basement windows recall the passing Federal style and display an elegant four-sided enframement enhanced by a keystone at the center of the top jamb and square impost blocks down the side jambs. Elegant "vermiculation," a rough-surfaced, twisting, "wormlike" surface, decorates the keystones and impost blocks on the basement windows in some houses. A freestanding white-marble porch with handsome fluted Doric columns shields the front doors, and rather than the usual iron railings of the period the stoops have massive white-marble balustrades, a glance backward to the Renaissance tradition. All the houses, but one, retain the original iron front fences with handsome anthemia, Greek keys, and lyres.

This blockfront, Nos. 1–13 Washington Square North, is one of the first monumental row house streetscapes in the city and, in the nineteenth century, simply was known as The Row. A continuous cornice line, evenly aligned doors and windows, and a several-hundred-foot-long front fence make for the impressive continuous vista. The freestanding doorway porches and balustraded stoops enhance the impressively uniform vista by their contrast to the flat and plainly detailed street fronts. The twelve-foot-deep front yards, enclosed by a continuous iron fence and shaded by trees, and location facing Washington Square impart to The Row a patrician grandeur and detachment missing in the usual New York row house built close to the sidewalk on a narrow street.

The construction of The Row was an outstanding example of private planning in nineteenth-century America. The blockfront developed under the control of the Sailors Snug Harbor, a home for retired sailors and owner of several blocks east of Fifth Avenue and north of Washington Square. In 1831 James Boorman, John Johnston, and John Morrison leased the building lots of The Row from the Sailors Snug Harbor for 100 years and built up the blockfront between 1831–1833 in two remarkably uniform and complimentary rows of houses, Nos. 1–6 and Nos. 7–13 Washington Square North. Under the terms of the 1831 leases, the lessee agreed to build "a good and substantial dwelling house, of the width of said lot, three or more stories high, in brick or stone, covered with slate or metal," set back twelve feet from the front lot line, and "to be finished in such style as may be approved of by the "lessor." The lessee also had the right to build a private stable at the rear of each lot, provided it not become a "slaughter house, tallow chandlery, smith shop, forge, furnace or brass foundry, nail or other iron factory, or any manufactory, . . . trade or business which may be noxious or offensive to the neighbors." The carriage houses of The Row are known today as Washington Mews.

The Row has not escaped drastic change over the years. Today Nos. 1–6 Washington Square North, which still have their fine Greek Revival style interiors, are offices for the various departments of New York University, but Nos. 7–13 Washington Square North retain only their slightly modified side and front façades. Threatened with demolition in 1939 for a high-rise apartment building, public outcry led Sailors Snug Harbor to preserve much of the original façades but could not prevent the gutting of the interiors in the conversion to apartments. At that time, full size fourth-floor windows and plain copper cornice replaced the original balustrade along the roofline and the small attic windows, set into the fascia board above a fine taenia molding and hidden by screens in a Greek key motif.

On the other side of Fifth Avenue, Washington Square North developed over a thirty-year period, and until the early 1950s, displayed the city's row house architecture from the Federal style of the 1820s to the Italianate brownstone-front style of the 1850s. No. 20 Washington Square North, the first house to be built on Washington Square, is one of the city's few remaining Federal style mansions. Built in 1828–1829 as a country house for George P. Rogers, the house displays the arched front doorway, peaked lintels, and a rusticated basement with heavy window enframement so typical of the Late Federal style. The house originally occupied thirty-seven feet of the fifty-foot-wide lot, leaving a carriageway at its west side leading to a stable in the back, but it was enlarged several times to fill this space. The fourth floors, its round-headed windows, and the iron railings in the front yard date from Henry J. Hardenbergh's 1880 conversion of the house into fashionable apartments.

The several Greek Revival row houses on this side of Washington Square North were built one or two at a time and lack the monumentality of The Row. But, unlike The Row, which are offices and apartments, several of these houses remain in private hands. The construction of the banal No. 2 Fifth Avenue apartment tower in 1951–1952 destroyed Nos. 14–18 Washington Square North. No. 14 (1839–1840) was the original Rhinelander family mansion. Nos. 16–17 Washington Square North (1851–1852) were two identical Italianate style row houses and stylistically concluded this architecturally distinguished block. In this instance, the builder's concession to the public outcry was a five-story-tall neo-Georgian wing to the high-rise tower of dubious architectural harmony with the houses remaining on the blockfront.

To the north of Washington Square, Ninth, Tenth, Eleventh, and Twelfth streets are charming tree-lined streets whose row houses reflect all the early- and mid-nineteenth-century architectural styles. The several-hundred-foot-long row of Greek Revival dwellings on the south side of West Eleventh Street, between Fifth and Sixth avenues, built in several groups in the 1840s, is one of the finest early-nineteenth-century streetscapes in the area. The flat street fronts, modest door enframements and window details, and a fairly uniform cornice line unconsciously form a unified, nearly-500-foot-long streetscape. The iron front fences and stoop railings, nearly all of which remain on these houses, add elegance and visual excitement to this remarkable vista. Such a fortuitously

No. 27 East Eleventh Street (1844–1845), Greenwich Village. Except for the double front doors in the Italianate style, this handsome row house is an excellent example of the Greek Revival style. In the nineteenth century, New Yorkers often grew wisteria vines up the fronts of their houses on guide wires—introducing a feeling of the country to the city street without harming the brick façade of the house.

surviving row also gives the present-day viewer a glimpse of the beauty and dignity of the early-nineteenth-century New York streets before high-rise residential and commercial construction obliterated the once-numerous blockfronts of human scale.

Greenwich Village abounds in ordinary row houses, erected by architect-builders for the city's prosperous business and professional men. In the early nineteenth century, the differences between the houses of the rich, as seen on Washington Square North, and the houses of merely well-to-do families, as seen on West Eleventh Street, are less dramatic than they will be in the remaining decades of the nineteenth century. In 1899 Montgomery Schuyler wrote that "the type is the same, and that the mansion was for half a century and more merely a more expensive expansion and elaboration of the smaller house." The row houses on West Eleventh Street are narrower and not built as deeply nor as tall as the mansions along Washington Square North. In the Greek Revival era, the ordinary row house had flat pilasters to support the entablature of the doorway, rather than costly fluted freestanding columns in a doorway porch, and wood or local brownstone trim rather than the costly white marble.

In the 1830s and 1840s, visitors to New York mentioned the restrained life style and handsome, but not extravagant, houses of the city's rich families. "The upper classes live in a more simple form, wanting some of the most refined improvements of high English life," wrote one Englishman in the 1840s. This situation "might be expected in a country where labor is comparatively high, and the fortunes, though great, still not often as princely as in the mother country." Few New Yorkers lived in palatial mansions until the Industrial Revolution and Civil War-induced boom piled up great fortunes and the rising tide of immigration offered ample supply of low-paid servants to run the large mansions. Only with the new fortunes and lavish social activity of the 1850s and 1860s, did mansions line Fifth Avenue and an extravagant house became a prerequisite to patrician social standing.

Chelsea.

By the 1840s, row house construction had swept past 14th Street into the Chelsea area near the Hudson River. "The neighborhood which bears the name Chelsea is rapidly covering itself with new buildings," wrote one newspaper in 1846. "The arrangements made by the original proprietors of the land in that quarter are such that no building can be erected for any purpose which will make the neighborhood disagreeable, and it is becoming a favorite place of residence."

Chelsea originally was the eighteenth-century estate of Captain Thomas Clarke, with boundaries from the present-day 14th Street to 27th Street and from Seventh Avenue west to the Hudson River. Captain Thomas Clarke expected that his country estate would be his retreat in old age and, as a soldier, chose the name Chelsea from the Chelsea Royal Hospital in London, a home for old soldiers

(top) Fifth Avenue, about 1865, View South from 14th Street. Although the fine Greek Revival and Italianate style houses in the foreground have given way to office buildings and stores, the First Presbyterian Church and Church of the Ascension in the distance still grace lower Fifth Avenue.

(bottom) London Terrace (1845–1846), north side of West 23rd Street, between Ninth and Tenth avenues, in 1922. This 800-foot-long terrace, designed by Alexander Jackson Davis, was demolished in the 1920s for the mammoth London Terrace apartment buildings.

and sailors. However, soon after buying the estate, Captain Clarke died. His widow, nevertheless, built the estate's mansion, which once stood on 23rd Street, 200 feet west of Ninth Avenue, surrounded by terraced grounds and sitting on a hill overlooking the Hudson River. Several generations later, the estate passed to Thomas Clarke's grandson, Clement Clarke Moore, a noted classical scholar, now remembered as the author of A Visit from Saint Nicholas. In the 1830s, Clement Clarke Moore mapped the estate into building lots and gave a full block to the General Theological Seminary, which is still in Chelsea.

An exceptionally fine row of Greek Revival style houses stands at Nos. 406–418 West 20th Street. These houses were built by Don Alonzo Cushman, a friend of Moore, who developed much of Chelsea. These houses are noted for the nearly original street fronts, particularly the fine cast-iron wreaths encircling the small attic windows in the cornice, and the iron stoop railings and areaway fences. No. 162 Ninth Avenue, at the southeast corner of 20th Street, is the generally forgotten 1834 mansion of James N. Wells, a builder, with a doorway porch with freestanding fluted white-marble Doric columns and pedimented lintels similar to the houses of The Row.

Brooklyn Heights.

In the eighteenth century, Brooklyn was a quiet farming area at the westernmost end of Long Island just across the East River from Manhattan. Many farms were held by families to whom the land had been granted in the seventeenth century under Dutch patents, and small villages, such as Flatbush, Bedford, and Bushwick dotted the countryside. However, Brooklyn's rural seclusion lasted only into the early nineteenth century. With the start of regularly scheduled ferry service between Brooklyn and Fulton Street in Manhattan in 1820, Brooklyn began its growth as a thriving autonomous city and as a desirable residential community.

On Brooklyn Heights, poised on a bluff overlooking the East River and the small city of New York clustered around the Battery, the several landowners divided their farms into row house building lots. Their names today are preserved in such Brooklyn Heights street names as Joralemon, Pierrepont, and Remsen. Well-to-do merchants, many of whom worked in Manhattan, built houses on Brooklyn Heights, attracted by the easy walk to the ferry to Manhattan and its spectacular view of New York Bay. The sight of the harbor from Brooklyn Heights, wrote one visitor in the 1830s, is "one of the most stunning views imaginable—the ferry-boats passing and repassing, the shipping, the harbour and the fortified islands in the vicinity, are all seen to great advantage."

By the 1820s, wooden and brick houses dotted Brooklyn Heights. "The houses in the principal streets have a particularly neat and elegant appearance," recalled one Englishman around 1830.

Cushman Row (1839–1840), Nos. 406–418 West 20th Street, Chelsea. This remarkably well-preserved row of Greek Revival houses, with fine stoop iron work, is one of the most impressive streetscapes in the city.

"They are chiefly built of wood, and painted white, with green latticed blinds on the outside. . . . For the entire length of some of the streets, weeping willows are planted on each side, which, independent of being very ornamental, offered a delightful shade to the fronts of the houses, and protect the foot paths even from the noon-day sun." On today's quiet, tree-lined streets, a few of these Federal style houses have survived to the present day, characterized by their pitched roofs and dormer windows, doorways set off with delicately leaded sidelights and toplights, and clapboard or Flemish-bond brick facades. One of the oldest and most beautiful dwellings on Brooklyn Heights is No. 24 Middagh Street (1824), at Willow Street, the former Eugene Boisselet house.

Although most houses built on Brooklyn Heights in the 1820s were frame, as befitted the then-rural community, Nos. 155, 157, and 159 Willow Street (1829) are three brick Federal style row houses. Nos. 155 and 157 Willow Street retain their original pitched roofs and dormers, which at No. 159 were replaced by a full third floor soon after the completion of the row. These houses are askew the present street line because of a slight change in the direction of Willow Street soon after their construction.

Although Brooklyn's population almost doubled between 1820 and 1830 from 11,000 to 20,000 persons, only Brooklyn Heights and the area around the ferry station resembled a city. In the mid-nineteenth century, George Hall, the first mayor of Brooklyn, recalled the city of 1823:

> The population of the city at that time consisted of about 20,000 persons; residing for the most part within the distance of about three quarters of a mile from Fulton Ferry. Beyond this limit no streets of any consequence were laid out, and the ground was chiefly occupied for agricultural purposes. The shores, throughout nearly their whole extent, were in their natural condition, washed by the East River and the bay. There were two ferries, by which communication was had with the city of New York, ceasing at twelve o'clock at night. . . . Of commerce and manufactures it can scarcely be said to have had any, its business consisting chiefly of that which was required for supplying the wants of its inhabitants. Sixteen of its streets were lighted with public lamps, of which thirteen had been supplied within the previous year.

In the following decades, Brooklyn grew rapidly and took on the appearance of a city. In 1834 Brooklyn received a city charter, the jurisdiction encompassing the present-day downtown, South Brooklyn, Navy Yard, and Fort Greene area. Its population, it has been noted, increased from 21,000 in 1830 to 48,000 in 1840 and reached 139,000 in 1850! Feverish land speculation and an almost never-ending building boom accompanied Brooklyn's growing population. "The rage for speculating in lands on Long Island is one of the bubbles of the day," declared Philip Hone in the prosperous mid-1830s.

MAP "B."

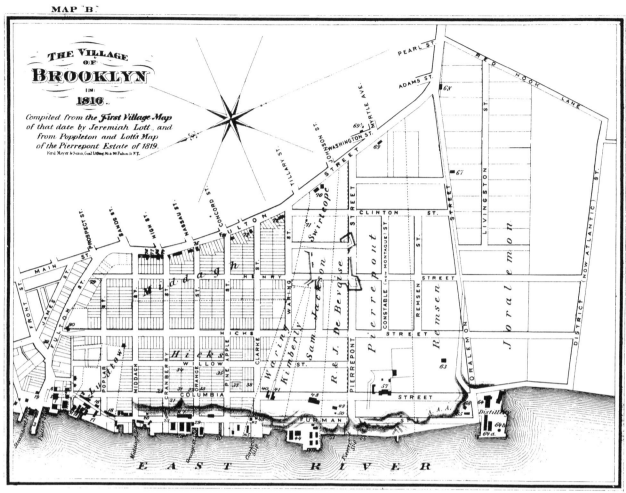

(top) Map of Brooklyn Heights in 1819, showing old farm boundaries, the then-recent plan of streets and building lots, and existing buildings.

(bottom) Nos. 43–49 Willow Place (ca. 1846), Brooklyn Heights, in 1936. This modest Colonnade Row is a delightful sight on secluded, one-block-long Willow Place. By the 1940s and 1950s, the block and Colonnade Row houses had run down badly. In 1972, however, three of the four Colonnade houses here had been restored.

Men in moderate circumstances have become immensely rich merely by the good fortune of owning farms of a few acres of this chosen land. Abraham Schermerhorn has sold his farm of 170 acres at Gowanus, three miles from Brooklyn, at $600 an acre; four years ago, having got out of conceit of it as a residence, he offered it for sale at $20,000, and would have taken $18,000; to-day he pockets $102,000, and regrets that he sold it so cheap!

In the 1830s and 1840s, handsome Greek Revival row houses filled many blocks of Brooklyn Heights. Construction first occurred in the northern portion of Brooklyn Heights, close to the ferry to Manhattan at the foot of Brooklyn's Fulton Street. The start of ferry service in 1836 from the foot of Atlantic Avenue in Brooklyn to South Ferry in Manhattan spurred development of the southern portion of Brooklyn Heights and adjacent South Brooklyn.

In Brooklyn Heights today, the Greek Revival row house together with the plainly detailed brick-front Italianate style dwelling of the 1850s recall the dignified streetscape of mid-nineteenth-century New York. On those blocks unmarred by high-rise construction, the basement-and-three-story row houses are tall enough to define the space of the city street but do not loom over the pedestrian and partially block the sun as happened in later decades. These streets take a special charm from the casual, unforced manner in which they were built up. The cornices are of varying heights, and the house fronts are shades of red brick or pastel paints and gently step in and out. Viewed today, with trees at the curb and occasional gardens in the front yards, some Brooklyn Heights blocks have the beauty and serenity, if not complete appearance, of the nineteenth century.

Joralemon Street, west of Hicks Street, is an unusually handsome block. The street slopes downhill toward the harbor, and twenty-four largely unaltered Greek Revival row houses remain on the north side of the street. Their stoops, doorways, and cornices rhythmically step down the slope giving a sense of motion to the block which reinforces the pedestrian's progress down the hill.

The best-known feature of Brooklyn Heights always has been the spectacular view of New York Bay and Manhattan from the edge of the bluff which gives the area its name. To take advantage of the view, fine dwellings were built along Columbia Street, later renamed Columbia Heights, at the edge of the bluff. In 1835 General Underhill built eight Greek Revival style row houses, known as the Colonnade Row, on Columbia Heights, between Cranbury and Middagh streets, overlooking the East River. A monumental three-story wood colonnade united the houses which cost $15,000 when new. Early on the morning of December 20, 1853, one of the corner houses caught fire and, according to contemporary newspaper accounts, "before the second house was on fire inside, the fire had extended the whole length of the block outside, front and rear." Not a trace of the Underhill Colonnade remains.

One did not have to be wealthy to live in a "Colonnade Row." Except for the bedraggled

Adams Street, Brooklyn, about 1890. These frame houses were built in the early nineteenth century when Brooklyn was a suburban village of several thousand residents across the East River from New York.

remnants of the city's first Colonnade Row on Lafayette Place in Manhattan, Nos. 43–49 Willow Place (1846) in Brooklyn Heights are the only remaining example in New York of this daring urban form. Square wood columns support a two-story-tall wooden porch which dignifies, but does not hide, the modest two-story-tall, narrow brick houses to which it has been added. An easily forgivable architectural fraud, the Willow Place Colonnade Row holds great appeal today because of its modest scale and the naïveté of its conception and execution.

Cobble Hill.

Brooklyn Heights largely was built up by the eve of the Civil War. Later houses in Brooklyn Heights were the extensive remodeling of earlier structures or were constructed on scattered vacant lots and one-time gardens. By the 1840s, row house construction extended beyond Atlantic Avenue, a fine shopping street, into what was then known as South Brooklyn. Since the area's renaissance, which began in the early 1960s, these blocks between Atlantic Avenue and Degraw Street have been known informally as "Cobble Hill," a name derived from "Cobleshill" or "Cobleskill," an eighteenth-century name for the area. These names originally referred to a steep hill near the old Red Hook Lane, a site close to the present-day intersection of Court Street and Atlantic Avenue. At that time, South Brooklyn was farmed productively under Dutch land patents of the seventeenth century. During the Revolutionary War, American troops transformed this prominent hill into "Cobble Hill Fort" or "Corkscrew Fort," consisting of three cannons on a platform surrounded by spiral trenches. After their victory over the American Army in the Battle of Long Island, the British Army captured the small fort and sliced off the top of Cobble Hill.

The area's earliest growth began in the 1820s. Henry Street was opened south of Atlantic Avenue in 1828 and, with the long-existing Red Hook Lane, linked Cobble Hill with Brooklyn Heights and the Fulton Ferry to Manhattan. The first newcomers to the area built suburban mansions on spacious grounds on the blocks west of Henry Street to enjoy a dramatic view of New York. By the 1830s, the small estates, none of which now remain, and the old farms were being broken up into building lots for row houses.

Cobble Hill's city development began at the start of ferry service in 1836 between the foot of Atlantic Avenue and South Ferry. The oldest standing house in Cobble Hill is No. 122 Pacific Street, a Greek Revival style row house built around 1833, with a mansard roof from the 1860s. By 1834, the grid street pattern was imposed from Atlantic Avenue south to Butler Street, later Harrison Street, now Kane Street. South of Butler Street, a partial grid coexisted for some years with the old country lanes. Although row house construction came in the 1830s and 1840s, it was not until the 1850s that

the area gained a citified appearance. Before that time, groups of urban row houses stood in surreal splendor in the open fields. The Reverend Sewall S. Cutting, pastor of the Strong Place Baptist Church, recalled the scene in the 1840s:

> On this side of Atlantic Street I recall no instance, in the streets running either way, unless near the river, where any street was built from one corner to another. In all the district from Atlantic Street to Carroll, the buildings were dwellings in detached clusters. Whole blocks were without a building on them, or with no more than two or three or four. Everywhere were footpaths across the blocks to make shorter routes to the South Ferry. My own family had been in 1845 the first to occupy a house in the row of houses on Harrison [now Kane], fronting Strong Place.

South Brooklyn's slow growth over several decades introduced a remarkable variety of architectural styles to Cobble Hill and its also-renamed neighbor to the south, Carroll Gardens. The row houses in Cobble Hill reflect the Greek Revival, Gothic Revival—some of the finest remaining examples in the city—Italianate, and Neo-Grec styles. Although Cobble Hill is a southern extension of Brooklyn Heights in its growth, few rich families crossed Atlantic Avenue and settled in South Brooklyn. Land prices in South Brooklyn remained at a reasonable level and permitted the construction of row houses for families of moderate means. Cobble Hill dwellings vary from the wide, basement-and-four-story-tall row houses along Clinton and Henry streets to the modest, basement-and-two-story-tall houses along delightful Tompkins and Strong places. Although Cobble Hill is a historic district and a pleasant neighborhood today, many row houses have lost their distinguishing detail around doorways, windows, and roofline in remodelings of recent decades.

The Decline of the Greek Revival Style.

The Greek Revival was the style for nearly all New York row houses from the early 1830s to the late 1840s and, on some houses, lasted into the early 1850s. In the 1840s, critics linked the style to the "paganism" of ancient Greece and argued that it was incompatible with a Christian nation's ideals. As the slavery issue intensified, other Americans recalled that man's earliest democracy in ancient Greece also had been cursed with the institution of slavery. "We are firm in the belief that the introduction of Grecian architecture among us has been a great mistake," declared one magazine in 1844. "Its edifices belong to another climate; they are the legitimate offspring of a remote age, an antagonistic religion, an obsolete form of government, and a widely different state of society from our own."

These attacks merely reflected a general dissatisfaction with the style. The very popularity of the Greek Revival contributed to its decline; excessive use had cheapened the style. In James Fenimore Cooper's *Home As Found* (1838), the Effingham family takes a boat ride up the Hudson River from New York. Passing numerous Greek Revival style country houses along the river, one character remarks that "an extraordinary taste is afflicting this country in the way of architecture . . . nothing but a Grecian temple being now deemed a suitable residence." His companion, James Effingham, replies:

> One such temple well placed in a wood, might be a pleasant object enough; but to see a river lined with them, with children trundling hoops before their doors, beef carried into their kitchens, and smoke issuing, moreover, from those unclassical objects, is too much ever for a high taste.

In its popularity, amateur architects and builders had adapted the style to uses for which it was inherently unsuited. In New York, banks, churches, schools, and occasional houses had templelike porticoes which added great cost to the building and blocked the sun from the front windows.

Another reason for the decline of the Greek Revival style was a shift in aesthetic values from the restrained forms and ornament and rational mood of the Classical tradition to the asymmetry, rich ornament, and emotional associations of the Romantic movement in architecture. The Greek Revival was a watershed style; often termed "Romantic Classicism," it combined severity and light-color materials of the Classical tradition with the association of ancient Greece. By the 1840s, the Romantic movement in architecture virtually replaced the Classical tradition. Buildings ideally evoked an association of a tantalizingly distant time or place and took on asymmetrically massed façades, rich ornament, and dark building materials which recalled the much-admired "picturesque" countryside.

In the cities, the planar red-brick front with severe white marble was the antithesis of the picturesque ideals of the Romantic movement in architecture. Although the asymmetrical massing of the country house was impossible to achieve on the twenty-five-foot-wide city lot, the heavy ornament and dark color front, also valued by the Romantic movement, were appropriate to the grand city row house and impressive streetscape increasingly valued at the time.

After decades of the restrained Federal and Greek Revival styles, New Yorkers of the 1850s welcomed the Romantic movement in architecture and the sweeping streets of grandly scaled and boldly ornamented row houses. These architectural ideals also complemented the unparalleled prosperity and social competition of mid-nineteenth-century New York and its residents. The Italianate style "brownstone-front" was the culmination of the Romantic movement in New York row houses. But before the opening of the Italianate style and the brownstone era, we shall discuss the Gothic Revival style row house of the 1840s which paved the way for its emergence.

Nos. 131 and 135 Hicks Street (1847–1848), Brooklyn Heights, in 1940. Gothic Revival row houses with shadowy brownstone fronts. No. 135 Hicks Street regained its cornice and casement-like windows in a 1969 façade restoration.

Chapter Three
Gothic Revival Style

The Gothic Revival style, which left its mark in the cities, villages, and countryside across the United States in the 1840s and 1850s, never was a popular style for New York row houses. The narrow city lot prevented the asymmetrical massing and picturesquely gabled roofline that was possible on the country house. Besides, a style so strongly associated with untamed nature seemed inherently unsuited for the town houses of bustling mid-nineteenth-century New York. Few Gothic Revival style row houses were built in New York in the 1840s and 1850s, and today only a ragged handful remain scattered throughout the city.

Despite its rarity in nineteenth-century New York, the Gothic Revival style was a crucial turning point in the architectural history of the city's row houses: it introduced those architectural ideals of the Romantic tradition that reached their fullest expression in the city's brownstone-front and Italianate style row houses of the 1850s and 1860s. Although the preceding Greek Revival style had recalled the ancient Greek city states, so distant in time and place, it marked only a partial acceptance of the Romantic movement's architectural ideals. In city row houses and country dwellings, the Greek Revival style still followed the Classical tradition in its symmetrical plan and massing and its restrained ornament and, therefore, often is termed Romantic Classicism. The Gothic Revival, on the other hand, recalled the far-away Middle Ages and, wherever possible, employed the asymmetrical massing, dark-color building materials, and rich ornament thought to complement the picturesque natural landscape. Only in city row houses did the Gothic Revival style rely solely upon dark-color materials and applied "Gothic" ornament for stylistic identification.

The Earliest Uses of the "Gothick" Mode in the United States.

The Gothic influence appeared on buildings in the United States several decades before its emergence as a serious style in the 1840s and 1850s. In the earliest years of the nineteenth century, leading American architects, then known for their work in the various styles of the Classical tradition, occasionally designed a building with such quaint "Gothick" touches as pointed-arch windows, castellated parapets, and decorative tracery. But, except for the playful appliqué of these Gothick details, these buildings, often churches, followed the Classical tradition in their symmetrical plan and massing. The pattern books of such British enthusiasts for the Gothick as Batty Langley and Horace Walpole provided a readily available source of inspiration for these details.

The first known American building in the Gothick mode was "Sedgeley" (1799), a country house built for William Cramon outside Philadelphia, designed by Benjamin Latrobe, then newly arrived from Great Britain. Like most early Gothick designs in this country, "Sedgeley" included the symmetrical plan and massing of the Classical tradition but was adorned with an overlay of medieval towers, pointed arches, and Gothick details largely taken from Batty Langley's books. Several years later, Latrobe's Gothick mode Bank of Philadelphia (1807), with a castellated roofline, a rose window, and a pointed-arch doorway, was completed at Fourth and Chestnut streets, under the direction of Robert Mills.

Other naïve Gothick designs appeared in the United States in these early years of the nineteenth century, most of them for Episcopal and Roman Catholic churches. Perhaps the first Gothick mode church in the United States was St. Mary's Chapel in Baltimore (1806–1808), designed by architect Maximilian Godefroy, recently arrived from France. Despite its superficial Gothick and picturesque touches, St. Mary's Chapel had "something of holiness, and quiet beauty about it, that excites the imagination strangely," wrote Mrs. Trollope in the 1830s, and is "more calculated, perhaps, to generate holy thoughts than even the swelling anthem heard beneath the resounding dome of St. Peter's." Other early buildings in the Gothick mode were Charles Bulfinch's Federal Street Church (1809) in Boston, John Holden Greene's St. John's Cathedral (1810) in Providence, Rhode Island, William Strickland's Masonic Hall (1809–1811) in Philadelphia, and Ithiel Town's Trinity Church (1814–1815) in New Haven, Connecticut.

Despite New York's conservative adherence to the Federal over the Greek Revival style for row houses until the early 1830s, the city saw many imaginative Gothick mode designs in the early part of the century. The city's first Gothick mode design was Joseph Mangin's Old St. Patrick's Cathedral (1809–1815) still standing at Mott and Prince streets. Although Old St. Patrick's Cathedral was a symmetrically massed building enriched by Gothick details, a guidebook to the city at the time described the church as a "magnificent gothic superstructure" and, quite significantly, added that "the gothic order seems to be the fittest for religious edifices." The popularity of Old St. Patrick's Cathedral probably encouraged other architects in the city to create Gothick mode designs for churches and buildings with religious associations. Among the city's other surviving buildings in this early Gothick mode are The Sea and Land Church, built by the Northeast Reformed Dutch (1817–1819) at Henry and Market streets, now overshadowed by the approaches to the Manhattan Bridge, and the General Theological Seminary's West Building (1835), a copy of the earlier East Building, built in 1827 but demolished in 1892.

The Romantic Movement in the United States.

In architecture, the Federal style dominated American buildings until the emergence of the Greek Revival style in the 1820s which, in the spirit of the rising Romantic movement, combined the emotional echoes of ancient Greece with the restrained ornament and symmetrical plan and massing of the Classical tradition. Only after the triumph of the Romantic movement in art and literature, which glorified pastness and untamed Nature, did the Gothic Revival emerge as a genuine architectural force in the United States.

In the 1830s and 1840s, literature produced Henry Thoreau, who left Concord to ruminate and write at Walden Pond; Washington Irving, who pictured a happy, rustic life along the Hudson River; and James Fenimore Cooper, who sang of the noble savage and the pioneer. In painting, such artists as Thomas Cole, Asher B. Durand, and others of the Hudson River School glorified the countryside and ignored the harsh realities of the contemporary urban and industrial scene.

As the Romantic movement flourished in American art and literature in the 1830s, certain architects who were tired of the Greek Revival style's transitional Romantic Classicism turned to the Gothic Revival style which idealized a long-gone Middle Ages and glorified picturesque Nature. Among the earliest buildings in the Gothic Revival style was "Glen Ellen" (1832), a castle outside Baltimore designed by Alexander Jackson Davis for Robert Gilman, complete with oriel window, octagonal corner turrets, and a medieval "ruin" for a gatehouse. Another striking Gothic Revival country house was Alexander Jackson Davis' dramatic "Lyndhurst" (1838), still standing in Tarrytown, New York, and now open to the public under the auspices of the National Trust for Historic Preservation.

In an America troubled by slavery and rampant industrialization, the Gothic Revival evoked the romanticized image of the Middle Ages pictured in the internationally popular novels of Ann Radcliffe, "Monk" Lewis, and particularly Sir Walter Scott. A Gothic Revival house recalled proud battles and the imagined chivalry and pageantry of medieval life, while a Gothic Revival style church soon seemed to be a more pious and "authentic" setting for religious services than buildings in a "heathen" Classical tradition.

In a complete swing away from the Greek Revival style's aesthetic ideals for simple, easily comprehended forms, the *North American Review* remarked in April, 1851, that "Gothic architecture appeals to the imagination, and fancy half supplies the deficiencies of the material scene. A Gothic building has always the charm of mystery." John Henry Hopkins, Bishop of Vermont and architect of several vaguely Gothic churches, similarly repudiated Greek Revival ideals and declared that "there is no style of architecture which admits of such variety, which is beautiful on any scale, and which is so little dependent on size for its effect. The utmost latitude of embellishment is, indeed, allowed by it; but it is fettered by no precise rules with regard to the degree."

A leading proponent of the Gothic Revival style in America was Andrew Jackson Downing whose *A Treatise on the Theory and Practice of Landscape Gardening* (1841), *Cottage Residences* (1842), and *The Architecture of Country Houses* (1850) did much to popularize the concept of the romantic Gothic

Trinity Church (1839–1846), Broadway and Wall Street, designed by Richard Upjohn. Trinity Church was one of the first major buildings in New York to employ the Gothic Revival style and brownstone façade.

residence wedded to the natural landscape. This harmony was to be achieved through irregularity of plan and massing, the interplay of light and shade, a varied roofline, the elimination of broad planar surfaces, and the use of dark façade colors. Downing's influential volumes were soon followed by many other books promoting the picturesque country house, among them, Gervase Wheeler's *Rural Homes* (1851), Lewis F. Allen's *Rural Architecture* (1852), Gervase Wheeler's *Homes for the People* (1855), and Calvert Vaux's *Villas and Cottages* (1857). All these books emphasized houses suitable for the country, since the Gothic Revival style posed a number of difficult, often insurmountable problems for the builder of city row houses.

The Gothic Revival Churches in New York.

The earliest Gothick mode designs in New York, we have noted, usually were for churches or church-related buildings. Likewise, the first buildings in fully developed Gothic Revival also were churches and rectories, because the style evoked strong religious associations. As Henry Cleveland, in 1836, wrote in the *North American Review:*

> . . . there is a style of architecture which belongs peculiarly to Christianity, and owes its existence even to this religion, whose very ornaments remind one of the joys of a life beyond the grave; whose lofty vaults and arches are crowded with the forms of prophets and martyrs and beatified spirits, and seem to resound with the choral hymns of angels and archangels . . . these are the characteristics of the architecture of Christianity, the sublime, the glorious Gothic.

Trinity Church (1839–1846) at Broadway and Wall Street, designed by Richard Upjohn, was one of the earliest Gothic Revival churches in New York. Architects praised Trinity Church for its richly ornamented design and its resemblance to a medieval church. "There are few things in architecture, that could hold out less promise of excellence" than the Gothick mode, wrote Arthur Gilman in the *North American Review* in 1844, but "it is evident, that a rapid advance has been made in an acquaintance with the true principles of the Gothic style. We are satisfied of this, when we see such edifices as Christ church, Brooklyn, and the new Trinity church in New York, rising, in almost mediaeval grandeur, upon our western shores."

Whatever the critical acclaim for Trinity Church, New York's Gothic Revival style churches of the 1840s and 1850s were but superficial copies of medieval churches. Trinity Church, however, boasted elaborate tracery, arched vaults, flying buttresses, medievally inspired sculpture, which did reflect the increasing maturity and architectural scholarship of the Gothic Revival style. At Trinity Church, these medieval features also reflected Richard Upjohn's leadership in the American "high church" movement of the 1830s and 1840s. But the medieval appearance of Trinity Church and the city's other Gothic Revival churches of the period was artful deceit. Because of the still influential Classical tradition and construction costs and capabilities in the period, Trinity Church was symmetrically massed, with a centrally placed tower, and the ceiling vaulting is of wood and plaster rather than genuine but costly stone construction.

Overwhelming praise nevertheless greeted the new Trinity Church. "Every day brings forth some new beauties . . . and crowds of spectators . . . visit, admire, and wonder at the magnificent edifice," wrote Philip Hone in 1846. "When completed, it will probably be the most elegant church edifice in the city, and undoubtedly the most costly one," one guidebook then declared. "The amount of its cost has never been publicly stated. The material of the building is a fine, reddish sandstone, nicely dressed. . . . Externally the building has a most imposing appearance. . . . It must be considered a noble specimen of architecture, and a fine ornament to that part of the city." Within a few years after the start of Trinity Church, many fine Gothic Revival style churches were built in the city, among them Upjohn's Church of the Ascension (1840–1841) at Fifth Avenue and West Tenth Street, James Renwick, Jr.'s, Grace Church (1843–1846) on Broadway at East Tenth Street, and Minard Lefever's Church of the Holy Trinity (1844–1847) at Montague and Clinton streets, one of his many Brooklyn churches.

The New Fashion for Brownstone in New York.

These Gothic Revival churches significantly were the first fine buildings in the city with full brownstone façades. Throughout the late eighteenth and early nineteenth centuries, brownstone was an inexpensive substitute for the classically correct granite, limestone, or marble. The luxurious Federal and Greek Revival style dwellings of the 1820s and 1830s, it will be recalled, employed these costly light-color building stones for basement and doorway trim on their red-brick fronts, and, in the patrician Bond Street area, occasional row houses sported extravagant marble or granite fronts. But on ordinary dwellings of that era, the builders usually employed the local brownstone for the basement's street front wall, the stoop, and the door and window details.

Trinity Church was the first of the major buildings in the city to exhibit a full brownstone façade. While discussing the architectural plans in 1838, the church's vestry selected dark brownstone over the gray limestone suggested by architect Upjohn. It is unlikely that the vestry chose brownstone over limestone solely to save money, as has been suggested, for with its extensive land holdings in Manhattan, Trinity Church was the city's wealthiest congregation. The good condition of the church's façade today is evidence that the brownstone was of the finest quality, properly cut in the quarry, and

⍟

carefully laid. More likely, the well-educated and well-to-do vestry members were acquainted with the rising Romantic movement and its architectural ideal that a house or any building harmonize with the form and colors of the natural landscape. "The practical rule . . . is, to avoid all those colors which nature avoids," declared Andrew Jackson Downing. "In building we should copy those that she offers chiefly to the eye—such as those of soil, rocks, wood, and the bark of trees—the materials of which houses are built. Those colors offer us the best and most natural study from which harmonious colors for the houses themselves should be taken."

Other congregations throughout the country soon fell under the spell of the Romantic movement and followed the lead of fashionable Trinity Church by selecting brownstone façades for their Gothic Revival style churches. In April, 1844, the *North American Review* discussed a church with a brownstone façade planned in Boston and noted that "the chocolate colored freestone of Connecticut and New Jersey is a far better material, being much softer and darker than granite." The article later suggested that a chapel, built of granite, at the Mount Auburn Cemetery should have been constructed of brownstone. The "shadowy repose" of brownstone, the article stated, was in far better taste than the "glaring uniformity" of granite. By the 1850s, brownstone was nearly a mandatory building material for wealthy city churches, and, in 1855, one magazine described James Renwick, Jr.'s, much-acclaimed white marble Grace Church on Broadway (1843–1846) as a "very showy building, very florid, and of bad white marble."

Dwelling Houses in the Gothic Revival Style.

Despite the notoriety of fashionable Gothic Revival churches and Andrew Jackson Downing's promotion of the style for country dwellings in the 1840s and 1850s, the Gothic Revival style never enjoyed widespread acceptance for private homes in New York. In a bustling and densely built-up city, it was difficult, if not impossible, to build an asymmetrically massed and picturesquely gabled house on the typical twenty-five by one-hundred-foot row house lot. The finest remaining Gothic Revival dwellings in New York, therefore, are the rectories of the costly churches built in the 1840s and 1850s. With a religious connection, relatively unhampered lot on the church grounds, and generous construction budget, a rectory could, in an uninhibited manner, employ the asymmetrical massing and the elaborate motifs inappropriate to or impossible for the ordinary row house. These rectories displayed the Gothic Revival style and the full brownstone fronts beginning in the late 1830s, whereas the row houses in the style did not appear until the mid-1840s.

An unusual rectory in the Gothic Revival style is No. 7 West Tenth Street (1839–1841), the

No. 7 West Tenth Street (1839–1841), Rectory of the Church of the Ascension, Greenwich Village. The rectory's brownstone front—perhaps the first in the city—was a startling architectural innovation at the time of its construction. Unlike the usual, later, flat-front Gothic Revival row house, No. 7 West Tenth Street relies on the asymmetrical massing of a pointed dormer window, chimney, and pitched roof for picturesque architectural effect.

rectory of the Church of the Ascension around the corner on Fifth Avenue. This virtually unchanged basement-and-two-and-one-half-story-tall rectory is one of the city's few surviving Gothic Revival row houses which demonstrates asymmetrical massing as well as applied medieval ornament. A pointed dormer projects on brackets from the façade at the second floor and thereby introduces to this twenty-five-foot-wide row house the massing so valuable to Romantic ideals in architecture. A large chimney and two small-pointed-arch dormer windows, set in the steep roof, make for a picturesque roofline silhouette.

The rectory's brownstone front, a daring innovation for the 1839–1841 period of construction, perhaps makes this building the first full brownstone-front row house in New York. Here, the brownstone front's rough texture is more appropriate to Romantic architectural ideals than the smooth-surfaced Classical brownstone fronts of nearly all row houses of succeeding decades. As with all Gothic Revival row houses, the Church of the Ascension rectory also relies heavily on its applied Gothic details, in this case, handsome drip moldings above the door and windows to strengthen its Gothic Revival style and cast picturesque shadows on the dark brownstone front. With its appropriate textured brownstone front and picturesque gabled roofline on its narrow city lot, the rectory, generally overlooked on this splendid block of West Tenth Street, ranks as one of the city's remaining architecturally distinguished row houses of the period.

Several blocks to the east at Broadway and East Tenth Street stands the handsome Grace Church Rectory (1843–1846). Built of a once-white but now-gray marble, this fine dwelling sits well back from bustling Broadway on spacious grounds enclosed by a handsome Gothic Revival fence. Because of these spacious grounds, the Grace Church Rectory avoids the design restraints of the usual narrow row house and has pointed-arch windows, a pointed-arch front entrance porch, and an unusually picturesque massing of bay windows, gables, and a roofline topped by pinnacles and clustered chimneys.

The Gothic Revival Style: The Row House Front.

Despite the restraints on design imposed by the row house lot and the style's religious associations, occasional Gothic Revival style row houses were built in New York from the mid-1840s to the late 1850s. A charming enrichment of the city streetscape, these houses were a fascinating attempt to adapt this romantic, essentially rural style to the constrained building lot of the grid-iron city plan that was the product of reason and real estate speculation. Although the applied Gothic Revival detail on these houses never proved highly popular and was soon forgotten, the Romantic architectural ideals,

(top) Cornice, No. 20 West 16th Street (ca. 1850). These pointed Gothic arches protrude about one foot from the row house front and make for an unusual cornice.

(bottom left) Doorway, No. 118 Willow Street (ca. 1845), Brooklyn Heights, with horizontal hood mold.

(bottom right) Doorway, No. 151 Avenue B (ca. 1850), with Gothic archway surmounted by horizontal hood mold.

first seen in these churches and row houses, strongly affected the design of New York row houses in coming decades.

On the Gothic Revival row house front, the door hoods, window lintels and sills, and roofline cornices significantly were more prominent than on the Greek Revival style front. This breaking of the previously planar row house front reflected the triumph of Romantic architectural ideals and their adaptation to the constraints of the city row house front. The usual Gothic Revival row house employed boldly projecting cornices, door hoods, and window lintels and sills as showy ornament and to cast picturesque shadows on the façade. "The strength and character of a building," wrote one architect then, "depend almost wholly on the shadows which are thrown upon its surface by projecting members."

Front doorways took several forms. The simplest treatment was a rectangular doorway "surmounted" or topped with a "horizontal hood mold," a horizontal form with rectangular "drip molds" at each end. Rather than a flat head, some doorways employed a low "Tudor" arch, sometimes supported on slender colonnettes. The most elegant doorway treatment combined just such a low Tudor arch surmounted by a horizontal hood mold. In these doorways, the "spandrel," or triangular space between the curve of the arch and flat hood mold, boasted elaborate carvings of leaves or the three-sided Gothic motif called a "trefoil." Andrew Jackson Downing significantly favored the square-headed door or window surmounted by the horizontal hood mold. "There is more domesticity in the square-headed window, and therefore, only introduce the arch in doors and windows of private houses in particular cases when the stronger indication of style is needed to give spirit to the composition." Presumably, it was for this reason, and the greater ease of executing the flat-headed rectangular opening rather than the arched opening, that the former became the most commonly used door and window form for the Gothic Revival row house.

The doors varied in the completeness of their Gothic forms and ornament. Although the front doors usually reflected the style by panels in some form of the pointed arch and occasional trefoils or quatrefoils, some Gothic Revival row houses were built with front doors in the Italianate style then coming into vogue. To enhance the picturesque shadows on the flat, brick row house front, the doorway was recessed more deeply in the Gothic Revival than in the Greek Revival style. Protruding from the façade, the clustered colonnettes, which usually supported the pointed-arch doorway lintel, increased the recessed depth of the front doorway and, in the words of one architect, gained "a depth of shadow and a quiet richness."

The windows of the city's Gothic Revival row houses also varied in their adherence to medieval precedent. In a concession to American building practices, the windows of most row houses were

Parlor, Grace Church Rectory (1843–1846), Broadway and East Tenth Street. The richly detailed bay window and beamed ceiling express an architectural extravagance and complete surrender to medieval inspiration rarely found in Gothic Revival row houses. Grace Church Rectory sits back from the street behind a Gothic Revival fence on ample grounds.

double-hung and had the small-sized panes of glass contemporary with the period. Occasionally, a row house employed outward-opening casement windows as a truly "medieval" form. In Brooklyn Heights, No. 131 Hicks Street retains its original small-paned casement windows, while its twin, No. 135 Hicks Street, only regained its casement windows in a 1969 façade restoration. In a compromise between construction practicality and architectural authenticity, some Gothic Revival and many Italianate style row houses of the 1850s achieved the appearance of casement windows by double-hung windows with thick vertical jambs and thin horizontal muntin bars.

Few row houses had what might be termed a Gothic cornice in form or detail. The architect-builder usually employed a cornice of the plain Greek Revival style or a boldly projecting cornice of the Italianate style supported by consoles or brackets. Not only did the Greek Revival and Italianate style cornices differ from the medieval details of a Gothic Revival dwelling, but their horizontal emphasis, characteristic of all classically inspired designs, also conflicted with the perpendicularity of the Gothic Revival style architecture.

The usual Gothic Revival cornice on a New York row house consisted of a row of pointed arches cut into the otherwise plain wood fascia board or brick façade. Though not completely Gothic in its style or simplicity, this cornice did employ the style's typical pointed-arch motif and, therefore, reflected the perpendicularity of true medieval design. For a remarkably picturesque effect, the wooden cornice at No. 20 West 16th Street has elaborate pointed arches which protrude about one foot from the façade; the twin house, No. 18 West 16th Street, has lost this charming wood cornice.

An important part of the Gothic Revival style was medieval ornament, ideally carved in stone. Aside from the ubiquitous pointed arch and horizontal hood-mold lintels, the most popular forms were the "trefoil," a three-lobed ornament, the "quatrefoil," a four-lobed ornament, and the "crochet," an elaborate projecting finial. Because the elaborate Gothic ornament was difficult to execute in stone, even in soft brownstone, stone carving was found only on the façades of the most expensive row houses. Wood and wood with plaster were used to simulate stone in the hallways and parlors, but this was not sufficiently durable for the façade. The Gothic Revival style row house, therefore, relied on its cast-iron stoop railings, front fences, parlor window balconies, and verandahs to display elaborate Gothic detail.

Virtually no Gothic Revival iron work survives in New York row houses except for occasional stoop railings and front fences. Before their demolition in 1955, the three-story-tall porches of the Rhinelander Gardens, at Nos. 102–116 West Eleventh Street, displayed the finest Gothic Revival style iron work in the city. Some Gothic Revival iron work still survives on a few row houses in Brooklyn Heights and Cobble Hill. Nearly all the stoop railings and areaway fences show the same elaborate *(top)* Verandah (*ca.* 1845), No. 36 Pierrepont Street, Brooklyn Heights. The verandah and fence here combine such Gothic Revival motifs as the pointed arch, trefoil, quatrefoil, and finial. The dappled pattern of light and shadow on the house in this photograph is fitting for the romantic inspiration of the Gothic Revival style.

(bottom) Iron Work (1848), No. 107 State Street, Brooklyn Heights. Although these houses have lost their protruding doorway and window details, they nonetheless retain handsome Gothic Revival parlor window balconies, stoop railings, and fences.

repeating pointed-arch pattern, perhaps all made at the same Brooklyn iron-work factories. In Brooklyn Heights, No. 107 State Street (1848), its façade details shaved off, retains a handsome parlor-window balcony with a quatrefoil design, and No. 36 Pierrepont Street (*ca.,* 1845), at the corner of Hicks Street, still is graced by a full-size porch of pointed arches, trefoils, quatrefoils, and finials.

Although most Gothic Revival style row houses continued the brick front with brownstone trim of earlier decades, some row houses of the late 1840s were among the first dwellings in the city to employ the then-daring full brownstone front. Among these in a Gothic Revival style which survive today are No. 16 Gramercy Park South (1844–1845); No. 28 East 20th Street, the Theodore Roosevelt House (1847–1848); No. 10 Fifth Avenue (1848–1849) at the northwest corner of West Eighth Street; and, in Brooklyn Heights, Nos. 131 and 135 Hicks Street (1847–1848).

The Gothic Revival Style: The Row House Plan and Interior Design.

The plan of the Gothic Revival row house matched that of the concurrent Greek Revival style. In interior design, Gothic forms were applied to what otherwise was a clean, smooth-surfaced interior in the Classical tradition. By the late 1840s, the budding showy taste of the 1850s and 1860s occasionally appeared on New York dwellings in elaborate mantels, doors, and ceiling plasterwork. This emerging taste worried many architects, and Gervase Wheeler gave this warning:

> The drawing room should be left as quietly simple with regard to architectural ornamentation as possible—nothing being worse taste than the overladen ornament of so-called Gothic rooms, in which the ceilings, cornices, and door and window casings are so heavy and clumsy as justly to disgust many with a style that seems to permit absurdities so monstrous.

These pleas for architectural simplicity were in vain. As already seen in the late Greek Revival style row houses of the 1840s, increasingly sophisticated machinery which could mass produce interior woodwork and papier mâché ornament at a low cost made possible the showy houses increasingly desired by well-to-do families in a wealthy and socially competitive city. In some Gothic Revival style dwellings, for example, the architect-builders employed wood and plaster to imitate the costly carved stonework, a practice condemned by Downing as "a glaring want of truthfulness sometimes practiced in this country by ignorant builders."

The ordinary Gothic Revival style mantel was white or black marble and consisted of a rectangular mantel shelf, supported by flat pilasters, and a hearth opening in the form of a low, pointed arch. Most mantels lacked the costly carved Gothic details and, except for the pointed-arch opening, were quite similar to ordinary Greek Revival mantels. But the cast-iron grate over the

(top left) Ceiling Centerpiece or Rosette, Willow Street, Brooklyn Heights, with quatrefoil and foliate forms characteristic of the Gothic Revival style.

(top right) Parlor Doors, No. 7 West Tenth Street, Rectory of the Church of the Ascension.

(bottom) Mantel, butler's pantry, Grace Church Rectory. Notice the shield and incised quatrefoils on the mantel and the handsome coal grate with Gothic arches and madonnas.

fireplace opening boasted pointed arches, trefoils, and figures of saints and thereby contributed elaborate medieval detail to the hearth in reasonably inexpensive cast iron. Only mantels in the finest dwellings carried carved medieval ornament.

Gothic Revival style mantels sometimes appeared in the parlors of otherwise entirely Greek Revival or Italianate style row houses—probably as a picturesque enrichment. A Gothic Revival row house did not always have Gothic Revival parlor mantels. According to the house's date of construction and the richness of its interior ornament, the parlor mantels sometimes were in a Greek Revival style of the 1840s or the elaborate round-arched Italianate manner of the late 1840s and 1850s. This free interchange of parlor mantels in different styles in the city's row houses of the 1840s and 1850s reflected the rising eclectic ideals in which the mixing of styles was thought to be picturesque and architecturally sophisticated. Also, it showed the freedom with which the Gothic Revival style was viewed in New York row houses. However, these stylistic developments did not influence the mantels of the basement, second, or third floors. The builder economized on these to afford a showy parlor floor and, on those less important floors, installed wood rather than costly marble mantels, usually in the declining, hence cheaper, Greek Revival style.

Row houses with nominally Gothic Revival street fronts often were Gothic in their interiors only as far as the parlor mantels. From a practical standpoint, the style was so infrequently used that most architectural ornament factories did not produce Gothic Revival interior fixtures, and, furthermore, the skilled workmen, who might have made many interior appointments by hand, had few opportunities to gain competence in the style. From the architectural side, the Gothic Revival in row houses was viewed mostly as a picturesque enrichment rather than a complete style, and it was thought unnecessary that the façade or interior design fully carry it out.

Interior doorways in Gothic Revival style row houses often were plainly molded, rectangular openings which lack Gothic pointed-arch form or applied ornament. When interior doorways did follow the Gothic Revival style, they took the same forms as front doors: slender colonnettes, rising to either a horizontal hood mold, or a low Tudor arch, or a Tudor arch surmounted by a horizontal hood mold, or a Tudor arch surmounted by a horizontal hood mold with elaborate spandrel carving. The doors themselves often had inset panels in the form of the pointed arch. Interior doorway moldings often were more intricately carved than exterior ones, simply because wood was easier to work than stone. Some builder's guides recommended elaborate doorways which were rarely, if ever, seen in a row house; for example, a doorway topped by an "ecclesiastical," high pointed arch with a Gothic finial at the top, or an arched doorway surmounted by a horizontal hood mold with a cornice of crenelation, the notched "castellated" motif imitating a battlement. These elaborate doorways

Mantel, parlor, Grace Church Rectory.
The front parlor mantel at Grace
Church Rectory enjoys a plasticity of
form and an elaborate carving found
only on the finest mantels of the mid-
nineteenth century.

showed the richness possible in the Gothic Revival mode and reflected the rising architectural grandeur of the 1850s.

The parlor-ceiling cornices of some Gothic Revival style row houses were a coved form edged by two plain moldings or, in a reflection of the rising Italianate style, an elaborate cornice of foliate forms. A plaster centerpiece, sometimes nominally Gothic in its trefoils or quatrefoils, dominated the center of the parlor ceiling. Looking back to the Middle Ages, some architects recommended a flat, beamed ceiling in Gothic Revival dwellings, but Andrew Jackson Downing preferred a vertical treatment. "The ceilings of rooms in the Gothic style are not treated as if supported on horizontal beams in the classical styles, because the principle of support is supposed to be perpendicular. Hence the ceiling is traversed by ribs, running down and resting on brackets, so as to convey the idea of vertical support." The complexity and cost of such a ceiling ruled out its use in most dwellings, and, moreover, this treatment would have dominated the parlor of a narrow New York row house and conflicted with the usual simple smooth-surfaced interior design to which people were accustomed.

The front parlor of No. 52 Livingston Street, in Brooklyn Heights, was remodeled in a Gothic Revival mode several years after the construction of the house. This once-rectangular parlor was converted into an octagon with niches at each corner, and beams radiate from the ceiling centerpiece to give the flat ceiling the appearance of medieval vaulting. The black-marble mantel typically has a shallow Tudor-arch hearth opening.

Manhattan.

Few Gothic Revival style row houses were built in New York, and only a handful of these remain, usually having lost much of their façade details. Among the city's finest row houses in this style were Nos. 10–16 Fifth Avenue (1848–1849), between West Eighth and West Ninth streets. These four houses boasted the then-daring brownstone front, horizontal hood molds for window lintels, and unusual crenelated roof cornices. Only No. 10 Fifth Avenue, at the northwest corner of West Eighth Street, has survived to the present day in any semblance of its original appearance. Although the street-level doorway has replaced the original stoop and all window lintels and sills have been shaved smooth with the façade, this house retains its original crenelated roofline and handsome quatrefoils cut into the stone above the parlor windows. To the north, Nos. 14–16 Fifth Avenue have lost all traces of original design, in a conversion to apartments, except for their five-story height.

Manhattan's unceasing development and rebuilding drastically has altered or demolished most of the city's nineteenth-century row houses. The survival of large portions of Greenwich Village or

(top left) No. 135 West Twelfth Street (1851), Greenwich Village. The front doors of this row house are nearly identical to a plate in D. H. Arnot's *Gothic Architecture Applied to Modern Residences,* 1851.

(top right) Doorways, from D. H. Arnot's *Gothic Architecture Applied to Modern Residences,* 1851.

(bottom) West 20th Street and Sixth Avenue, southwest corner, in 1854. A charming row of Gothic Revival row houses. Notice the miniature scale of the horse-drawn omnibus in relation to the modest row houses. Demolished.

Chelsea is one of the wonders of the city and presents a charming contrast of nineteenth-century streetscape and life style with present-day New York. Brooklyn, with its quieter history of growth, inevitably contains more of the city's surviving nineteenth-century neighborhoods and dwellings than does Manhattan, particularly for the Gothic Revival style row house.

Brooklyn.

In Brooklyn Heights, Nos. 131 and 135 Hicks Street are two of New York's finest remaining Gothic Revival style row houses. Built in 1848, No. 131 Hicks Street has a virtually unchanged façade, and No. 135 regained its original appearance in a 1969 facade restoration which added a cornice and casement windows copied from its twin, No. 131. The doorway enframements have a low Tudor arch, surmounted by a horizontal hood mold with elaborately carved spandrels, which is similar to a design in Arnot's *Gothic Architecture Applied to Modern Residences* (1851), and the original doors are deeply set into the façade to gain a large dark shadow. All the windows keep the typical horizontal hood molds. The stoop railings and areaway fence combine quatrefoils and elaborate pointed arches, and in the fence are rows of Gothic finials.

During the 1840s and 1850s, Gothic Revival motifs often were added to an earlier row house as a "modernization." In Brooklyn Heights, No. 52 Livingston Street originally was a Greek Revival style dwelling built in 1847 but gained a Gothic Revival style front and an already mentioned parlor, most likely after the construction of Minard Lafever's Packer Collegiate Institute across the street in 1854. Although this charming house presently suffers the indignity of a pink-stucco façade, modern aluminum window frames, and a floor added above the cornice, it retains a Gothic Revival style areaway fence and porch across the first-floor width, horizontal hood-mold window and doorway lintels, and an arched-pattern cornice.

Some Gothic Revival row houses remain in Cobble Hill, immediately to the south of Brooklyn Heights. Here, as throughout the city, the stone door and window lintels usually have been shaved flush with the façade, but traces of these stone lintels can still be seen in the otherwise brick fronts. Even these altered row houses display Gothic motifs in the remaining stone carving and iron work. The only nearly intact Gothic Revival style row house in Cobble Hill is No. 271 Degraw Street (1850). A three-sided bay window, extending up the entire front of the façade, breaks the usual flat-face row house pattern and achieves an unusual sense of asymmetry for its twenty-two-foot-wide front. Though presently painted a stylistically inappropriate white color, this house retains much of its original Gothic applied detail, including a fence in an arched pattern with rows of finials, horizontal hood

(top left) Back Porch, No. 36 Pierrepont Street (*ca.* 1845), Brooklyn Heights. Notice the handsome Gothic Revival touches.

(top right) No. 271 Degraw Street (*ca.* 1850), Brooklyn. The front of this house, though painted an inappropriate light color, retains virtually its original appearance.

(bottom left) No. 167 State Street (*ca.* 1848), Brooklyn Heights, a handsome Gothic Revival dwelling house, although much façade detail has been removed.

(bottom right) Nos. 54–56 Union Street (1847–1848), Brooklyn. The original real estate advertisement for these forlorn row houses read: "New and Genteel Houses, at low rent . . . some in full Gothic style. . . ."

molds for door and window lintels, and a repeating arch pattern for the frieze of the cornice.

What is one of the city's most imaginatively designed surviving Gothic Revival row houses, in both its formal composition and its applied stylistic detail, stands largely overlooked at No. 154 Court Street (1854). Although a store-front remodeling on this commercial street destroyed the basement and first floors, the intact second and third floors give a good idea of the house's original appearance. Within the constraints of the twenty-foot wide lot, this house gains a striking asymmetry with a two-sided projecting bay, a flat recessed portion, and a balancing stepped-out square portion. The unusual brick cornice has a row of dentiling above the corbels, recalling the arched frieze usually cut into the wood fascia board. Horizontal hood molds rise in a peak over the modestly pointed window heads, an apparently now-unique form of window in the city.

The Decline of the Gothic Revival Style.

Even in its modest heyday, architects and magazine articles criticized the Gothic Revival style as unsuitable for city row houses and for American dwellings in general. "We know of no successful efforts in Gothic street architecture, in England or in this country," observed one magazine in the mid-1850s. "We have no models in antiquity of this kind except collegiate buildings. . . . We are of the opinion that the Gothic style, if used at all in cities, should be kept sacred."

The pervasive "sacred" associations and difficult asymmetrical massing of the Gothic Revival style had provided somewhat of a challenge even in building country houses, and by the 1850s the style's vogue declined on all dwellings. After all, the style had no roots in America where, in contrast to Great Britain, there were no actual medieval structures or ruins to inspire study or to provoke the imagination. "The Gothic style is altogether an exotic in America, where, so far from bearing any historic associations and sentiment, it is quite an alien. . . . There being no examples of it in former buildings, no wonder, therefore, that anything can be palmed off upon the American public as Gothic," wrote one British magazine in the early 1850s.

Some American critics also linked the style with aristocratic British ideals and considered it distinctly foreign to the American spirit. In the 1870s Mark Twain attacked James Dakin's unusual Gothic Revival style Louisiana State Capitol (1849) in Baton Rouge:

> By itself the imitation castle is doubtless harmless, and well enough; but as a symbol and breeder and sustainer of maudlin Middle-Age romanticism here in the midst of the plainest and sturdiest and infinitely greatest and worthiest of all countries the world has ever seen, it is necessarily a hurtful thing and a mistake.

Rhinelander Gardens (after 1854), Nos. 102–116 West Eleventh Street, Greenwich Village, in 1937. Deep front yards and dazzling Gothic Revival cast-iron porches made this row of ordinary brick houses one of Greenwich Village's visual treats. Demolished in 1955.

The Gothic Revival never shook off this foreign connotation. "Many persons of pure taste are frightened when the idea of 'Gothic' is presented to them as a style suggested for their house," complained one architect.

American builders had other reasons for resisting the Gothic Revival style, even in the simplified appliqué form. The style was not suited to large-scale construction for middle-class housing, because pointed arches and stone carving, even with sham materials, were time-consuming to execute and hence more expensive than the massive rectangular Greek Revival style forms. The Gothic details, furthermore, required considerably more knowledge of a past style to execute with any degree of accuracy, and, before Arnot's *Gothic Architecture Applied to Modern Residences* (1851), no builder's guides offered line drawings of Gothic Revival style forms and details.

The Gothic Revival style finally died, as did the nearly concurrent Greek Revival, as a consequence of the shift in taste around 1850 away from relative architectural simplicity to the flamboyant forms and ornament of an eclectic Italianate style, more appealing to a nouveau riche society eager to flaunt its taste and wealth. Our surviving legacy of Gothic Revival style forms is hard to find in the row houses of the city but holds undeniable charm for anyone who has once fallen under its spell. Nowhere are these architectural testaments to man's unfulfilled romantic yearnings more appealing than when chanced upon around some city corner in present-day New York.

Fifth Avenue, In 1859, View South from 37th Street. By the eve of the Civil War, "a continuous line of magnificent mansions" lined the two miles of Fifth Avenue from Washington Square to the foot of Central Park at 59th Street. The elegant row houses and mansions ranged in price from $20,000 to $200,000 and $300,000 and dazzled sophisticated New York with their richly ornamented façades and resplendent parlors. However, some New Yorkers complained that "nearly all the houses are built on the same [Italianate] design, which gives to it an air of sameness and tameness that is not pleasing." Nearly all the mansions and churches on midtown Fifth Avenue were demolished over the years for department stores and office buildings. The Empire State Building now rises just beyond the spire of the Brick Presbyterian Church in the foreground on this engraving.

Chapter Four

The Italianate, Anglo-Italianate, and Second Empire Styles

The late 1840s and early 1850s were years of architectural ferment in New York. After decades in restrained red-brick-front Federal and Greek Revival style row houses, New Yorkers now yearned for picturesque and impressive dwellings which would reflect the city's unparalleled wealth, social competition, and the rising Romantic movement in architecture. The Italianate style appeared in New York in the late 1840s, and in the years before its demise in the mid-1870s the city's row houses attained a remarkable splendor and architectural flamboyance.

The last great New York dwelling in the Greek Revival style was the John Cox Stevens mansion (1845–1847) on College Place at Murray Street. Designed by Alexander Jackson Davis, the white marble mansion, known as "Stevens' Palace," boasted ample landscaped grounds, a monumental semicircular portico supported by two-story-tall Corinthian columns, a central hall beneath a dome, and immense, lavishly decorated parlors for frequent entertaining. The Stevens mansion was "the most elegant Grecian mansion in New-York . . . without doubt," declared one magazine, and Philip Hone wrote that "the house is, indeed, a palace. The Palais Bourbon in Paris, Buckingham Palace in London, Sans-Souci at Berlin, are little grander than this residence of a simple citizen of our republican city."

In the very richness of its Greek Revival style and its palatial scale, the Stevens mansion heralded the architectural ideals and social currents soon to replace the Greek Revival style and the long-lived Classical tradition of architectural modesty in the city's row houses. Only one or two years after completion of the Stevens mansion, brownstone-front Italianate style mansions of unmatched grandeur were rising on Fifth Avenue in the vicinity of 14th Street. At the same time, occasional row houses had adopted daring brownstone fronts and the Italianate style, and those row houses which still employed the Greek Revival style evidenced an increased scale and greater richness in their Greek forms and ornament and sometimes occasional touches of the emerging Italianate style.

In Greenwich Village, the block of East Tenth Street, between Fifth Avenue and University Place, still reflects the architectural ferment of the late 1840s and early 1850s. Nos. 6, 8, 10, 12, 14, and 24 East Tenth Street are Greek Revival row houses built in the 1840s, presently in varying states of original condition. On the other hand, Nos. 4 and 18 are Gothic Revival, which first introduced the architectural ideals of the Romantic movement to the city's row houses. The round forms of the incoming Italianate style appear on doorways, stoop iron work, and cornices at No. 16 East Tenth Street (1846) and No. 20 (1848). Not everyone admired the simultaneous popularity of these three architectural styles or their eclectic mixing on one house. "The present age is distinguished . . . by too cosmopolitan a taste for variety of styles, with a view to the production of novelty and picturesqueness," wrote M. Field in his *City Architecture* (1853). "We should eschew all unpure, mixed, and transition styles, and for city architecture should adopt the Italian."

The Background of the Brownstone Era.

Although the Romantic movement encouraged the fashion for brownstone fronts and Italianate style on New York row houses, the increasingly sophisticated machine technology, the city's rising wealth, and an opulent and competitive social scene offered further incentive, and indeed the means, to encourage the spread of this showy style to nearly all the city's row houses in the 1850s.

Advancing technology first influenced the construction and architectural treatment of the city's row houses in the 1830s. Factory-made stoop railings and areaway fences occasionally appeared on Greek Revival row houses, and, in the interior, some doors, moldings, and ceiling plasterwork were machine-made. By the 1840s, iron stoop railings, fences, and interior details generally were machine-made and purchased at local factories.

Before this time, marble, fine woods, iron work, and ceiling ornament were hand-hewn and, therefore, only available in the most costly dwellings. With the improved capabilities and economies of machine manufacture, showy materials and elaborate ornament began to appear in the houses of the city's well-to-do middle class and, despite the savings, retained the status connotations of hand-labor days. The technology of the period also brought unparalleled comfort to many New Yorkers through previously unavailable indoor flush toilets, hot and cold running water, forced hot-air heating, and numerous kitchen improvements.

The scale and elaborate ornament of New York row houses mirrored the growing affluence of America's most prosperous city, and foreign and domestic trade remained the foundation of its prosperity. By 1860, more than one-third of the nation's exports and more than two-thirds of its imports, as measured by goods' value, passed through New York. Along the East River, New Yorkers admired the swift clippers and international packet ships; dry goods and foodstuffs filled merchants' warehouses and often overflowed onto the sidewalks; and the renowned East River shipyards built some of the finest ships in the world. "One needs to come down to the river quays to see the greatness of New York City," wrote one Scottish visitor in the late 1840s.

Long the unquestioned leader of American trade, New York became the nation's financial and business center in the 1850s and 1860s. Banks and insurance companies proliferated in size, assets, and numbers, and one British businessman described New York as "now the largest—indeed *the* money market of the States." In turn, the city's array of financial services strengthened its trade position because, as one visitor noted, its financial market "offers facilities to merchants which cannot be afforded by any other city." At the same time, this activity attracted the main offices of the nation's corporations, paving the way for the city's concentration of corporate headquarters in later years.

In the mid-nineteenth century, New York also became a leading manufacturing center. The city's rail and water transport routes offered quick connections to raw materials as well as to markets for the finished goods, and a rising tide of immigrants provided ample cheap labor. In 1850 the value of the city's manufactured goods totaled approximately $105,000,000. By 1860 the figure had risen to $160,000,000, and by 1870 it more than doubled to $333,000,000.

In these decades of unparalleled prosperity, New York's population tripled in just thirty years—from 313,000 in 1840, to 515,000 in 1850, to 814,000 in 1860, and to 942,000 in 1870! A nearly continuous building boom accompanied this rapid growth in population.

These thriving trade, financial, and manufacturing activities brought great wealth to many families. Reveling in their newly won riches, these families flaunted their prosperity and sought concomitant social recognition from the city's longer-established Dutch and mercantile families. New York's affluent middle class imitated the city's rich families as best they could in houses, carriages, parties, and clothing. Although visitors to New York pointed out its showy social scene as early as the 1820s, the mid-nineteenth century brought an unmatched extravagance and competition to the game.

New York's social life was "in a state of constant fluctuation, in accordance with the fluctuating fortunes of commercial life. Its doors are guarded, but they never seem to be closed, and you have a constant stream flowing in and out," wrote one Englishman in the 1840s. After the Civil War, New Yorkers themselves openly criticized the extravagant life styles and social competition of the "shoddy aristocracy . . . tossed to the surface in the convulsions of the society caused by the war." New York "'Society' is constantly shifting—it is a kaleidoscope," lamented one magazine. "Few, if any, of the leaders of ten years ago remain; all are gone—gone, and none know whither, or care. 'Society' is too eager, too busy, to stop and shed a tear upon ruined fortunes or blasted hopes."

By the 1850s, the wealth and social ambitions of some families in New York had exceeded even the scale and architectural treatment of a row house mansion in the Bond Street or Washington Square North tradition. Following the lead of John Cox Stevens' "Palace" on College Place, families built freestanding town mansions on Fifth Avenue near 14th Street and Madison Square. Those families unable to afford a mansion and costly grounds lived in palatial brownstone-front Italianate style row houses whose height, depth, and rich architectural embellishment surpassed that of all earlier dwellings. Although only a few families lived in these town mansions or splendid twenty-five- or thirty-foot-wide row houses, tens of thousands of more modest Italianate style row houses throughout the city did aspire to a similar grandeur of scale and embellishment in their street fronts and interiors.

In such an extravagant and frantic social setting, the tastefulness of one's dwelling was an object (top) Philadelphia Athenaeum (1845–1847), one of the first palazzo-inspired buildings in the United States.

(bottom) John Cox Stevens Residence (1845–1847), College Place and Murray Street, southeast corner, Alexander Jackson Davis, architect. In the 1840s, College Place, now West Broadway, was an elegant residential backwater adjacent to the verdant onetime Columbia College campus. By 1850, stores and warehouses had invaded the area, and, in the mid-1850s, Columbia College sold its pleasant campus for warehouse building lots and moved uptown to East 49th Street. In the mid-1850s, John Cox Stevens' lovely but short-lived mansion was demolished and warehouses were built on the site.

of great concern. Women's magazines, led by *Godey's Lady's Book,* and books purporting to be guides to good taste in interior decoration first appeared in the 1850s. Few Americans better understood or profited more from the social importance of the home at that period than Samuel Sloan of Philadelphia, author of several books on city and country house architecture in the 1850s and 1860s. He realized that "taking advantage of every novelty, which fancy introduced into the architecture of the day, and which fashion stamps with her signet, our merchant princes, ever desirous of surpassing their neighbors, grasp with avidity, and without delay make use of, the newest designs." In the early 1850s, Sloan boldly stated:

> A man's dwelling at the present day, is not only an index of his wealth, but also of his character. The moment he begins to build, his tact for arrangement, his private feelings, the refinement of his taste and the peculiarities of his judgment are all laid bare for public inspection and criticism. And the public makes free use of this prerogative. It expects an effort to be made, and forms opinions upon the result.

The Background of the Italianate Style.

The inspiration for the Italianate style in New York row houses was the fifteenth-century Italian city palace or *palazzo*. In 1829 the British architect Charles Barry probably made the first use of the *palazzo* or *Cinquecento* mode for the Traveler's Club (1829–1831) on London's Pall Mall. Barry again employed the richly decorated *palazzo* mode for the Reform Club (1838–1840) and later for government offices in the Whitehall area. About the same time, graduates of the famed École des Beaux Arts in Paris adopted the *palazzo* mode for government buildings, because its monumental scale and rich classical ornament were deemed suitable to express the dignity of the French government. Designs for large public buildings in Berlin, Vienna, and other European capitals soon reflected this mode.

In the United States, Arthur Gilman probably was the first American to recommend the *palazzo* mode as an alternative to the Greek Revival style in an 1844 article in the *North American Review.* In the following years, an occasional building in the Renaissance *palazzo* mode began to appear in American cities. The Philadelphia "Athenaeum" (1845–1847), designed by John Notman, was one of the first *palazzo*-mode buildings in this country and still stands on the east side of that city's Washington Square. In her *History of Architecture* (1848), Louisa Caroline Tuthill mentioned the Philadelphia Athenaeum and expressed the rising concern for the architectural treatment of the city streetscape. "This building is a beautiful specimen of street architecture. Where the space for an edifice in the city is necessarily very limited, the best possible way of rendering it ornamental, is to

(top) A. T. Stewart Store (1845–1846), east side of Broadway, between Chambers and Reade streets, in 1850. The first palazzo-inspired building in New York and one of the first department stores in the world. Though now altered into several discount stores and threatened with destruction, the A. T. Stewart Store still projects the elegance and dignity which electrified New York 130 years ago.

(bottom) Brooklyn Savings Bank (1846–1847), Fulton and Concord streets, Brooklyn, Minard Lafever, architect. One of the first palazzo-mode buildings in New York. Demolished.

decorate the doors and windows, the cornice and balustrade."

Another equally early building in this Renaissance mode was the A. T. Stewart Store (1845–1846) in New York at Broadway and Chambers Street, later *The New York Sun* building. New Yorkers marveled at its splendor, one of the first department stores in the world. The "splendid edifice . . . is nearly finished. . . . There is nothing in Paris or London to compare with this dry goods palace," wrote Philip Hone in 1846. The A. T. Stewart Store immediately became the shopping mecca of New York's well-to-do families, and its fame and grandeur helped to spread the daring *palazzo* mode throughout the city.

The A. T. Stewart Store also became a landmark on Broadway, then New York's street of fashionable shops and hotels. In an anonymous article in *Harper's*, George William Curtis declared:

> A few years ago, when a man returned from Europe, his eye being full of the lofty buildings of the Continent, our cities seemed insignificant and mean. . . . But the moment Stewart's fine building was erected, the difficulty appeared. That tyrannized over the rest of the street—that was a key-note, a model. There had been other high buildings, but none so stately and simple. And even now there is, in its way, no finer street effect than the view of Stewart's building seen on a clear, blue, brilliant day, from a point as low on Broadway as . . . Trinity Church. It rises out of the sea of green foliage in the [City Hall] Park, a white marble cliff, sharply drawn against the sky.

The article concluded that we "will look up to the beautiful buildings in Broadway and long not for Italy and an Italian beauty, but be gratefully contented for what we are." Today, this onetime "most magnificent dry-goods establishment in the world" is divided into several discount department and appliance stores.

Across the East River, Minard Lafever's Brooklyn Savings Bank (1846–1847) at Fulton and Concord streets displayed the *palazzo* mode tempered with some Greek Revival details. Although the bank was demolished in 1936 for Cadman Plaza park at the foot of the Brooklyn Bridge, a print in Lafever's *The Architectural Instructor* (1856) shows that, as originally built, it exhibited many Renaissance *palazzo* motifs later to be seen in New York's Italianate style row houses. In *The Architectural Instructor*, Lafever described the Brooklyn Savings Bank as in the "Italian style" and noted that the fronts of the adjoining dwelling houses were designed to harmonize with the bank.

The Appearance of the Palazzo Mode on New York Dwellings.

The *palazzo* mode won immediate acclaim in New York and throughout the United States for commercial and public buildings, and by the late 1840s daring mansions and row houses in the city

Herman Thorne Residence (1846–1848), south side of West 16th Street, just off Fifth Avenue, Trench and Snook, architects, in 1854. The Thorne residence probably was the first Italianate style dwelling house in New York. Later, New York Hospital built its facilities on the residence's grounds, which stretched through the block to West 15th Street, and used the former mansion for administrative offices. Since the early 1960s, the Chelsea House apartment building has occupied this site. West 16th Street, off Fifth Avenue, nonetheless, has a number of well-preserved late Greek Revival, Gothic Revival, and Italianate style row houses.

occasionally employed its domestic offshoot, the Italianate style. Several years later, the Italianate style replaced the long-lived Greek Revival style on New York row houses, and, in 1854, one magazine stated that "the Grecian taste . . . has within the last few years been succeeded and almost entirely superseded, both here and in England, by the revival of the Italian style."

The first Italianate style dwelling in New York very likely was the Herman Thorne mansion (1846–1848) on the south side of West 16th Street, just off Fifth Avenue. Designed by Trench and Snook, the Thorne residence employed the brownstone front, fully enframed and boldly ornamented front doorway and windows, and the prominent cornice so common to Italianate style row houses throughout the city in subsequent years. In 1847 one magazine described the then unfinished Thorne mansion as "unquestionably the finest private dwelling in the country . . . it has an air of unostentatious magnificence that no town house in the Union can pretend to." This magazine further realized the importance of the mansion's brownstone front and Italianate style to the architecture of the ordinary row house and declared that "we are glad for the sake of our domestic architecture, that Col. Thorn [*sic*] has erected a noble mansion in 16th street. It will help vastly to ornament our growing town and to improve the taste and knowledge of our builders."

Throughout the 1850s, magazines and guide books to the city pointed out Herman Thorne's "elegant mansion" and particularly its "ample courtyard." The Thorne mansion "has the advantage of standing back in an inclosed fore-court, with double gates and a carriage-drive sweeping under a portico, of the Tuscan order," wrote one magazine. "On each side of the entrance door is a niche, with a bronzed figure of a Mercury, holding a lamp; there are also two recumbent figures of dogs on the landing before the door. A pretty white marble basin and fountain stand in front of the portico." Newspapers and magazines also enthusiastically reported Herman Thorne's earlier life in Paris and hoped that he and his new mansion would introduce finer social as well as architectural practices to New York. "The social career of Colonel Thorn [*sic*] has been so frequently the theme of remark . . . particularly his magnificent mansion in Paris," declared one magazine in the late 1840s.

> His brilliant entertainments, elegant equipages and princely expenditure attracted the attention of that vast metropolis, the modern Babylon of more than ancient grandeur, not merely that they were unrivalled in their kind, but for the singular phenomenon that an American, a republican, an unsophisticated Yankee, should have ventured into the proud domain of aristocratic splendor, and taken the prize in a costly race with the nobles and millionaires of Europe.

Another early mansion to introduce the *palazzo* mode to New York was the Richard K. Haight residence (1848–1849) also designed by Trench and Snook at the southeast corner of Fifth Avenue and 15th Street. Old engravings and photographs show a freestanding brownstone mansion of plain Italianate style with

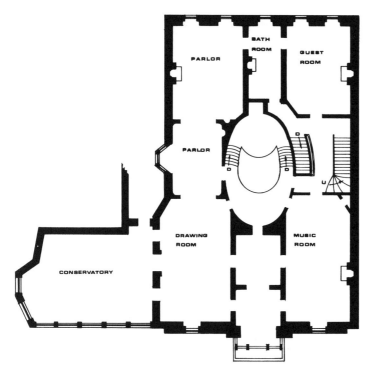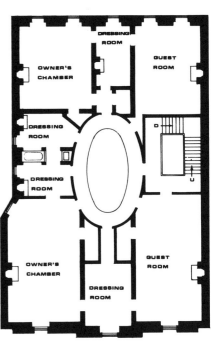

(top) Fifth Avenue, in 1865, West Side, View South from the Northwest Corner of 21st Street. Mansions, club houses, and churches of celebrated grandeur and extravagance rose on Fifth Avenue between Washington Square and 23rd Street in the 1850s. The immense building in the foreground is the Union Club, completed in 1855 by Thomas & Son, architects, at a total cost of nearly $200,000. All the buildings in this photograph are gone today except for the First Presbyterian Church, its tower seen in the hazy distance.

(bottom left) Plan, Henry Parish Residence, No. 26 East 17th Street, off Fifth Avenue, R. G. Hatfield, architect. First floor, 1848 plan. Demolished.

(bottom right) Plan, Henry Parish Residence, Second floor.

a rusticated basement, impressive stoop and doorway, fully enframed windows, and a classical balustrade at the roofline. The Haight mansion was "Palladian" in style, declared one magazine, and "though it may have been since exceeded in richness of decoration, we doubt if it has been in good proportion, and purity of design." In the mid-1850s, another magazine praised the "chaste and elegant house of Mr. Haight" and declared that "if it has a fault, it is its over-refinement. Every window and doorway indicates a careful study, which is refreshing after the hurried and careless treatment which is stamped on almost all our architecture. It is a pure specimen of Italian architecture."

The sumptuous parlors of the Haight mansion more than compensated for any simplicity in its street-front appearance. In New York, "the house most elegantly fitted up is unquestionably that of Mr. Haight," wrote one visitor in the early 1850s, "with an Italian winter garden, playing fountains, large saloons in the Parisian fashion, a drawing room in the style of the Taj Mahal at Agra, a splendid library, etc., etc. You perceive at once that the owner of the house has travelled all over Europe, and likes to be surrounded with the recollections of everything he has seen abroad."

In a crowded city of twenty- and twenty-five-foot-wide row houses and traffic-filled streets, the spacious grounds and outbuildings of the Haight mansion were a startling sight. "A lower range of offices, and a stable-yard entrance is seen down the street; while there is also another arched entrance for carriages between two projecting columns, on the right," noted one magazine. Perhaps the most unusual feature of the Haight mansion was a greenhouse or "winter garden" at one corner of its grounds. The "large winter-garden," according to one Englishwoman, was,

> a glass building with a high dome; a fine fountain was playing in the centre, and round its marble basin were orange, palm, and myrtle trees, with others from the tropics, some of them of considerable growth. Every part of the floor that was not of polished white marble was thickly carpeted with small green ferns. The *gleam* of white marble statues, from among the clumps of orange-trees and other shrubs, was particularly pretty; indeed, the whole had a fairy-like appearance about it.

When the 14th Street area lost its residential fashion after the Civil War, a large addition and another floor were built on the Haight residence, and in 1871 the splendid mansion became one of the city's first apartment buildings.

Another mansion to introduce the Italianate style to the New York row house was the Henry Benkard residence (1849–1850) at the northwest corner of Fifth Avenue and 15th Street. The Benkard mansion reflected the Italianate style row house on the scale of a mansion: a rusticated basement, brownstone front, fully enframed windows, and a cornice supported by modillion blocks. As with all Italianate row houses, the front doorway of the Benkard mansion was unusually grand; the round-headed double doors were enframed by Corinthian columns and a horizontal entablature and *(top)* Richard K. Haight Residence (1848–1849), Fifth Avenue and 15th Street, southeast corner, Trench and Snook architects, in 1854. Demolished.

(bottom left) Van Buren Residence (1849–1850), north side of 14th Street between Fifth and Sixth avenues. The Van Buren residence outlasted the other extravagant mansions erected in the Fifth Avenue and 14th Street vicinity in the 1840s and 1850s. It disappeared as recently as 1927 for an ordinary row of two-story-tall store buildings.

(bottom right) Henry Benkard Residence (1849–1850), Fifth Avenue and 15th Street, northwest corner in 1854. Another mansion to introduce the Italianate style on New York dwelling houses. Demolished.

were approached from the street by two curving and balustraded stairways. In 1865 the Manhattan Club purchased the Benkard mansion for $110,000 and stayed there until 1890, when it moved uptown to the A. T. Stewart mansion at 34th Street.

These Fifth Avenue mansions introduced an unparalleled grandeur of scale and richness of ornament to the city's row houses. One of the largest and most showy mansions of this period was the Henry Parish residence at No. 26 East 17th Street, near Fifth Avenue. The British visitor Isabella Lucy Bird visited the Parish mansion and described its sumptuous interior in considerable detail:

> At one house which I visited . . . about the largest private residence in the city, and one which is considered to combine the greatest splendour with the greatest taste, we entered a spacious marble hall, leading to a circular stone staircase of great width, the balustrades being figures elaborately cast in bronze. About this staircase was a lofty dome, decorated with paintings in fresco of eastern scenes. There were niches in the walls, some containing Italian statuary, and others small jets of water pouring over artificial moss.
>
> There were six or eight magnificent reception-rooms, furnished in various styles—the Mediaeval, the Elizabethan, the Italian, the Persian, the modern English, &c. There were fountains of fairy workmanship, pictures from old masters, statues from Italy . . . porcelain from China and Sevres; damasks, cloth of gold, and *bijoux* from the East; Gobelin tapestry, tables of malachite and agate, and 'knick-knacks' of every description. . . . I saw one table the value of which might be about 2000 guineas.

The twenty-three-year-old Miss Bird declared that on the second floor "the bedrooms were scarcely less magnificently furnished than the reception rooms." Although she felt that such Fifth Avenue mansions as the Parish residence "were rather at variance with my ideas of republican simplicity . . . and surpassed anything I had hitherto witnessed in royal or ducal palaces at home," she nonetheless wrote of the Parish mansion that "there was nothing gaudy, profuse, or prominent in the decorations or furniture; everything had evidently been selected by a person of very refined taste."

In the 1850s and 1860s, New Yorkers believed that the Italianate style brownstone-front dwellings were in better architectural taste than the city's earlier Federal and Greek Revival dwellings. Compared with the grandly scaled and richly ornamented Italianate style row houses, the city's late-eighteenth- and early-nineteenth-century Federal style row houses indeed were plain in appearance. "The old three story brick dwelling houses," observed one magazine,

> although spacious and comfortable in their construction, were entirely destitute of all architectural embellishments; they had no dressings to their windows, and the fan-light over the door . . . were all that our best houses could boast of in the way of external ornament. Now, the humblest of our city dwellings, however, make a gratifying display of knowledge and taste in their frontage.

Another magazine wrote that the "cheapest 'colony houses' [tenements] of the present day . . . are elegant structures, externally, compared with the city residences of our wealthiest families but few years since." Many residents of a proud and wealthy New York agreed with Louisa Caroline Tuthill that "the recent evidences of improving taste and public spirit of the citizens, offer the most certain promise that at some future day New York will equal in splendor the proudest cities of the old world."

The Emergence of the Italianate Style in New York.

By the early 1850s, nearly all the city's architects and builders had adopted the shadowy brownstone front and the showy Italianate style for row houses. However, no New York row house style had a precise beginning or end, and the row houses of the late 1840s and early 1850s reflected a transition between the Greek Revival and Italianate styles ordinarily showing the ideals of both the preceding and the succeeding styles. The Greek Revival style, it will be remembered, first appeared as Ionic colonnettes in Late Federal doorways. When builders adopted additional Greek motifs, such as heavy pilasters supporting an entablature for a doorway enframement or the fret and anthemion for iron work, the style became more Greek than Federal; hence, the term Greek Revival. Nevertheless, the new style did not exist in a vacuum any more than did its predecessor. It, too, was subject to inevitable modification stemming from changes in aesthetic values, in taste, and in construction technology. A row house seldom reflected a pure style; it often showed occasional forms and motifs of a past mode as well as signs of the style which eventually would succeed it.

On the New York row houses, the Greek Revival did exist as a "pure" style from the early 1830s to the early 1840s. However, by the mid-1840s the influence of the Romantic movement, which led to the Italianate style, appeared in a preference for dark brownstone over the customary limestone or marble in doorway enframements and window details and in a breaking of the façade's planar unity with somewhat heavier sills and lintels.

In the late 1840s, the rising Italianate influence sometimes appeared on Greek Revival row houses as an elaboration of the Greek façade forms. The pilasters of the doorway porch sometimes gained Corinthian capitals, an inset panel running vertically the full length of the pilasters, and occasionally a triangular pediment imitating the peaked roof of an ancient Greek temple in place of the usual rectangular entablature. One or two rows of dentils often were added to the doorway entablature for additional richness. At the same time, specific Italianate style forms and motifs also appeared on the otherwise Greek Revival row house front. Doorways incorporated such forms of the Italianate style as round-headed double doors or an arch set into the horizontal entablature, and stoop and areaway fence iron work employed a simple oblong form with rounded ends.

Brownstone and the Brownstone-Front Row House.

Local brownstone was a regular building material in New York City and environs long before it achieved overwhelming popularity and fashion in the middle of the nineteenth century. Half a mile north of the Battery, at the intersection of Broadway and Fulton Street, is St. Paul's Chapel (1766), the oldest church on Manhattan Island, which is sturdily constructed of Manhattan schist and brownstone.

Despite its humble background as an inexpensive local substitute for marble or limestone, brownstone came to epitomize luxury and architectural sophistication on New York mansions and row houses in the late 1840s. In 1848 and 1849, the newly-finished and extravagant Thorne, Haight, Benkard, Parish, and Van Buren mansions on or near Fifth Avenue introduced the shadowy and impressive brownstone front for dwelling houses to a startled New York. At the same time, and indeed several years earlier, occasional Gothic Revival and Italianate row houses were built with brownstone fronts. Except for an occasional rectory, the earliest remaining brownstone-front dwelling in New York probably is No. 16 Gramercy Park South (1844–1845), an unusually wide Gothic Revival style row house, remodeled in 1888 by Stanford White for The Players, a private club.

In the late 1840s and early 1850s, New Yorkers and visitors to the city admired the "unostentatious magnificence" and "refinement" of its brownstone-front mansions and row houses, and within several years nearly all New York's large row houses were built with the fashionable brownstone front. "Brownstone has now, as all our town readers know, come to be the favorite building material for shops, churches, and residences . . . the prevailing tint of New York is fixed," one magazine declared in the early 1850s. On the eve of the Civil War, one magazine wrote that "brown sandstone houses are the rage among the new rich men" and noted the "brownstone blocks . . . looming up in palatial display everywhere in the city," and in the late 1860s one newspaper reported that within the Fifth Avenue district nearly all the row houses were fronted with handsome brownstone. The brownstone front was so popular for dwellings in New York for so many years that, even now, any row house in New York, even an early-nineteenth-century, red-brick-front Federal house or white-limestone-front dwelling of the 1890s, still is popularly termed a "brownstone."

Brownstone quarries were close to New York, and water routes offered a quick and relatively inexpensive transport to the city. The brownstone most often used in New York came from a "belt" about twenty miles long centered at Portland, Connecticut, a town named for the famous British quarry town. Barges carried the stone down the Connecticut River to Long Island Sound and then to New York. The other major brownstone quarries were near Little Falls, New Jersey, on the Passaic River, near Paterson. The brownstone for Trinity Church in New York came from these New Jersey

(top) "Range" of Brownstone-Fronts, Nos. 322–350 West 46th Street, about 1900. Occasionally the much-admired monumental streetscape vista was a monotonous rather than elegant sight. Demolished.

(bottom) "Brownstone Front." The fashionable brownstone front was actually a four- to six-inch-thick veneer of brownstone over a brick house. As on many buildings, the brownstone front on this Brooklyn Heights corner house is spalling badly.

quarries, whose stone had a lighter shade than the Connecticut variety.

Brownstone is a soft, close-grained triassic sandstone or freestone. When first cut the stone is pink, but it soon weathers to an even, rich, chocolate brown because of the presence of hematite iron ore. Advancing technology partly was responsible for the widespread popularity of brownstone for New York row houses, because the invention of steam-channeling or steam-cutting processes lowered the cost of all cut stone and brought the fashionable soft brownstone within reach of even middle-class row house owners.

Nineteenth-century New Yorkers and magazines referred to the city's brownstone row houses as "brownstone-fronts," for they actually are brick houses whose street front has a four-to-six-inch-thick brownstone facing or veneer. The back-yard walls of a brownstone-front row house are ordinary brick. The architectural deception of the brownstone front clearly appears on corner houses where the narrow twenty- to twenty-five-foot-wide street front has the brownstone facing, and the fifty-foot-long side wall around the corner is brick.

Besides echoing the dark browns, grays, and greens of the rugged landscape, the smooth brownstone front also enhanced the much-desired monumentality of the row house front and streetscape. Stone was considered a more dignified building material than brick or wood, and brownstone's smooth surface visually united the houses along the street and called attention to the elaborate doorway and window ornament. New York builders minimized the seams between slabs of brownstone much in the way that builders of Greek Revival style row houses put lampblack in the mortar to minimize its whiteness between the bricks. Builders used "as large slabs" of brownstone "as could be procured, and the joints narrowed till they were as nearly as possible imperceptible, the assumption of the builder apparently being that the whole brown-stone veneer should seem to be a single sheet," wrote Montgomery Schuyler in the 1890s. "In the later works of the brown-stone period, this assumption comes so near being made good that in the first floor there are no joints visible, great slabs of veneer stretching from opening to opening and one or two joints that could not be obviated being concealed by mouldings tacked on."

Over the years, the brownstone fronts of some row houses have scaled badly and the elaborately carved doorways and window details have crumbled and occasionally fallen off. The durability of brownstone long has been a problem on New York's row houses. On the brownstone-front north side of City Hall, declared one magazine in the 1850s, "decay is visible in almost every part, and many of the stones are miserably peeled and mutilated." This same article then wondered if New York's architects and builders ever examined brownstone and other building materials with regard to their "absolute or comparative fitness and durability." In the mid-nineteenth century, several purportedly scientific articles recommended various treatments to preserve brownstone fronts, among them a yearly oiling with linseed, to prevent the stone from "drying out" and to keep out harmful moisture.

Brownstone, like all sandstone, is a soft building material, but when properly cut and laid it does not deteriorate any more than other building stone. The brownstone façade of Trinity Church, for instance, remains in good condition today. However, to last brownstone must be cut across the grain and laid ashlar, i.e., with the grain running perpendicular to the building façade. Nevertheless, even with the aid of steam channeling equipment, New York builders often ignored these time-consuming quarrying and construction methods. Although this distinction about the grain of the stone, in the words of one architect, "seems to the careless reader a merely whimsical objection," it "is in truth a very important matter, as any upright and well-informed builder will confess." When cut and laid with the grain, brownstone crumbles and scales, because water seeps into the exposed pores of the thin brownstone blocks and, upon freezing, expands and splits the stone into large, thin sheets. Had the stone been cut and laid across the grain in the first place, the deterioration of most brownstone fronts, then and now, would be minimal.

Although the fashion for brownstone emerged in the late 1840s, ordinary brick was an acceptable material for row house fronts until the eve of the Civil War. After that, the brick front was relegated to the modest middle-class and working-men's dwellings, which have disappeared largely from Manhattan but remain in sizable numbers in several areas of Brooklyn. "Houses built of stone, or having stone fronts, are the only kind which meet with favor from the moneyed portion of our community," declared one newspaper in the 1860s. "Brick is getting too common for first-class fashionable circles, and are left to be occupied by the more humble of the people."

The only exception to the brownstone hegemony in New York row houses was costly, smooth-surfaced "pressed brick" or "Philadelphia brick." Whereas New York and Boston fell under the spell of the brownstone front, fine row houses in Philadelphia usually were built of this pressed brick. Ordinary brick had a rough, textured surface and varied in color, but the pressed brick had a smooth surface, much like that of stone, and a uniform dark red color. During the 1850s and 1860s, a veneer of pressed brick on a row house front apparently cost as much as brownstone—or four times the cost of the ordinary rough-surfaced brick front.

In the manufacture of pressed brick, the clay was ground into fine particles and put into molds whose sides first had been dampened. Enormous pressure acted on the molds and compacted the clay into a solid brick, which then was burned in a kiln. The pressed brick was longer and narrower in size than the usual brick, and, according to one architectural journal, the usual dimensions were 8½ inches long, 4¼ inches broad, and 2½ inches thick. Pressed brick was popular in New York, particularly on

Anglo-Italianate style row houses, and an outstanding example of its use with brownstone trim is "The Triangle" (1859–1861) on Stuyvesant Street between Second and Third avenues, attributed to James Renwick, Jr.

During the rage for brownstone fronts, occasional white-marble-front dwellings were still built in New York, the most famous being the A. T. Stewart mansion at Fifth Avenue and 34th Street. Another marble-faced dwelling of the period was the John Taylor Johnston residence (1856), a basement-and-four-story-tall row house in a simple, but impressive, Italianate style which stood at No. 8 Fifth Avenue, at the southwest corner of Eighth Street, until its demolition for an apartment building about 1950. However, white marble never was a popular façade material on the city's row houses of the 1850s and 1860s. Besides its high cost, the usual light color was at variance with the dark building materials favored by the Romantic movement, and marble was too hard to take the elaborate foliate carving which so delighted New Yorkers in the mid-nineteenth century.

The Italianate Style: The Monumental Streetscape.

During the brownstone era, an important architectural theme was the monumental streetscape formed by a several-hundred-foot-long row of nearly uniform row houses. The boldly protruding stoops, richly ornamented doorways, smooth brownstone fronts, and heavy cornices receded into the distance for an impressive vista. The row house of the 1850s and 1860s was at least several feet taller than comparable row houses of earlier years, which enhanced the monumentality of the streetscape, because of a higher basement, taller ceilings on all floors, and often an additional floor. By then the city's fine row houses rose to four stories and a basement and, in some cases, five stories and a basement.

Although the higher ceilings and additional floor indeed made for an impressive dwelling house and matched the lavish life style of well-to-do families, economic necessity also encouraged the increased height of the city's dwellings. A large portion of the price for a row house in a fashionable location was the cost of the lot, and a sharp increase in the price of land convenient to downtown Manhattan, beginning in the 1850s, forced the builder to construct row houses several feet narrower in width to prevent a substantial rise in house prices. Whereas the luxurious row houses of the 1820s and 1830s on Bond Street or around St. John's Park were twenty-seven, twenty-nine, even thirty feet wide, the fashionable brownstone-fronts of the 1850s in the Fifth Avenue and Madison Square district rarely exceeded the standard twenty-five-foot width. The row houses of middle-class families shrank from the comfortable twenty-five feet of the early nineteenth century to twenty and eighteen feet. Single-family dwellings for lower middle-class and prosperous workingmen's families, if they were built at all, were fourteen or twelve and a half feet wide. The high ceilings of the mid-nineteenth-century row houses brought back some of the spaciousness of the wider houses of earlier decades and, with the greater depth and additional floor, regained some of the space lost because of the narrower lot.

As the width of row houses decreased and their height increased simultaneously, the awkward proportions of the individual house front presented a serious architectural problem. On the eve of the Civil War, costly New York row houses were twenty-two to twenty-five feet wide and fifty to sixty feet tall—or a height twice its width. In the sixteen- and eighteen-foot-wide row houses, the proportions of the individual fifty- or sixty-foot-tall houses were even more awkward—often a height two and a half or three times its width. In *City Architecture,* M. Field devoted several pages to the means of "creating harmonious proportions in the elevations of city buildings, which, from economy of ground plot, are necessarily too narrow for a good proportion, and would appear likely to fall unless propped up by their neighbours."

Field recommended string courses, six-or-so-inch-wide bands across the street fronts between some floors, which introduced a strong horizontal line to the façade and divided it into reasonably square portions to "counteract the excessive height of numerous stories." Since the late eighteenth century, the city's row houses commonly had a white marble or brownstone string course between the basement and first floor, but for the exceptionally tall and narrow mid-nineteenth-century row house Field suggested a "three-fold" division of the façade, consisting of a string course between the rusticated basement and first floor and another between the top floor and the next-to-top floor.

The builders of New York row houses apparently disregarded this common-sense advice about street-front proportions; only occasionally did a brownstone-front row house have a string course between the top floor and the next-to-top floor. Indeed, in the quest for an impressive street front, the city's architect-builders often unconsciously magnified the already-awkward proportions of the individual row house. Starting with the tall parlor windows, which commonly dropped to the floor, the windows, as well as ceilings, became successively shorter with every floor, and cornices often were so prominent that they accentuated this narrow and visually tapering form.

Though acknowledged at the time, the awkward proportions of the individual row house front were not an overriding concern of the city's architects, because the monumental streetscape vista was as important a consideration to row house architecture as the appearance of the individual row house. While awkward for the appearance of the individual dwelling, the tall and narrow proportions of the row house street front made for an unusually impressive streetscape when part of a long row of similar, if not identical, dwellings.

Before the late 1840s and the appearance of the Italianate style row house, New York architects and builders rarely considered the architectural impact of the row house front on the streetscape appearance. Le Roy Place on Bleecker Street (1826–1827), the Colonnade Row on Lafayette Place (1832–1833), and The Row on Washington Square North (1831–1833) were acclaimed at the time of construction for their impressive streetscape appearance, but they failed to introduce the monumental streetscape ideal to the city's row houses.

New Yorkers were, nevertheless, aware of impressive row house vistas in the 1830s. When the full third floor and flat roofline of the Greek Revival replaced the pitched roof and dormer-window roofline of the Federal style in the early 1830s, New Yorkers, it will be recalled, praised the change as a "style less tawdry and more in consonance with the rules of good taste" and were glad that the "old, ugly, and absurd custom" of buildings of different heights on the same blockfront now "is avoided." The Federal and, to a lesser extent, the Greek Revival style were unself-conscious vernacular styles that did not even aim for an architecturally or socially pretentious row house streetscape, and, from a practical standpoint, few architects and builders in the early-nineteenth century could afford to build a row of eight or ten identical dwellings at once.

By the late 1840s the term "street architecture" had appeared in books and magazine articles on architecture, and the monumental streetscape became an important architectural consideration in the design of city dwellings. In the tradition of the patrician "terraces" in London and Bath and New York's Le Roy Place and Colonnade Row, the individual row house was subordinated to the dignity of the entire row or blockfront. In the 1840s, the Anglo-Italianate style, a variation on the Italianate style specifically suited to the impressive row or terrace, appeared on New York row houses. Even in a several-hundred-foot-long block of Italianate style row houses, the street fronts often are virtually identical. The facades are a uniform distance from the street and form a continuous smooth plane, and the cornice level often changes only a few times, in most cases for a shift in ground elevation.

Very rarely did just one or two architect-builders construct all the houses on one side of the street in the mid-nineteenth century. Normally, a block was filled up by various builders, a few houses at a time, over a period of years. To gain the monumentality of the planar façade expanse and uniform or nearly uniform cornice line, each builder consciously maintained the street-front design, cornice line, and string courses fixed by the earlier row houses on the block.

The two-hundred-foot-long blockfronts of the city's avenues, between two crosstown streets, were particularly suited to an impressive streetscape. Eight to ten row houses filled an avenue blockfront and, before the days of automobile traffic, the wide avenue offered a setting of greater dignity and better scale for the tall row houses than the narrow crosstown street.

For a particularly impressive effect on the two-hundred-foot-long avenue blockfront, Field

No. 462 West 23rd Street (ca. 1860), Chelsea, in 1915. A good example of the brownstone-front Italianate style row house of the 1850s and 1860s that once dominated midtown Manhattan from 14th Street to Central Park. Built as a fine one-family residence on once-fashionable West 23rd Street, this brownstone-front—though still well maintained—had become a boarding house by 1915. Notice the discreet sign "The Oxford, Furnished Rooms" on the parlor window balcony and the milk bottle on the window sill of a top floor room.

recommended that "the corner houses of the block may be higher and more decorated than the rest." In the 1850s, such ornamental treatment was limited to quoins, a vertical row of rustication blocks, at the corner from the basement floor to the roofline. An unusually rich architectural feature in the Renaissance tradition, quoins turned the eye inward to the center of the blockfront and emphasized its horizontality, an important quality in Renaissance architecture. With the appearance of the Second Empire style in the late 1850s, the corner houses often gained a steep mansard roof, much in the manner of corner pavilions, to enhance the impressive blockfront composition.

The Italianate Style: The Row House Front.

Besides the monumental building front and streetscape, the other striking feature of the New York row house front in the mid-nineteenth century was its bold forms and elaborate ornament. The Italianate row house, a distinctly urban style, gained its picturesque appearance through bold façade forms and ornament, which cast deep shadows on the brownstone front, and, unlike the preceding Gothic Revival style, avoided any attempt to gain the asymmetrical massing better suited to country dwellings. "The very plainest modern style may, by judicious treatment, be made to develop such features as will necessarily render it picturesque," declared one magazine. The city house may "in the first place . . . present an unusual variety of outline, through the medium of projections and recessions . . . and impart to it certain broad effects of light and shade. Second, to enrich it with appropriate details which, while they pleasingly attract the eye, at the same time arouse curiosity."

Bold ornament on the row house also enhanced the impressive streetscape. The cornices, doorway porches, and stoops, when lined up, led the pedestrian's eye down the sweeping vista. M. Field objected to architects' plans which considered row house design in terms of a single house viewed from directly across the street and not as a part of the streetscape as seen by the pedestrian. Because New Yorkers usually saw row houses at an angle from the sidewalk or street and as part of the blockfront, Field recommended that architectural plans and "views of street buildings should always be taken *obliquely,* and show the neighbouring houses as well, because they in fact assist to support them, and form part of the general effect." Only ornament boldly projecting from the street front could be seen clearly from such an angle, and the building thereby avoids "the meagerness presented by naked walls and unbroken surfaces."

In this period of social upheaval and rapid accumulation of wealth, the bold forms and lavish ornament of the Italianate style reflected the social ambitions of New York's well-to-do families better than the modestly ornamented and planar fronts of earlier styles. The "curved and flowing lines and a profusion of delicate ornament in relief" on an Italianate style dwelling produced "a very ornate

St. Luke's Place (early 1850s),
Greenwich Village. Despite the
overwhelming popularity of the
brownstone front in New York after
1850, fine row houses were built with
red-brick facades and brownstone trim
until the Civil War years. The row
houses along St. Luke's Place are
unusually well-preserved and attractive.

and elegant effect," wrote Andrew Jackson Downing. Likewise, Samuel Sloan declared that "fashion in all its gaudy glare of ornament kept exclusive ability to astonish and confound the luckless lookers-on at all this palatial effort of accumulated wealth, to let its bursting pride be seen and felt." At the same time, some New Yorkers considered a showy row house front a moral as well as an architectural imperative. "Nothing denotes more greatly a nation's advancement in civilization than the ornate and improved styles of its architecture, and the erection of palatial private residences," declared one newspaper in the extravagant Civil War years.

Reveling in these new architectural ideals after decades of simplicity and restraint, some New York builders decorated the brownstone-front row houses with too much, and often poorly composed, carved ornament. Though advised by architects that "ornamentation should be given rather to display some portion of the design than to hide it," house buyers admired showy row house fronts and parlors, and the machine technology of the era manufactured the requisite ornament at a cost low enough even for middle-class dwellings. Although New York's brownstone-fronts of the 1850s and 1860s may be overly elaborate for some tastes today, they must be viewed as a reflection of architectural ideals, society, and technology in that confident era.

Doorway. The front doorway was the most striking feature of the Italianate row house façade. "The doorway is the most indispensable feature of the structure, and therefore calls loudly for adornment, and should generally be distinguished by more impressive decoration than any other feature," wrote one magazine. On a fine brownstone front, rounded consoles, faced with acanthus leaves, supported a heavy and protruding "door hood" or "door cover," usually a modestly rounded form but sometimes flat-headed or with a triangular pediment. On either side of the deeply recessed doorway, pilasters decorated with recessed panels and circles for the full length rose to the consoles and the door hood. Round-headed double doors, with heavily molded panels of circular forms at the lower part of each door and windows at the upper half to light the foyer and stair hallway, replaced the single front door with two sidelights and a top light which was characteristic of the earlier Federal and Greek Revival styles.

On large dwellings, a stone arch below the console-supported door hood and above the double doors repeated the form of the round-headed double doors and introduced another arch to the doorway. For additional richness, an elaborately detailed keystone marked the top of this arch, and small consoles with their scrolled sides facing the street supported each end as it sprang from the door jamb.

The bold forms and elaborate ornament of such a doorway treatment were too costly and of too large a scale for the modest, often brick-front, middle-class row houses of the period. On these

(top left) Iron Work Advertisement (*ca.* 1850). Iron work of all kinds in the Italianate style offered to builders.

(top right) Console or scrolled bracket, supporting a doorway hood, No. 212 Columbia Heights (*ca.* 1860), Brooklyn Heights. Notice the deep picturesque shadows cast by the console.

(bottom left) Freestanding Doorway Porch, No. 210 Columbia Heights (*ca.* 1852), Brooklyn Heights. A type of doorway porch generally found only on the finest Italianate style row houses.

(bottom right) Doorway, No. 212 Columbia Heights (*ca.* 1860), Brooklyn Heights. A heavy door hood supported by consoles is the usual doorway style on Italianate mode dwelling houses in New York.

houses, the door hoods often were a modest projecting rectangular form, supported on unornamented brackets or modestly embellished consoles. The front double doors on these houses usually were flat-headed rather than the costly round-headed form but were embellished with circular panels.

Besides the elaborate forms and ornament which made for a showy appearance, the large door hood and consoles cast the fashionable picturesque shadows on the dark row house front, and the deeply recessed doorway introduced a mysterious dark volume to the façade. This doorway, wrote one magazine, presented an "opportunity for the greatest beauty and grandeur of light and shade."

The profusion of arched and rounded consoles on the Italianate doorway reflected the newly fashionable love of circular forms so evident in the row house fronts and interiors of the period. "The new element of beauty . . . is the use of the circle, subordinate to, and contrasting with, the horizontal or straight line. This is seen chiefly, in the round arch, which appears in doors and windows," observed one architect. Circular forms, it was thought, complemented the Romantic movement in architecture, because the circle "addresses itself more to the feelings and the sense, and less to the reason and judgment."

Although doorway treatment usually was a rounded hood supported by consoles, the doorway porch, with two freestanding columns supporting a triangular pediment or rectangular entablature, appeared on some of the city's finest brownstone-fronts. Because a freestanding doorway porch cast even greater shadows than did a console-supported hood, it often was considered aesthetically superior to the usual doorway hood. "The portico," declared one magazine, "yields the greatest scope for design and decorative effect, as it produces the broadest and deepest shadow, while the cylindrical surface of the columns gives the highest lights." A freestanding porch also was closer to the Renaissance *palazzo* inspiration of the Italianate style row house than the usual rounded doorway hood. To enhance this Renaissance feeling and make for an even more showy doorway, builders occasionally added rustication blocks around the round arch over the doors beneath the porch.

The freestanding doorway porch was more difficult to construct than the rounded doorway hood and, consequently, was found only on the most expensive dwellings in the city. During the 1830s and 1840s, only the finest Greek Revival style dwellings, such as The Row along Washington Square North, employed the doorway porch, and nearly all other row houses had the simple doorway enframement of rectangular pilasters and entablature flush with the façade. Nineteenth-century photographs of long-gone Italianate brownstone-front dwellings along Fifth Avenue show doorway porches which stand two or three feet from the façade.

Stoop. The stoop of an Italianate row house was several feet higher and wider than that of a similar row house of preceding years. The stoop was an "important accessory, worthy in all respects, of the best efforts of the architect," wrote architect David H. Arnot, because it offered an "imposing mode of access" and "a degree of stateliness" to "the principal floor by an adequate ascendency over the sidewalk and its daily crowds." Besides this much-desired architectural grandeur, the higher ceilings of the basement floor forced the stoop's increased height. In an unexpected benefit, these large stoops set the row house back several feet farther from the street than in earlier years. Very often the areaways in front were planted with shrubs and flowers or wisteria which climbed up guide wires just in front of the façade to the cornice.

The cast-iron stoop railing was one of the first elements of the New York row house to evidence the emerging Italianate style. As early as 1846 and 1847, the stoop railings, front fences, and window balconies of some otherwise Greek Revival and Gothic Revival row houses had shown an Italianate inspiration in simple oblong forms with rounded ends. Several years later, the elliptical loop iron work often looked like a twisting rope or appeared with its center adorned with other circle-inspired or foliate forms. The iron work "of lofty size and excellent workmanship" on fine New York row houses excited "much surprise" in one Englishman in the 1850s. The elaborate stoop railings and front fences, marble or brownstone "flight of steps . . . marble pillars and façade, and lamps of bronze and plate glass, make a very imposing entrance to the house of a *republican aristocrat.*"

By the mid-1850s, the stoop railings and areaway fences of large brownstone-fronts were a thick handrail and round balustrade more in keeping with the style's inspiration in Renaissance Italy. On some row houses, these were cast-iron finished as brownstone. The balustrade motif sometimes appeared on row house fronts cut into the stone under those occasional parlor windows which did not drop to the floor.

In the 1850s and 1860s, the city's modest brick-front row houses rarely employed the balustrade for stoop railings and areaway fences, because it was too expensive a feature and of too large a scale for these small dwellings. Instead, these houses employed the oblong loop iron work which now provides an important clue to identifying them as Italianate style. Just as these houses employed an ordinary brick front rather than expensive brownstone, they eliminated such costly ornament as the console-supported rounded door hood and massive cornice. Over the years, any alterations on these houses generally have removed original façade details and further simplified the street front. Judging only from the street front, these houses often appear to be Federal or Greek Revival style. But the loop pattern of the stoop railing and areaway fences often survive to the present day and identify the house as the Italianate style of the 1850s and 1860s.

Cornice. A striking feature on the Italianate row house was a boldly protruding cornice supported by rectangular brackets or the familiar rounded consoles. A projecting roofline was "one of the simplest, cheapest, and most effective modes of giving force and spirit to any building," wrote Andrew Jackson Downing. The cornice cast deep picturesque shadows on the façade and set a definite upward limit on the house necessary to good proportion. On New York row houses, cornices were many pieces of wood, a single piece of pressed metal, or occasionally stone.

Window Treatment.   The street-front windows enhanced the monumentality and elegance of the row house. Windows were longer and often wider than in preceding years, and, continuing the precedent of the Greek Revival, the front parlor windows usually dropped to the floor. "The nearer a window-sill approaches the floor," wrote one magazine in 1850, "the more cheerful a room will look: placing the sill even with the floor, seems almost essential to the elegance of a drawing room; while the opposite treatment gives the appearance of confinement and gloom."

During the 1850s, several-foot-high, cast-iron guard railings or a low parlor-window balcony shielded the parlor from the view of passersby. By the 1860s, most brownstone-front row houses abandoned ornamental guard railings and balconies and relied more on wooden interior shutters to shield the parlor from view. The window sill often became a one- to two-foot-deep shelf supported on stone or cast-iron consoles with a foot-high balustrade around its edges.

Window treatment was another of the early elements of the row house front to show the emerging Italianate style in the 1840s. On some Greek Revival and Gothic Revival row houses of the period, the window lintels and sills protruded several inches from the previously planar façade and often rested on modest brackets. As early as 1836, one magazine lamented row house fronts "which are generally so plain as to be painful to the eye" and recommended "the appropriate ornament of windows, a rich heavy cornice above them and a moulding extending sometimes down their sides. This contributes very greatly to relieve the plain surface, and give it a finished and elegant air." With the triumph of the Italianate style in the late 1840s, windows gained boldly projecting lintels and sills and, in some cases, vertical side jambs for a full enframement on all four sides. This four-sided window enframement cast even greater shadow on the brownstone front than did just bold lintels and sills and increased the window's shadowy depth into the façade.

Richly ornamented brownstone-fronts usually did not have the blinds or outside shutters so popular in the Federal and Greek Revival row houses. When closed, the blinds eliminated the picturesque shadow of the deeply set windows and, when open, reduced the visual impact of the bold lintels and sills and interfered with the increasingly popular complete window enframement. Shutters appeared on the fine Italianate style row houses only when the family was away for the summer in the country or the house otherwise was empty.

In the late 1840s and 1850s, advancing technology permitted ever larger panes of glass in

Elevation of the Principal front.
Phillips & Tabor. 12ᵗʰ st. V. no.

0   10   20   30   40

(top) Window Enframement, at "The Triangle" (1860–1861), Stuyvesant Street.

(bottom left) No. 21 Fifth Avenue (1851), southeast corner of Ninth Street, "Mark Twain House," in 1952. The "early Romanesque" mode of the 1850s. Demolished.

(bottom right) Nos. 12 and 14 West Twelfth Street (1848–1849), Greenwich Village, Alexander Jackson Davis, architect, elevation drawing of 1847. Possibly the first Anglo-Italianate "English Basement" Row houses in New York. Demolished in 1958.

windows. In the early nineteenth century, New York row houses had small-size window panes, six over six, as in the late eighteenth century. By the late 1840s, the windows in fine row houses were large panes of glass, about fifteen inches wide and thirty inches long, in ordinary double-hung windows or, in a nod to the medieval precedent of the Gothic Revival, with genuine outward-opening casement windows or double-hung windows simulating casement windows. By the mid-1850s, windows in fine New York row houses were single sheets of fashionable plate glass. In 1846 Philip Hone marveled at the plate-glass windows at the A. T. Stewart Store but considered them nonetheless a "useless, piece of extravagance . . . which must have cost four or five hundred dollars each, and may be shivered by a boy's marble or a snow-ball."

Although New York mansions and fine row houses adopted the fashionable plate glass for street-front windows in the mid-1850s, the city's modest brick-front dwellings employed casementlike windows, with large-sized panes of glass, well into the 1860s. But even when street-front windows of a showy brownstone-front were plate glass, the back windows overlooking the garden, and therefore not visible to the street, were cheaper, large-size panes of glass introduced in the late 1840s. In a statement typical of an era which glamorized the brownstone-*front* row house, the architectural plans for a detached double house designed by Samuel Sloan read: "All glass, in the first story front and sides, is the best American crown glass, the rest may be of an inferior quality."

In the nineteenth century, the homeowner in a fashion-conscious New York naturally wanted his house to reflect the latest architectural fashion and contain all modern conveniences. With the advent of plate glass, many New Yorkers modernized the street fronts of their Federal and Greek Revival row houses by replacing the small panes of the 1830s and 1840s or the larger panes of the late 1840s and 1850s with a single sheet of plate glass.

Today, the usual aim of a brownstone restoration is to point out the dwelling's venerable age. Occasionally small-paned "Colonial" glass—similar to or even smaller than that found in the city's late-eighteenth- and early nineteenth-century Federal style dwellings—is installed today in some mid-nineteenth-century Italianate row houses. Particularly susceptible to these spurious restorations are those modest row houses whose brick fronts and restrained ornamental detail are the manifestation of architectural economy rather than any connection with the earlier simplicity of classical tradition. The cornice, supported on simple brackets, the oblong looped iron work on the street front, and the round-arched, white-marble parlor mantels and showy ceiling plasterwork in the interiors definitely prove the dwelling's Italianate style.

Nos. 220 and 222 Fifth Avenue (1851–52), between West 26th and West 27th streets, in 1881. These two florid Anglo-Italianate dwelling houses—one altered into a shop on the first floor—epitomized the extravagance of Fifth Avenue in the 1850s and 1860s and the elegant city residences of the famed "Upper Ten Thousand." Such richly ornamented brownstone-fronts led visitors to proclaim Fifth Avenue a "street of palaces." Demolished.

The Anglo-Italianate Style.

As the Italianate style emerged in New York in the late 1840s, occasional row houses also adopted the handsome and practical Anglo-Italianate style. The Anglo-Italianate or English basement-style row house was known for its two- or three-step stoop at the front doorway rather than the immense ten- or twelve-step stoop popular at the time; it also formed planned monumental streetscapes and had an unusual floor plan which better handled the problem of rising land costs and increasingly narrow building lots.

The first Anglo-Italianate dwellings in New York very likely were Nos. 12–14 West Twelfth Street (1848–1849), demolished in 1958 for the construction of the Church House of the First Presbyterian Church. An 1847 elevation of these two houses drawn by Alexander Jackson Davis survives in Avery Library, and a leading architect like Davis, who disliked the ubiquitous stoop on New York row houses, might have originated the style.

By the mid-1850s, row houses from middle-class blocks of Chelsea to the patrician Madison Square area adopted the Anglo-Italianate style. "Many of the new blocks on the Fifth Avenue constructed in this manner, though of even a smaller frontage, have a very imposing and elegant appearance, while the interiors are finished with a degree of splendor which could not have been indulged in by their owners in houses of greater extent," declared one magazine. However, Anglo-Italianate row houses rarely were built in Brooklyn where full-sized building lots were much cheaper than in Manhattan.

Dwellings of this style usually were a basement-and-four-stories tall and sixteen to eighteen feet wide. The basement and first story were faced with the familiar rusticated brownstone, and the doorway and single window at the side were round-headed and often enframed by a bold molding. Above the basement and first story, the street front was smooth brownstone or a dark red "Philadelphia pressed brick" with window details in handsomely contrasting brownstone. The windows of the second-floor parlors dropped to the floor and often opened onto a cast-iron balcony which, along with the roofline cornice, helped to unify the row visually.

In the parlors, such decorative details as mantels and ceiling plasterwork were the same in an Anglo-Italianate row house as in the Italianate, but the floor plan was significantly different from that of other New York row houses at the time. An elliptical stairway occupied the center of the house rather than climbing straight to the upper floors along the six- or seven-foot-wide side hallway. The stairway thereby made use of the poorly lit and ventilated center of the house, and, with the side-stair hallway eliminated, the front and back rooms filled the full width of the house. "It has been found that quite as spacious rooms may be had in a [Anglo-Italianate] house of twenty feet front, as

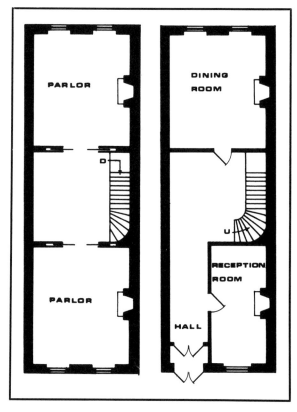

(top) Anglo-Italianate Terrace, south side of East 16th Street, between Second and Third avenues, in 1854. Several houses in this row still stand.

(bottom left) Anglo-Italianate Doorway, No. 29 Stuyvesant Street (1860–1861), "The Triangle." Though employing the richly carved stonework and elaborate iron work of the era, the stoop of an Anglo-Italianate doorway has four, five, or six steps rather than the ten or twelve steps of the Italianate style dwelling house.

(bottom right) Plans, first and second floor of a typical Anglo-Italianate style row house.

in the old style of houses built on a full sized [twenty-five-foot-wide] lot," observed one magazine several years after the style's appearance.

With this new floor plan, room use in the Anglo-Italianate row house differed somewhat from the Italianate dwelling of the period. The front room of the basement floor still was an informal dining room and the back room a kitchen. On the first floor, the small room at one side of the front door hallway was an office or waiting room for guests, and the back room overlooking the garden likely was the formal dining room. On the second floor, the front and back rooms, occupying the full width of the house, were twin parlors with an anteroom and stairway in the center, making "a suite of three handsome rooms when the sliding doors are thrown open." The parents' and childrens' bedrooms and servants' quarters occupied the upper floors.

Although the Anglo-Italianate dwelling offered an imaginative solution to the problem of costly city land in the 1850s, it never neared the popularity of the Italianate style and, with the emergence of the fashionable mansard roof in the 1860s, lost favor on New York row houses. Anglo-Italianate dwellings were built in Manhattan from the Washington Square area into the East and West Thirties and Forties, but like the Italianate style dwellings most of these have been demolished in the continual rebuilding of midtown Manhattan. Today, the few surviving Anglo-Italianate row houses are found on West Ninth, Tenth, and Twelfth streets off lower Fifth Avenue in Greenwich Village and on several handsome blocks of Chelsea.

The Second Empire Style.

A variation on the Italianate style for the New York row house was the Second Empire or mansard roof style. Inspired by the Paris of Emperor Louis Napoleon and Baron Haussmann, the style epitomized the elegance and sophistication of Second Empire France and was the national rage in the United States in the late 1860s and early 1870s. So complete was its conquest of American architecture that, in 1868, Samuel Sloan confidently stated that "the French Roof—or, as it is often called, the Mansard—was and is in great request. Public and private dwellings, and even stables, are covered, with this new roof; and no man who wants a fashionable house, will be without it."

In New York, architects and builders often abandoned the Italianate style and built rows of brownstone-front dwellings with the fashionable mansard roof. On the New York row house, the Second Empire style usually involved only the addition of a mansard roof above the cornice of an otherwise Italianate dwelling. Inspired by mid-nineteenth-century Paris and the classicism of the École des Beaux Arts, the Second Empire style's background matched the heavy forms and elaborate ornament of the Italianate style. Because the Italianate and Second Empire were contemporary and

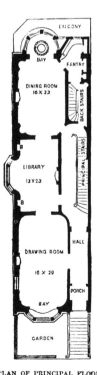

CHAMBER PLAN.

(top left) Hart M. Schiff Residence (1849–1850), No. 32 Fifth Avenue, southwest corner of Tenth Street, Detlef Lienau, architect, in 1854. The first house in New York with the Parisian-inspired mansard roof. Demolished.

(bottom left) Curving Stairway running up the center of an Anglo-Italianate style row house of the 1850s on West 20th Street in Chelsea. A skylight, with stained glass, partly lights the stairway in the daytime.

(right) John A. C. Gray Residence (1856–1857), No. 42 Fifth Avenue, between West Tenth and West Eleventh streets, Calvert Vaux, architect. Another early house with a mansard roof. Demolished.

architecturally similar, the interior design and plan of row houses in each style were the same. They were so similar in appearance that the Second Empire or mansard roof style also was known as the "Franco-Italianate" style.

The Background of the Second Empire Style: The Paris of Louis Napoleon.

In 1852 Louis Napoleon, then prince-president of France, made himself the country's emperor and ruled until 1870, when the defeat of France in the Franco-Prussian War cost him his throne. As Emperor Napoleon III his ambition had been to regain the royal splendor of his famous cousin Napoleon I, and that of the earlier French kings. Under his sponsorship, Baron Haussmann rebuilt large parts of Paris in a manner suitable to the emperor's aspirations by cutting tree-lined avenues through Paris' medieval maze of streets and by lining the new avenues with handsomely designed, uniform apartment buildings. The avenues formed monumental vistas, often focusing on notable, newly constructed public buildings.

Visconti and Lefuel's addition to the Louvre in the 1850s, designed to connect with the Tuileries, was Napoleon III's first public works project of architectural significance. Several hundred years earlier the Louvre had served exclusively as a royal palace, but by the nineteenth century it housed several other functions, including the principal public art collection in France. When Visconti died in 1852, H. M. Lefuel assumed the commission. Lefuel's 1853–1857 extension to the Louvre recalled the original Louvre, begun in the sixteenth century under King Francis I, but its richly applied ornament reflected the nineteenth-century Renaissance ideals then sweeping Europe and America as the *palazzo* influence in commercial buildings and city houses.

Lefuel's extension to the Louvre raised the mansard roof to international prominence. Steeply sloped on each side of a building, the mansard roof was named for one of Louis XIV's royal architects, François Mansart, and created fully lit attics with high ceilings without the cost or trouble of building another full floor. For this practical consideration, the mansard had been used in France for several centuries on all types of buildings. In the 1850s, it soon spread throughout the world because of its fashionable Parisian connotations and striking appearance. The mansard roof was the most identifiable and, on New York row houses, the only characteristic of the Second Empire style.

The Appearance of the Second Empire Style in the United States.

Several years before the remarkable rebuilding of large parts of Paris spread the mansard roof throughout the world, it already had appeared on an occasional building in the United States. In 1847–1848, Charles Lemoulnier, an architect recently arrived from Paris, introduced perhaps the first mansard roof in the United States on the Deacon mansion at Concord and Washington streets in Boston's then rural South End. The mansion was two stories tall with projecting end pavilions and had a handsome mansard roof. Its splendor and walled gardens excited much comment at the time of its construction—particularly the several entire rooms brought from the Hôtel de Montmorency in Paris.

Several of the earliest Second Empire houses in the United States were built in New York. The city's first house with a mansard roof was the Hart M. Schiff mansion (1849–1850), No. 32 Fifth Avenue at the corner of West Tenth Street. Schiff, a French banker, recently had arrived in America, which, in the words of one magazine, "may account for the owner's adoption of a style of building which would remind him of the courtly formality, and solid gentility of the olden time in his native country." Detlef Lienau, a Danish architect who had come to the United States in 1848, gave the three-story-tall, freestanding mansion a high mansard roof and dormers which excited great curiosity in the city. The Schiff house is "a mixture of French and Italian, with a remnant of the Gothic principle," declared one magazine authoritatively in the early 1850's. The unfamiliar mansard roof led some critics to view this Parisian-inspired style as a picturesque mode better suited to country than city houses. The Schiff house is "built something after the fashion of an old French chateau on a small scale," one magazine observed incorrectly. "We like it, but prefer it for a country rather than a city house. Its roof and dormers are picturesque, and the combination of the brown stone with the brickwork [is] very pleasing."

Following the Schiff mansion, occasional architect-designed dwellings in the city were built with mansard roofs in the 1850s and early 1860s before the rage for the Second Empire style swept the nation. One notable mansard roof dwelling was the John A. C. Gray house (1856–1857), No. 42 Fifth Avenue between West Tenth and West Eleventh streets, designed by the firm of Vaux and Withers. John A. C. Gray was a vice president of the old People's Bank and a commissioner of Central Park, and through this latter position he no doubt met architect Calvert Vaux. Overlooking the grounds of the Church of the Ascension on one side, the Gray house was a basement and four stories tall, the top floor incorporated within the striking mansard roof. Vaux's design continued the usual row house plan, with rooms off a long hallway, except for a three-sided bay window on the first floor and small windows for dressing rooms and bathrooms on the upper floors facing the church grounds. The cost of this fine town mansion and its desirable lot was $30,000.

Though much admired for their elegance and unusual rooflines, these town mansions in Boston and New York did not themselves lead to the sudden vogue for the Second Empire style on the eve of the Civil War. The Second Empire style did not reach American architects directly from Paris but, according to Henry-Russell Hitchcock, came indirectly from the Parisian-inspired hotels built in London in the mid-1850s. Although Americans had little contact with French architectural developments in the

1850s a number of British architectural publications, widely read in America, kept American architects fully informed of events in England.

In the socially and economically unsettled mid-nineteenth century, Americans admired Paris, where the internationally popular Empress Eugenie presided over a lavish court and Baron Haussmann was building his impressive avenues. After thousands of Americans visited the successful international exhibitions in 1855 and 1867, Paris was popularly synonymous with technological progress, as well as sophistication and elegance in the arts and society.

In this background of a rising taste for all things Parisian, several large commissions in the Second Empire style on the East Coast in the late 1850s helped to raise the style to national prominence. In 1859 and 1860, James Renwick, architect of Grace Church on Broadway and the Smithsonian Institution in Washington, D.C., designed the most notable of these Second Empire buildings—the Charity Hospital on Blackwell's Island, now known as Welfare Island, in New York's East River; the old Corcoran Gallery on Pennsylvania Avenue west of the White House in Washington, D.C.; and Vassar College's Main Hall in Poughkeepsie, New York, modeled after the Tuileries in Paris.

In the 1860s, architects and builders throughout the United States adopted the Second Empire style with an enthusiasm that was matched throughout the Western world. Farmhouses, freestanding villas, fine row houses, and even carriage houses sported the fashionable mansard or "French" roof. "We see this wonderful power of fashion in the sudden and universal application of the mansard roof among us," wrote one newspaper in the late 1860s.

> A very short time ago nobody seemed to know that buildings had roofs, and that roofs were not necessarily a thing to hide but to be seen and ornamented; although Mr. Calvert Vaux had taught us better in a neat design for a residence on Fifth Avenue. . . . Suddenly, however, a sort of roof epidemic seemed to seize us; and now no building, great or small, can be a building without its "French roof."

The Second Empire Style: The Row House Front, Plan, and Interior Design.

The architect-builder in New York, like his fellows in other large American cities, adapted the style of Louis Napoleon's Paris to contemporary row house forms, construction materials, and local workmen's skills. However, such distinctive features of the New York row house as the brownstone front and the stoop, though distinctly un-Parisian, were so popular that their disappearance for an architectural fad proved unlikely.

The row house front of the Second Empire style was brownstone and occasionally in combination with the even less Parisian pressed brick. In either case, the basement was the familiar boldly

No. 35 West Twelfth Street (*ca.* 1840), Greenwich Village. This narrow house originally was twenty-five feet wide. In the 1860s, half the house was sheared off for an adjacent building and the mansard roof was added to make up for the lost space.

rusticated brownstone. In New York, the Second Empire row house continued the local tradition of the elevated parlor floor and high and wide stoop with a classically inspired balustrade railing. The front doorway had the heavy, rounded hood, supported by consoles or occasionally a freestanding doorway porch.

Street-front windows of the Second Empire row house, as in the Italianate style, at the least have boldly protruding lintels and sills or are fully enframed. Below the mansard roof, the usual acanthus-leaf–faced consoles supported a heavy cornice. The salient feature of the Second Empire row house was the steeply sloped mansard roof, pierced by two or three dormer windows and decorated with a picturesque cast-iron railing, known as a "cresting," at the street-front edge of the roof. At a time when high ceilings and a usual fifth floor gave fine New York brownstone-fronts awkwardly narrow proportions and a looming presence over the streets, the mansard roof gave the roofline a picturesque look and offered the space of another floor without the visual impact of the basement-and-four-story-tall façade.

The mansard roof makes the Second Empire a simple style to identify, for it was difficult and economically foolhardy to remove in later renovations. But the presence of a mansard roof on a row house does not necessarily mean Second Empire. In the 1860s, these "French" roofs were added to many Federal and Greek Revival row houses to "modernize" them and add another floor in a city of always scarce housing and high rents. These modernizations usually are easy to detect, because the builder rarely updated the plain Federal or Greek Revival doorway, window lintels, or cornice to conform with the showy Second Empire style. Throughout Greenwich Village and Brooklyn Heights, the trained eye picks out mansard roofs over Flemish-bond brick fronts, a dentiled cornice, or a Greek Revival doorway.

In Greenwich Village, No. 35 West Twelfth Street offers a most unusual case of such a row house alteration in the 1860s. This curious house is thirteen feet wide, a basement and two stories tall, and it has a mansard roof with a single dormer window. When completed in 1840, the house was twenty-five feet wide and a basement and two stories tall. In 1867 the property changed hands, and the eastern half of the house was cut off to give more width to an adjoining house, now the site of an apartment building. With half of the house shorn off, the mansard roof and single dormer probably were added to this strangely attractive house to regain some of the lost space.

Row House Floor Plans.

The New York row house of the 1850s often continued the same interior plan as the row house of the 1840s. The first floor consisted of identical front and back parlors, separated by sliding double doors,

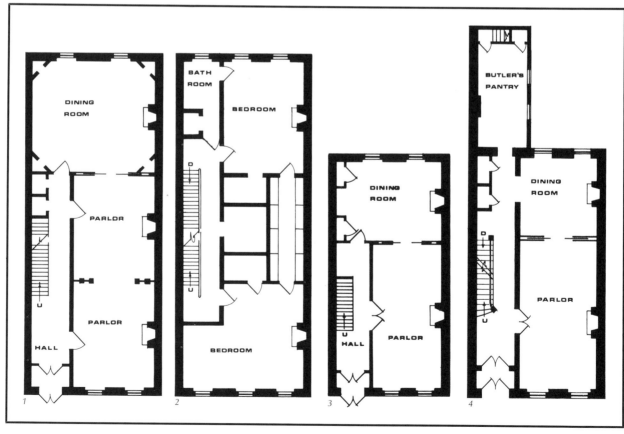

(top) The Hatch Family, Eastman Johnson, 1871. An elegant mansion's library in post-Civil War New York. The Hatch residence, though sadly altered, still stands at the northeast corner of Park Avenue and 37th Street.

Plan 1. Triple parlor arrangement of the 1850s. First floor.
Plan 2. Triple parlor arrangement of the 1850s. Second floor.
Plan 3. Front and back parlor arrangement of the 1860s and 1870s. First floor.
Plan 4. Front and back parlor arrangement, with butler's pantry, of the 1860s and 1870s. First floor.

an open archway, or a screen of Corinthian columns, and an eight- to ten-foot-deep "tearoom" across the back of the house overlooking the yard. The tearoom usually was a wooden extension on the basement and first floors only and did not reach to the second and third floors.

By the 1850s, large brownstone-fronts adopted a new floor plan whose grandeur reflected the increasing wealth and social activity of New York families. A full-sized third room, fifteen to twenty feet deep and a regular part of the house structure, replaced the eight-foot-deep tearoom extension. This third room was the dining room for all meals except breakfast, a function made practical only after the invention of the dumb waiter around 1850. No longer did the servants have to carry plates and food up and down the narrow stairway between the kitchen in the basement and the dining room on the first floor. A small butler's pantry with the dumb waiter occupied the space behind the stairway and near the dining room.

Under this new floor plan, the old back parlor, which had looked into the tearoom or an open back porch, was a center room without its own windows. Because sliding doors separated this center room from the back dining room, it became essentially a part of the front parlor whose windows faced onto the street. To enhance this impressive union of the front and back parlors and increase the light and ventilation in the center room, only a shallow arch at the ceiling or a screen of Corinthian columns rather than solid parlor doors separated the two rooms. The front and middle rooms had become a single thirty-five- to forty-foot-deep parlor, but separate fireplaces, two sets of ceiling centerpieces and moldings, and separate doorways on the side hallway in each room maintained the old idea of distinct front and back parlors.

Even when a full-sized third room replaced the eight- to ten-foot-deep tearoom, few builders reduced the dimensions of the front and center rooms, which formed an impressive double parlor. The fine brownstone-fronts of the 14th Street and Madison Square areas in the 1850s and 1860s attained truly monumental dimensions—twenty-two, twenty-five, or thirty feet wide, a basement and four stories tall, and sixty or sixty-five feet deep. Fourteen-foot-tall ceilings and elaborate architectural ornament in the parlors complemented these patrician dimensions. Because the third room was a regular part of the house structure and not merely an extension of the basement and first floor, the bedrooms on the upper floors were correspondingly deeper, and identical pairs of washrooms and storage closets for each bedroom occupied the center ten feet of these floors.

The first floor parlors, though impressive for occasional entertaining, were poorly lit and ventilated from the front and back windows. As the price of land in a fashionable neighborhood convenient to downtown Manhattan continued to rise, only the most expensive row houses were built with the twenty-five-foot width necessary for the proper scale, lighting, and ventilation of these

James Lancaster Morgan Residence (1869–1870), No. 7 Pierrepont Street, Brooklyn Heights, about 1880. A fine post-Civil War brownstone-front with a fashionable mansard roof. Notice the carriage stone at the street curb in front of the stoop and, in the street, the special pollution problems of a horse-powered city.

sixty-foot-deep dwellings. In the 1860s, the floor plan of most New York row houses again changed, and the double parlors were replaced by one large parlor with one fireplace and marble mantel in the center of one long wall and a large double doorway opposite, opening onto the side hallway. With a single thirty- to thirty-five-foot-deep front parlor and dining room overlooking the back yard, the depth of fine row houses dropped from sixty feet to a more reasonable fifty or so. Under this floor plan, the butler's pantry sometimes moved from behind the stairway and became a small extension to the back of the house.

During these changes in the plan of the first floor in the 1850s and 1860s, the basement and upper floors remained the same—except to incorporate the era's advances in heating and indoor plumbing. However, on the second floor of large houses, the front room often took the full width of the house and was a family sitting room or library. The back room, separated from the front room by closets and dressing alcoves with wash basins, was the parents' bedroom and had a bathroom with toilet, tub, and shower. The third and fourth floors included childrens' bedrooms and several small servants' rooms.

In an era of large families and several live-in servants, the sixteen-room, five-story-tall brownstone-front combined grand parlors for entertaining and spacious living quarters for the family and, with its many floors, offered privacy for parents, children, and servants. Nevertheless, the five floors with high ceilings were problems in themselves, and in 1874 one architect complained that a town house was "little else but a string of stairs, with more or less extended landings. . . . Up and down, up and down, the women folk are perpetually toiling as in a treadmill . . . in the fruitless and health-destroying labor of carrying themselves from floor to floor."

Interior Design.

Although the Italianate and Second Empire row houses boasted front doorways, windows, and cornices of unparalleled richness, it was in the parlors and dining room that these houses fully expressed the bold forms and lavish ornament inherent in the styles. The wood and plaster of the interior were far easier to work than the brownstone of the street front. "We must peep within the palaces if we would comprehend the full extent of their splendor. Their lavish adornment is a marvel even to traveled eyes," wrote one newspaper describing the dwellings rising along Fifth Avenue after the Civil War.

The front parlor epitomized the family's roots, refinement, and social position—real or imagined. "Was there ever an American woman who, furnishing a house, did not first lay aside the money for the parlor?" asked a book about housekeeping in the 1870s. "A parlor must be, even if after it there comes

(top left) Hallway, James Lancaster Morgan residence, first floor, about 1880. Notice the heavy curtains shrouding the doorways and the richly stenciled ceiling with gas chandeliers.

(top right) Parlor (*ca.* 1865), South Oxford Street, Fort Greene, Brooklyn. This Italianate brownstone-front was a run-down rooming house before a 1970 renovation. Notice the elaborate white marble mantel, front windows which drop to the floor, gilt pier mirror and curtain valances, and double doors leading into the front hallway.

(bottom) Front Parlor, James Lancaster Morgan residence, about 1880.

the deluge." Parlors of New York brownstone-fronts were renowned for Brussels carpets, stamped leather or velvet wallpaper, overstuffed sofas and chairs, and gilt mirrors in profusion. Even before the spendthrift years following the Civil War, one British visitor to New York typically declared: "It is said in France that no orders sent to Lyons for the furnishing of private mansions are on so grand a scale as those from New York."

In the 1860s, magazines and newspapers often lampooned the many New York families who spent one-third of their income to rent a house at a fashionable address, bought showy furniture for the parlor and dining room, and then occupied the basement and several bedroom floors, which guests never saw, in genteel squalor. Fine furnishings for the parlors were surprisingly expensive. In the 1870s, Goodholme's *Domestic Cyclopedia* advised its readers that parlor furnishings in a $5,000 to $6,000 house should cost about $600. At that ratio, the parlor furnishings for a $25,000 brownstone—a good, but not exceptional, house in Manhattan—cost about $3,000, or more than the value of some workingmen's dwellings.

During the daytime, mahogany shutters and heavy draperies in the parlors were closed lest the sun fade the furniture, and some women "were always uneasy when their visitors sat down on a sofa or an ottoman, and could not forbear inviting them to change their seats and take chairs." After all, "the more the damask-covered seats were used, the sooner they would wear out."

Despite its grand architectural features and expensive furnishings, the parlor was silent and empty except for such formal moments as the morning calls, an evening party, or the fifteen minutes while guests gathered before a dinner party. Theodore Roosevelt remembered the parlor of his boyhood home, an 1848 brownstone-front near Gramercy Park, as a "room of much splendor . . . open for general use only on Sunday evening or on rare occasions when there were parties."

Fireplace. Although a wood- or coal-burning fireplace no longer heated New York row houses in the mid-nineteenth century, the fireplace mantels nonetheless remained the most important decorative feature of the showy parlors and dining room. The fireplace "has become the central point of the decorative treatment of the chamber, the gathering-place of family and friends," wrote one magazine in the early 1870s, "and the very word 'fireplace' has become in northern countries, suggestive of, almost synonymous with, the most heartfelt associations of domestic happiness and regard." In the late 1840s, the basically rectangular mantels of the Greek Revival style, with flat pilasters and horizontal entablature, took on boldly carved rococo features and appeared in some of the city's late Greek Revival and early Italianate style dwellings. At the same time, an elaborately ornamented, white-marble Italianate or "Renaissance" mantel, with a round-arched fireplace opening, appeared in row house parlors and remained the overwhelming fashion into the 1870s.

(top) Bedroom, James Lancaster Morgan residence, about 1880. As in all nineteenth-century row houses, the mantel, doorway, and ceiling ornament were simpler in the upstairs bedrooms than in the first floor parlors.

(bottom) Back Parlor, James Lancaster Morgan residence, about 1880. Notice the front parlor through the open sliding parlor doors.

Italianate mantel shelves had a scalloped edge and, in large houses, were supported by an acanthus- or oak-leaf–faced console at each end. During the 1850s, the parlors of the finest dwellings had statuary mantels, i.e., maidens standing on each side of the mantel carrying the shelf on top of their heads like the ancient caryatids. A handsome rope molding, like that found around the front doorway or on iron work, edged the round-arched fireplace opening. An ornamental keystone marked the top of the arch, and, aside from stylized round forms, popular designs included the Renaissance-inspired scallop shell, large pieces or baskets of fruit, shields, and the heads of beautiful women. The latter ranged from demure young ladies to Indian maidens with headdresses to lusty Marie Antoinette-like coquettes. In the 1850s and 1860s, richly carved leaves and fruit filled the spandrel or triangular area at each side of the arched fireplace opening. However, architectural taste changed after the Civil War, and mantels thereafter rarely carried elaborately carved foliate forms. Then, the keystone often consisted of stylized round forms, and the spandrels had several layers of triangular moldings.

The parlor mantels were the largest and most elaborately detailed in a New York row house, and the others were a simpler design, a cheaper marble, and, for several years after the emergence of a new architectural style, the passing and therefore cheaper style. As the Italianate mode emerged in New York in the late 1840s and early 1850s, the mantels on the upper floors were the declining Greek Revival style. By the 1860s, the Italianate style was firmly established in New York, and the mantels on the upper floors were a simple Italianate style but with modest forms and ornament. Although nearly all parlor mantels then followed the round-arched-opening Italianate style, they varied greatly in the quality of the carved ornament and marble. Elaborate, carved ornament did not necessarily indicate a good mantel; the foliate or stylized forms often were cut shallow and, therefore, were somewhat indistinct in form and detail.

The finest marbles were pure white and unmottled, with a lustrous sheen, whereas less expensive marble had a generally grayish tint, numerous gray streaks, and a dull finish. White marble was the usual but not the only choice for row house mantels in the 1850s and 1860s. Rose, brown, black, and even dark green marble sometimes appeared in rooms other than the parlors, particularly in the family dining room in the basement floor. Occasionally a mantel mixed two colors of marble, such as black with pink trim or black with white trim.

Some "marble" mantels actually were a "marbelized" slate or wood. Slate was easily enameled or painted to imitate marble, and, in manufacture, slate's softness allowed it to be cut quickly into slabs, polished to a smooth surface, or carved into bold and elaborate forms. Samuel Sloan praised "the high perfection which may be attained in the enamelling or marbelizing of slate. By this process

beautiful imitations of the richest and most expensive foreign marbles . . . may be produced in a manner so perfect as to challenge detection after the closest scrutiny." Sloan unequivocally stated that "mantels finished in this style are unequalled, attain a very high polish, retain their beauty much longer than common marble, and . . . possess the desirable quality of cheapness."

Though generally scorned then and now for the masquerade of an ordinary material as a costly one, the marbelized mantel must be viewed as the product of the same technology which brought such conveniences as central heating and plumbing to most New York dwellings and made fine materials and elaborate ornament available to the middle class. "We are bound to express our admiration of the unwearying industry and sleepless energy, by means of which difficulties of no ordinary kind have been overcome," declared one magazine in the 1860s. "A rude material has been exalted into one distinguished by artistic beauty. Refined taste has been bestowed on the production of articles for daily use, which can be sold to the public at the most moderate prices."

The improving capabilities of stone cutting and carving machinery indeed made possible the bold forms and elaborate ornament of Renaissance style mantels, and, except for occasional Italian imports in the finest dwellings, most mantels in New York row houses were factory-made in this country. In 1853 the *Godey's Lady's Book* magazine visited the J. and M. Baird marble-mantel works in Philadelphia and described "the operations of sawing, rubbing, cutting, and polishing, as we saw them performed at this establishment." After the blocks of marble arrived at the factory from the quarry, they were stored temporarily in the yard. "You are struck with the vast amount of the various kinds of marble which is piled up around you; those in the yard having the rough, uncouth exterior of the quarry, each awaiting their turn to be polished and made acceptable to genteel society." From the yard, the blocks of marble went to the "sawing room" where they were cut into slabs of the desired thickness by long strips of iron using sand and water for additional cutting friction. Afterwards, the slabs of marble went to the "rubbing department" where a "lap-wheel," ten feet in diameter and driven by an upright shaft at a thousand feet a minute, eliminated planar imperfections and gave the marble an even surface.

In the "stonecutter's department," workmen carved elaborate forms and ornament into the marble with steel tools and wood mallets. "The skill of the workmen displayed in this room is of the very highest character of art. Bouquets of flowers, wanting nothing but color to make them appear perfectly natural, are gradually developed by the artistic touch of the workmen." The Renaissance style mantels came in six, eight, or ten pieces, and the workmen next evened the seams between the pieces and drilled a few small holes in the marble where the mantels were to be joined together and securely fastened to the chimney breast.

The last step of mantel manufacture was the "polishing department," where steam-driven machinery was used on the flat mantel shelves and rectangular side pieces while workmen polished the elaborate ornamental keystones and consoles by hand. Afterward, the various pieces were crated together and shipped to their destination. In the Baird factory mantel-showroom, "we saw some patterns which are held as low as ten dollars each, while others are held at a thousand and upwards the pair. The elaborateness of carving on some indicated the highest elevation of the chisel; not a few, indeed, were exquisite specimens of the Phidian art."

The elaborate mantel only hinted at the extravagant forms and ornament in the parlors of fine New York brownstone-fronts. A large overmantel mirror in a wide, gilt frame filled the width of the protruding chimney breast and rose five, six, and even eight feet from the mantel shelf to the cornice at the ceiling. Although overmantel mirrors and the accompanying pier mirrors between the two street-front windows appeared in some parlors during the early nineteenth century, they were a part of nearly all parlors by the 1850s and the emergence of the Italianate style. "The use of large mirrors have [sic] become much more fashionable among us; and, in fact, there is no finer decoration for our saloons [parlors]," wrote one newspaper in 1851. The gilt-framed overmantel mirror was not only another showy touch for parlors but it made the somewhat narrow rooms appear to be wider than they were. A large marble or bronze clock customarily was placed on the center of the mantel shelf along with other decorative objects to be reflected in the mirror.

Ceilings. "The beautiful hard-finish ceilings of a house in the city, which have thus far satisfied the most fastidious taste have been spurned, and the parlors are now finished in Papier Mâché of the most costly and beautiful description," observed one New Yorker in the 1840s. The extravagant plaster ornament of parlor ceilings in most Italianate row houses again reflected the era's fondness for showy applied ornament and the pervasive influence of machine technology.

In large row houses, a several-foot-wide "centerpiece" or "rosette," often vaguely baroque or rococo in feeling and relying on vigorous foliate forms, adorned the center of the ceiling. Made of plaster or papier mâché, these centerpieces weighed over one hundred pounds and often served a functional as well as decorative purpose. The gaslight which hung from the "rosette" gave off an unpleasant odor of gas, so small holes were worked into the centerpiece to trap part of the rising fumes and carry them into the chimney flue and out-of-doors.

A cornice of several inch-wide moldings and occasional foliate forms ornamented the corners where the walls met the ceiling. Like the centerpiece, the plaster or papier-mâché cornice was purchased at a factory by the linear foot and glued into place at the house. Only the simplest coved moldings in the bedroom floors were run by hand in wet plaster. Inch-thick moldings, which divided

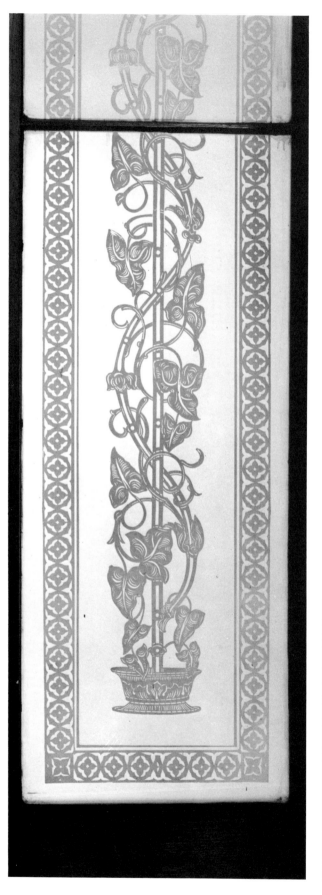

(left) Etched Glass, Remsen Street, Brooklyn Heights. Etched glass, with naturalistic or animal designs, often appeared in the upper part of doorways in mid-nineteenth-century New York row houses.

(top right) Mantel, Parlor, West 20th Street, Chelsea. A round-arched mantel of the 1850s with fine grape bunches and vines in the arched spandrels. The ceiling centerpiece and cornice are reflected in the mirror.

(bottom right) Mantel, Parlor, Willow Street, Brooklyn Heights. A transitional mantel of the late 1840s and early 1850s which combines the rectangular form of the Greek Revival mantels with rococo-inspired ornament forecasting the Italianate style.

the ceiling into several panels, cast small shadows on the ceiling and broke up its vast expanse. Often they were gilded to stand out more boldly from the white-painted or frescoed ceiling. In the heady post–Civil War years, Samuel Sloan warned that "when gilding is employed, it should be used sparingly; for, if overdone, that which would have been elegant will become gaudy and vulgar."

Visual necessity, as well as the showy taste of the period, led to the bold forms and elaborate ornament on parlor ceilings in the mid-nineteenth century. With the impressive twelve-, fourteen-, even sixteen-foot-tall parlors in fine brownstone-fronts, the ceiling and its details were farther from view than ever before and, at the same time, had to stand out from the boldly colored and patterned wallpaper then in vogue. "The great obstacle to perfection in the finish of a Drawing Room of the first class will be found in nine cases out of ten in the enrichments not having sufficient relief, the effect being very meagre on a lofty ceiling," wrote Samuel Sloan.

After the Civil War, some brownstone-fronts evidenced a taste for relative simplicity in interior design which forecast the Neo-Grec mode popular on New York row houses in the late 1870s and early 1880s. Parlor ceiling cornices relied on rounded coves formed by several moldings rather than foliate forms and screens of earlier years but still employed fine centerpieces, gilt moldings, and occasional frescoes for ornament.

The interior design of small brick-front row houses was more modest than that of fashionable brownstone-fronts. These houses continued the classical tradition of architectural simplicity into the 1850s, and their parlor ceilings employed the relatively simple plaster centerpiece and cove-form cornice. Their marble mantels reflected a simple Italianate mode, but the parlor-floor doors remained rectangular with simple moldings, often with the "Greek ear." Because the elaborate parlor mantels and arched parlor doors were of too large a scale or too costly for these small row houses, builders looked for other ways to ornament parlors in the late 1850s and 1860s. Relatively inexpensive machine-made plaster or papier maché ornament offered one way, and an elaborate foliate screen, for instance, often replaced the simple coved form for cornices.

Doors.   In the 1850s and 1860s, the sliding parlor doors of large and small New York row houses had frosted-glass windows with elaborate etched foliate designs. After the Civil War, large row houses had the mahogany, black walnut, or rosewood sliding doors popular in the 1870s and 1880s. Doorknobs throughout the house then usually were white porcelain, but in some large brownstone-front dwellings doorknobs on the parlor floor were white porcelain with painted flowers, glass with silver granules blown in, silver plate over brass, or an extravagant solid silver.

Heavy wood moldings framed all doors and windows of mid-nineteenth-century row houses. The Italianate style's fascination with circular forms appeared as shallow, arched doorways or an elegant

Parlors in an Anglo-Italianate Style Row House, West 20th Street, Chelsea. View from the back parlor through the square stair hall into the front parlor. A particularly elegant and spacious ensemble of rooms.

half-circle doorway arch in first-floor parlors. Only costly dwellings had the arched doorway, which was more difficult to execute than the flat-headed, rectangular doorway found on the less important bedroom floors of these row houses.

In the mid-nineteenth century, mahogany, black walnut, and rosewood replaced the light-color mahogany, oak, and satinwood for parlor woodwork in fine dwellings. Only these dark woods effectively contrasted with the thick doorway and window moldings, richly decorated ceilings, and the bright colors then popular for wallpaper and carpets. Black walnut was the most popular wood of the era for its deep color, ease of taking elaborate carving, and resistance to wear. In the parlors with mahogany or black-walnut woodwork, the doors emphasized the fine finish of the wood with large, simply molded, rectangular or circular panels or a juxtaposition of different woods or stains in the same place. But the parlors of most row houses in the mid-nineteenth century had pine woodwork which was painted a light color or given the imitation graining of a more costly wood.

Floors. The original pine floors of New York's brownstone-fronts were seemingly out of character with their lavish mantels, gilt mirrors, and richly ornamented ceilings. In Federal and Greek Revival dwellings, floors in the parlors were handsome one-foot-wide, one-inch-thick, light-color planks. By the mid-nineteenth century, the floors of New York row houses were four- to six-inch-wide pine planks, occasionally laid over an even cheaper subflooring because of the nearly universal fashion for wall-to-wall carpets.

Before the mid-nineteenth century, carpets were handmade and had been available only to the wealthy. In 1844 Erastus Bigelow invented a machine which wove ingrain carpets, and in 1848 a power loom for Brussels and tapestry carpets. Carpets dropped dramatically in price but still retained their earlier status connotations. By the 1850s nearly every middle-class family proudly put a thick, floral-patterned carpet in the parlor. However, a carpet was something of a problem. It rested on a pad of woven grass called "China matting," which gave off an unpleasant musty odor in damp weather. Carpets also had to be taken up once or twice a year to be cleaned. To cut down on soil and postpone this cleaning, a linen cloth usually was placed beneath the dining-room table to catch bits of food, hence a popular name the "crumb cloth" or "drugget." The maid swept off or shook out the crumb cloth after each meal.

Hardwood floors in New York row houses of the 1850s and 1860s usually date from the late nineteenth or early twentieth century when softwood floors and wall-to-wall carpets had lost favor. In the mid-nineteenth century, only an occasional row house was built with hardwood floors, but stairways always were hardwood for practical reasons.

Room Shape. Within the constraints of the row house width, the parlors emphasized vistas to gain

J. & F. W. Ridgway, Plumber, No. 145 Broadway (1844). Notice the Greek Revival style bathroom equipped with sink, toilet, tub, and shower.

a spatial dignity commensurate with the lavish ornament and monumental street fronts of the period. Doors, windows, mantels, and the overmantel mirror fell on axes, and the pier mirror set between the two street-front windows of the front parlor, and often a mirror between the windows of the back parlor, made for a long vista down the length of the house. The large overmantel mirror was opposite the double doors from the hallway into the parlor and enhanced the width of the house.

At the same time, the shape of the parlor was more complicated than in previous years. The chimney breast stood out boldly from the wall, the elaborate mantel protruded one or two feet further into the room, and the heavy plaster cornice at the ceiling emphasized the breaks in the previously rectangular room shape. In the 1860s, a bay window in the back parlor added a polygonal extension to the end of the room and, in the words of Samuel Sloan, was "an addition to a house which should never be dispensed with . . . for there is nothing that gives more *life* to a room, than this pretty feature, and certainly the space it adds is an acquisition, which those who once enjoy the privilege it gives of trivial view, will not readily relinquish." Nevertheless, a bay window on the street front of an Italianate and Second Empire row house was rare in New York, because it interrupted the monumental streetscape of flat-front row houses.

Entrance Hall. The small foyer between the two sets of round-arched double doors shrank from the comfortable five- to six-foot length of earlier decades to an awkward few feet where guests merely might receive shelter from bad weather. The foyer floor usually was either all white marble, a pattern of black and white rectangular tiles, or occasionally encaustic tiles, a dull-finish tile in an elaborate pattern, usually a dark red, yellow, or black and imported from England. A floor of highly decorated encaustic tiles often cost more than one of marble, and, according to Samuel Sloan, "for stores, vestibules, entries, outside verandahs, green houses, churches, and in fact every place where beauty, taste and economy are objects to be attained, there is nothing that can be more suitable than the Encaustic Tiles."

The long stair hallway on the first floor usually had a softwood floor, covered by carpet, white and black marble, or the encaustic tiles of the foyer. As late as the 1860s, the stairs in New York's brownstone-fronts curved gracefully at the top and bottom, and, in an era of hand labor, this handsome sweeping stairway, with statue niches and mahogany handrail emphasizing its curved form, could be afforded in the ordinary row houses. After the Civil War, the straight flight of stairs with right-angled corners was considerably cheaper to construct, and the large brownstone-fronts of the 1860s were the first houses in the city to include stairs that went straight up to the second floor with only a superficial curve at the various turns of the handrail.

The huge newel post at the foot of the stairway usually was an elaborate polygonal or a

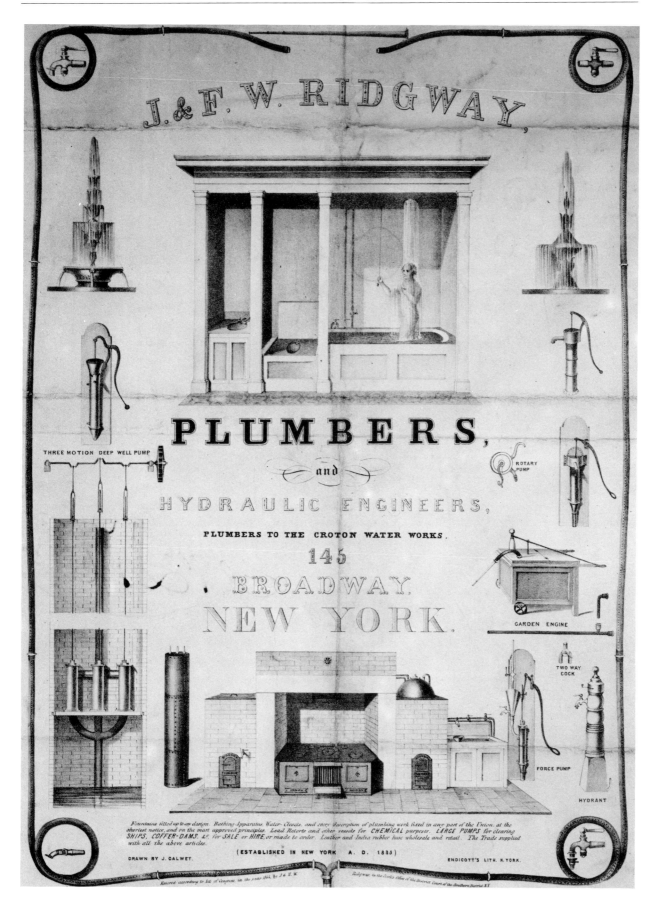

Renaissance-inspired baluster. The newel post, like the simpler balusters of the handrailings, usually continued the mahogany or black walnut of the parlor doorway moldings. For a particularly lavish effect, newel posts sometimes combined inlays of rosewood or butternut with black walnut or an ebony inlay with mahogany. A round or rectangular skylight, often of stained glass, partly lit the stairwell. "The light descending in full stream from above distributed and broken by innumerable angular surfaces and the brilliant contrast of the dark wood with the mellow hue of the walls and floors cannot fail to produce one of the most pleasing subjects of internal picture," wrote one New Yorker in the 1850s.

Kitchen.   In the mid-nineteenth century, the kitchen of a New York row house included many of the appliances of a kitchen today—though in a far simpler form. In the 1840s, a coal- or wood-burning stove replaced the hearth for cooking and, by the 1860s, included ovens, broilers, storage space, as well as the elaborate floral ornament that denoted modernity and good taste to the era. The stove, which sat in a large brick hearth along the wall, nevertheless had to be fed by hand, banked at night, and emptied of ashes several times a day.

As early as the 1840s, iceboxes appeared in New York dwelling houses and were described as "large wooden boxes, standing on feet, and lined with tin or zinc, being generally inter-lined with charcoal, and having at the bottom a receptacle for ice, and a drain to carry off the water that drops from it as it melts; a vessel being always set underneath to catch the droppings." The icebox indeed lessened the problem of food preservation, but the servants had to empty the water pan every day and keep the drainpipe to the floor pan free of the sawdust in which the iceman packed the ice. By the 1870s, iceboxes often were fine pieces of furniture with mahogany cabinets and brass or silver-plate hardware, and in occasional row houses a water pipe passed through the icebox and provided cool water in the summer.

The kitchen also was the sitting room for the servants, and a thoughtful lady of the house provided a table, a rug or piece of carpet, some magazines and books, and a good light. In mid-nineteenth-century New York, wealthy families hired six or seven servants—a cook, waiter, parlor maid, upstairs maid, laundress, houseman, and likely a coachman. Middle-class families had to make do with only three servants—a cook, waiter, and maid. The servants worked six days a week and received several dollars a week, plus room and board, for work which began an hour before the family awoke and ended after its members were asleep.

Few streets in New York had alleys in back of the houses. To the health and comfort of the block's residents, the family horses and conveyance were kept in a private carriage house or stable in a less fashionable street nearby. The service entrance to the house was the door to the basement under the stoop, and throughout the day cries of street vendors filled the air and tradesmen's wagons lined the curbs of even the city's finest streets.

Bedroom Floors. While lacking the impressive mantels, woodwork, and ceiling height of the parlor and dining room, the bedrooms on the upper floors of a brownstone-front epitomized the comfortable life style of wealthy New York families 100 years ago. In the second-floor parents' bedroom, the furnishings included a double bed, bureaus with mirrors, a dressing table, several chairs, a wall-to-wall carpet, and usually the desk where the lady of the house wrote notes, paid bills, and gave the cook instructions for the day's meals. By the 1860s, bedrooms in fine New York dwellings had large closets instead of wardrobes and elegant marble and mahogany wash basins with hot and cold running water set into alcoves instead of the old-fashioned washstand with basin and pitcher. Each family bedroom floor also included a fully equipped bathroom.

The renowned comfort of a New York brownstone-front did not extend to the servants' quarters on the top floor. In winter, a coal grate was the only source of heat, and, instead of a bathroom, the servants used the washstand with water pitcher, basin, and chamber pot. The complaints about unwashed, even malodorous, servants probably were accurate, because the "help" washed in a tub or sink in the kitchen about once a week.

Different ceiling heights throughout a row house of the period reflected the importance attached to the various floors. In a basement-and-four-story-tall dwelling, basement ceilings typically were nine feet high, the first floor an imposing fourteen feet high, the second floor eleven feet, the third floor ten feet, and the fourth floor nine feet. It is a noteworthy comparison that the ceilings in today's so-called luxury apartment buildings rarely reach nine feet, a height reserved for the nursery and servants' rooms on the fourth and top floor of the city's fine mid-nineteenth-century dwellings.

Mechanical Equipment of Row Houses.

In the 1840s, advancing technology dramatically increased the comfort of New Yorkers living in fine row houses. In terms of such equipment as indoor plumbing and central heating, the New York row house of the 1840s more closely resembled a dwelling of the early twentieth century than one of the 1830s, just one decade earlier. "Within the past few years, more regard than formerly has been paid to domestic conveniences," wrote Minard Lafever, "and many valuable improvements have been introduced, which are beginning to be considered indispensable, even in ordinary dwellings. Among these the supplying of water to the several stories, the various modes of warming, and also of ventilating." A new "desirable dwelling house in East Sixteenth-st. near Union-square," according to an 1846 real estate advertisement included "Croton water, range, boiler, bath, water closets, double

(top) Bedroom, second floor, Dean Street, Boerum Hill, Brooklyn. In most mid-nineteenth century row houses, the front bedroom on the second floor stretched across the full width of the house and had an arched niche for the double bed.

(bottom left) No. 301 Hicks Street, Brooklyn Heights (*ca.* 1862). A pleasant brownstone-front of the 1860s which still stands, though sadly altered.

(bottom right) Back Yards, looking toward Madison Square from a rear window of No. 28 East 28th Street, about 1855. Notice the back porches, clothesline posts, and rude wooden extensions in the back yards. In the distance, a carriage house stands around the corner from the magnificent Iselin residence facing Madison Square.

flight of stairs, furnace, dumb waiter from basement to attic, gas, and every other improvement introduced into modern built houses of the first class."

The opening of the Croton reservoir system in 1842 guaranteed a constant supply of wholesome water to New York and for the first time made possible indoor plumbing for the city's dwelling houses. As early as 1788, one New Yorker observed that "a want of good water is a great inconvenience to the citizens; there being few wells in the city. . . . Several proposals have been made by individuals to supply the citizens by pipes; but none have yet been accepted."

Before the availability of Croton water, most New Yorkers drank a hard and brackish water drawn from city pumps, known as "tea water pumps," at most street intersections. In a growing city, where continual construction disturbed the ground and subsoil, the water from city pumps was unpleasant tasting, often polluted, and scarce during summer droughts. Graveyards posed a particular threat to New York's water supply, and in 1829 the city banned the common practice of building burial vaults under the street. In 1823 the city forbade any burials in the built-up portion of the city. In the early nineteenth century, well-to-do New Yorkers drank barreled spring water brought into the city from then rural midtown and upper Manhattan or rain water which drained from the roof into a large brick cistern in the backyard.

The early nineteenth century saw several unsuccessful schemes to bring good water to New York, among them the drilling of artesian wells in the city and the cutting of a canal from the Housatonic River in New Jersey and bringing water into the city by pipes under the Hudson River. An inadequate and contaminated water supply slowed New York's emergence as a modern city by contributing to low standards of public health, which led to the numerous yellow-fever epidemics, and by hampering efforts to put out the frequent fires of the era.

After the disastrous fires in lower Manhattan in 1833 and 1835 and several summers of droughts, New Yorkers voted approval of the Croton water system in 1835. At a cost of $12,000,000, the city dammed the Croton River in upper Westchester County and built a solid masonry water conduit forty-five miles long to the city's 150,000,000-gallon receiving reservoir at 86th Street, later a part of Central Park. Amidst great fanfare, water was introduced into the Croton Distributing Reservoir at Fifth Avenue and 42nd Street on July 4, 1842. "Nothing is talked of or thought of in New York but Croton water," wrote Philip Hone several months thereafter. "Fountains, aqueducts, hydrants, and hose attract our attention and impede our progress through the streets. . . . Water! water! is the universal note which is sounded through every part of the city, and infuses joy and exultation into the masses."

Before the introduction of Croton water in 1842, bathing and toilet facilities were almost unknown in New York row houses. "Another defect in the American establishments is the want of *cabinets de (top left)* Walker's Patent Improved Hot Air Furnace," for Heating Churches and other Public Buildings, Dwellings, Stores, &c." (*ca.* 1850)

(top right) Toilet Shower Baths (*ca.* 1850).

(bottom) Wash Basin, with original brass faucets (*ca.* 1855), South Portland Avenue, Fort Greene, Brooklyn.

toilette," observed James Fenimore Cooper in the 1820s. "They are certainly to be found in a few houses, but I have occupied a bed-room five and twenty square, in a house, otherwise convenient, that had not under its roof a single apartment of the sort." Toilet facilities consisted of chamber pots in the pantries between the front and back bedrooms and a "bathing house" or privy in the back yard. In 1836 the luxurious Astor House hotel, on Broadway at Vesey Street, created a sensation because of the toilets and provisions for bathing on every floor.

After a plentiful water supply was assured in the mid-1840s, newly built row houses included one or two bathrooms, and in 1841 George Templeton Strong typically declared: "Tried our new bath room last night for the first time, and propose to repeat the experiment this evening. It's a great luxury—worth the cost of the whole building." The city tax for introducing Croton water to a row house was $10 a year in a basement-and-two-story-tall dwelling and $12 a year in a basement-and-three-story-tall house. Often the second-floor hall bedrooms in the back of the house became the family toilet and bathroom, and handsome marble wash basins soon appeared in the old pantries between the front and back bedrooms or in a niche in the wall in the bedroom itself.

The city's finest dwellings, old and new alike, soon included elaborate bath and toilet facilities. In an extreme example, Robert Griffith Hatfield's plan of 1848 for the lavish Henry Parish mansion at No. 26 East 17th Street, near Fifth Avenue, included seven toilets and eleven tubs and wash basins. However, the high cost of pipes, valves, and fixtures, not yet mass-produced, limited nearly all row houses of the 1840s and 1850s to far more modest bath and toilet arrangements. Even the magnificent basement-and-four-story-tall brownstone-fronts of the 1850s originally had only one or two large bathrooms for the entire family; the servants still used the earlier chamber pots and bathed in a tub in the kitchen. In houses with a bathroom in the 1840s, hot water often had to be carried upstairs from the kitchen where it was heated in a "log boiler," at the back of the kitchen stove, by the hot air and smoke passing up the chimney.

During the 1860s, dramatic improvements in toilet and bathing facilities appeared in New York row houses. Large row houses had bathrooms on the several bedroom floors. When the "circulating boiler" or hot-water system replaced the old log boiler arrangement, hot water was available directly from the tap in the bathroom and bedroom wash basins throughout the house. The circulating boiler was a thirty- to forty-gallon copper tank next to the always lit stove which kept the water nearly at the boiling point. When hot water was drawn from the pipe coil, cold water entered, thus making for an automatic hot-water system.

As plumbing arrangements in the city's dwelling houses improved and expanded, New Yorkers' attitudes toward the bathroom also changed. "What was known a few years ago, even as a luxury, is

WALKER'S
PATENT IMPROVED HOT AIR
FURNACE,
For Heating Churches and other Public Buildings, Dwellings, Stores, &c.
SOLD BY GEO. WALKER, 292 BROADWAY, N. Y.

FIGURE 1, INTERIOR VIEW.

The objects aimed at by the patentee, in the construction of his Hot Air Furnace, are,

1st. By means of one fire, to produce a mild, uniform and agreeable temperature throughout several apartments, and to warm a whole house sufficient for sleeping rooms, or to keep plants of all kinds in the coldest weather.

2nd. To avoid all dust and gas, and to keep the apartments well ventilated by means of a constant supply of fresh air from without.

3rd. To be simple, so that any one capable of managing a stove can take care of it.

FIGURE 2, GROUND PLAN.

4th. To be economical in point of fuel.

5th. To be durable, so as not to require frequent or expensive repairs.

The Furnace is constructed of cast iron, is placed in the cellar and enclosed in brick walls, in such a manner that there is very little heat wasted by escaping into the cellar or chimney flue. Consequently all the fuel consumed is made available to heating the apartments; and in no case where they have been erected, have they failed to give entire satisfaction.

Orders or letters of enquiry, from any part of the United States or Canadas, will be promptly attended to.

RECOMMENDATIONS.

REFERENCES.

TOILET SHOWER BATHS.

This new and valuable improvement received the FIRST PREMIUM of the American Institute, (*A SILVER MEDAL*,) at the late Fair as the

BEST SHOWER BATH YET INVENTED.

It is now offered to the public as a most complete article of furniture in the shape of a

WASH STAND,

From which it may be converted into a SHOWER BATH complete in one minute, by turning the crank at the side; thus affording all the facilities for shower-bathing without requiring any extra room. They are furnished in various styles, of Mahogany, of Black Walnut, and of Painted Wood.

Cut No. 1 represents the bath ready for showering, 2 as wash stand, and 3 closed.

For sale, at Wholesale and Retail, at the sole Agency, by

SMITH, TORREY & CO.
50 Maiden Lane and 33 Liberty-St.
NEW YORK.

now a necessity," remarked Samuel Sloan. By the 1860s, house buyers wanted lavish bathroom appointments to complement the splendor of the rest of the house. "Now the polished metal tub and tubular shower, with silver, marble, and walnut setting, are esteemed necessary for comfort, in very moderate houses." However, such splendid "conveniences of plumbing have been over-done," one magazine reported.

> Frequently a marble slab basin or an enamelled bath is seen with invisible inlet or outlet for water, and only a fancifully enriched plated knob, perhaps over the centre of the affair. In perplexity this is pulled at, but it will not draw out. A lucky turn to the right sends a rush of hot water streaming into the basin or bath. This is soon too hot, and you look in vain for some friendly tap of a cooler element. Another turn of the knob, and, with a gurgling swirl, the water as quickly disappears, and all is empty, whilst vexation and embarrassment disturb all ideas of comfort.

Improved heating arrangements was the other major advance in comfort for the New York row house in the 1840s. During the eighteenth and early nineteenth centuries, the wood-burning fireplace heated the city's dwellings. During the 1820s, well-to-do families began to burn coal in grates, because it gave a more constant heat with less tending than wood fires. "Coal is here only burned by the opulent," declared one Englishman in New York in the 1830s, "and although fashion has declared in favor of its use, yet wood is the chief, and indeed, almost the only fuel consumed here; it is certainly much healthier and cleaner, than its sable substitute but the matter of dollars and cents has its share of influence."

By the 1830s and 1840s, coal was available to New Yorkers at a reasonable cost because of the opening of the Erie Canal in 1825 to the Great Lakes coal fields, the completion of the Delaware and Hudson Canal in 1828 to the Pennsylvania coal fields, and the growth of the railroad network in the 1830s. Philip Hone believed that coal offered a nearly unlimited source of cheap fuel for heating dwellings and, in 1839, noted in his journal that since 1820 the output of the Pennsylvania coal mines had grown from 365 tons to over 1,000,000 tons. The reduced size of the fireplace opening and appearance of ornamental cast-iron fireplace grates at that time indicated the triumph of coal over wood for heating the city's row houses.

By the 1840s, forced hot-air heating systems appeared in some New York dwellings. "In many houses, the open stoves, and their unblazing anthracite coal, are now banished, and plain marble slabs, perforated for the passage of hot air substituted in their rooms," recalled one Englishman in the 1840s. In this period, the coal-burning furnace sat in the cellar in a brick vault about six feet by nine feet. Wide wooden troughs brought outside air into the brick vault, where it was heated by contact with the hot surface of the furnace and then forced through tin pipes to the upper floors.

Often, a small jet of water in the furnace vault restored some humidity to the air after its heating. These tin air ducts, which varied in diameter depending on the room size, led to an elaborate cast-iron or brass floor or wall register. In the 1840s and 1850s, the hot-air system usually heated only the basement and first floors, while the upstairs bedroom floors still relied on coal grates in the fireplaces. By the Civil War, improved furnaces in fine brownstone-fronts often heated the entire house.

The operation of the hot-air furnace was fairly simple. Every morning a servant raked out the furnace and threw away the ashes, stoked it with coal twice a day, and at night banked the cinders and partly closed the damper to ensure constant fire and even heat.

Only a few contemporary sources mention the heating of the city's dwellings. But in the 1840s one Englishman was already voicing an apparently deathless British criticism of American central heating:

> The method of heating in many of the best houses is a terrible grievance to persons not accustomed to it, and a fatal misfortune to those who are. Casual visitors are nearly suffocated, and the constant occupiers killed. An enormous furnace in the cellar sends up, day and night, streams of hot air through apertures and pipes, to every room in the house. No spot is free from it, from the dining-parlour to the dressing closet. It meets you the moment the street-door is opened to let you in, and it rushes after you when you emerge again, half-stewed and parboiled, into the wholesome air.

Contrary to these complaints about constant heat, the hot air furnaces of the 1840s actually sent up uneven blasts of scorching air, mixed with some gas and soot, rather than a pleasant, even flow.

Greenwich Village.

Though best known for its outstanding Federal and Greek Revival dwellings, Greenwich Village has some of the finest Italianate and Anglo-Italianate style row houses remaining in Manhattan. The handsome Italianate style once stretched from Greenwich Village, through present-day midtown Manhattan into the East Sixties and Seventies. But the nearly complete rebuilding of midtown Manhattan in the last 100 years and the continual alteration of row houses in fashionable Greenwich Village and on the East Side have destroyed or drastically changed most of the brownstone era's splendid buildings.

In the mid-nineteenth century, lower Fifth Avenue and adjacent Ninth, Tenth, Eleventh, and Twelfth streets were among the most fashionable in the city and, therefore, saw some of the earliest and most spectacular Italianate, Anglo-Italianate, and Second Empire dwellings in the city. Although lower Fifth Avenue, south of Twelfth Street, always has retained its distinguished residential tradition,

(top) Double Parlors, Salmagundi Club (1852–1853), originally the Irad Hawley residence, No. 47 Fifth Avenue, between East Eleventh and East Twelfth streets. The last mansion of the 1850s and 1860s standing on Fifth Avenue today. A dazzling display of marble mantels, Corinthian columns, rosewood doors, and ornamental ceiling plasterwork. The Salmagundi Club, surprisingly, was only a typical residence on Fifth Avenue, easily surpassed in size and ornament by the Thorne, Haight, Parish, and Stewart mansions.

(bottom) Statuary Mantel, Salmagundi Club, front parlor (1852–1853).

the mid-nineteenth-century mansions and row houses, which gave the area its original fashion, largely have disappeared in the past fifty years. Today, the handsome Church of the Ascension, the First Presbyterian Church, and high-rise apartment buildings from the building booms of the 1920s and 1950s line Fifth Avenue in the several blocks north of Washington Square.

Only the Salmagundi Club, at No. 47 Fifth Avenue, remains to give an idea of the original character and scale of the area and to offer a glimpse into the life style of the city's richest families in the 1850s and 1860s. The house was built in 1852–1853 for Irad Hawley, president of the Pennsylvania Coal Company, which had its coal yards about a mile to the west near the Hudson River. With its boldly rusticated basement, high balustraded stoop, and lavish door hood supported on consoles, the Salmagundi Club is a wide, mansion-sized version of the era's fine Italianate style brownstone-front row house. The parlor floor epitomizes the splendor of the Italianate style in the elaborate white-marble "statuary mantels," plaster ceiling ornament, rosewood doors, and two pairs of Corinthian columns between the identical front and back parlors. The dining room, overlooking the back yard, originally was in the Gothic Revival style and is now the Club's art gallery.

Although the opulence and grand scale of the Salmagundi Club amaze the visitor today, No. 47 Fifth Avenue apparently was not that extraordinary a dwelling for Fifth Avenue in the 1850s and 1860s. Newspaper articles and guidebooks often described mansions built on lower Fifth Avenue but never mentioned this fine building.

The blocks of Ninth, Tenth, Eleventh, and Twelfth streets adjacent to Fifth Avenue retain much of their low-rise residential character and offer a complete display of row house architecture of the 1830s, 1840s, and 1850s. Some Italianate and Anglo-Italianate row houses on these blocks occupy the site of earlier houses. Among the finest surviving monumental Anglo-Italianate streetscapes in the city is the row comprising Nos. 20–38 West Tenth Street. These five-story brownstone-front dwellings were built in 1856 (except for No. 38, which was completed in 1858) and traditionally are attributed to James Renwick, Jr., architect of numerous Anglo-Italianate rows in the city. The rusticated first floors have the typical round-arched single window and doorway, approached by a several-step-high stoop with handsome railings and areaway fences. A continuous cornice, unfortunately missing on several of the houses, and a virtually complete cast-iron balcony in front of the second-floor parlors' French windows give this distinguished row an impressive visual unity. Surprisingly, the individual houses of the Renwick Terrace are not uniform in width but vary from eighteen to twenty-two feet.

Other fairly intact Anglo-Italianate row houses in the lower Fifth Avenue area are: Nos. 54–58 West Ninth Street (1853); No. 31 West Ninth Street, which shows the original appearance of the three-house group Nos. 29–33 (1854) and is attributed to James Renwick, Jr.; Nos. 19–23 West Ninth

Renwick Terrace (1856), Nos. 20–38 West Tenth Street, Greenwich Village, attributed to James Renwick, Jr. A distinguished terrace of Anglo-Italianate brownstone-fronts. Although several houses have lost considerable original façade detail, the rusticated ground floors, cast-iron balcony in the front of the second floor parlor windows, and the cornice unify this range of dwelling houses.

Street, also attributed to James Renwick, Jr.; Nos. 24 and 28 West Twelfth Street, an early pair of brownstone-front dwellings (1851–1852); and Nos. 48–52 West Twelfth Street (1854) whose unusual doorways have small columns supporting an arch.

Some row houses in Greenwich Village reflect the transition from the Greek Revival to the Italianate style which occurred in the late 1840s and early 1850s. In the West Village, Nos. 58–62 Morton Street (1847–1849) freely combine the Greek Revival and Italianate styles. At No. 62 Morton Street, the best-preserved house of the row, the stoop and areaway iron work is Greek Revival, but the double front doors are Italianate in form and ornament. A triangular pediment above the entablature of the pilastered doorway enframement reflects the elaboration of Greek Revival forms and the plasticity of façade features increasingly fashionable in the late 1840s. The elaborate cornice treatment combines a row of egg-and-dart molding, modillion blocks, and taenia molding.

Even after the appearance of the fashionable brownstone-front in the late 1840s, fine row houses were built with a conservative brick front and brownstone trim into the late 1850s. The nearly intact Nos. 3–17 St. Luke's Place in the West Village combine the old-fashioned red-brick front with such fashionable features of the Italianate style as a bold cornice, a door hood supported by consoles, and a high rusticated basement. This handsome curved row was built in several sections during the early 1850s following a master design. Originally facing St. John's Cemetery of the Trinity Parish, these houses were owned by prosperous merchants, many of whose offices and warehouses were just to the west along the Hudson River or about a mile to the south in lower Manhattan. In 1898 Carrère & Hastings transformed the old cemetery into the landscaped Hudson Park, which featured Italian Renaissance-inspired terraces, a reflecting pool, and even a country "cottage." This is now a playground named James J. Walker Park, in honor of that former mayor who lived at No. 6 St. Luke's Place.

At any time of the year, St. Luke's Place is one of the most beautiful streets in New York. Set back from the largely traffic-free street by tree-shaded and attractively planted front yards, the well-preserved, warm, red-brick and brownstone-trim fronts enjoy an open, several-hundred-foot-long vista past the playground which is nearly out of sight below the street level and behind a handsome iron fence.

A walk down St. Luke's Place toward the Hudson River is a visual and architectural pleasure seldom equaled in the city. Starting at Seventh Avenue South, several five- and six-story-tall, old-law tenements greedily step out to the lot line and block the sun. Then one approaches a curve in the street, typical of the West Village, which conceals the rest of the block from view. As one turns this curve, the fifteen-house-long row of St. Luke's Place begins and slowly unfolds its full length and

St. Luke's Place (early 1850s),
Greenwich Village. View toward the
west. Block-long St. Luke's Place is one
of the loveliest streets in New York.
Well-planted front yards and trees
along the curb enhance the mellow red-
brick and brownstone-trim façades,
which are virtually unchanged from the
1850s.

exceptional charm to the pedestrian. The trees in front yards and boldly protruding door and window
details cast romantic shadows on the muted red-brick street fronts. The high stoops, with their intact
cast-iron railings, boldly step out from the red-brick fronts into the handsomely planted front yards
and beckon the eye down the full length of this magnificent row.

Lower Second Avenue.

In an ever changing New York, "The Triangle" on Stuyvesant Street and its unusually handsome setting
have retained much of their original dignity through the years. This group of Anglo-Italianate row
houses, attributed to James Renwick, Jr., stretches from Nos. 23–35 Stuyvesant Street around the
point of the triangle to include Nos. 112–128 East Tenth Street. It is a stunning architectural solution
to this strangely shaped intersection of East Tenth and Stuyvesant streets, between Second and Third
avenues. As individual buildings, the row houses of The Triangle are fine examples of the
Anglo-Italianate style and, except for a few missing iron railings, have nearly the same appearance
today as when they were completed in 1861. The contrast in color and texture between the
soot-darkened, red, Philadelphia pressed brick and dark brownstone window trim and rusticated first
floor is a striking sight at any distance. Heavy cornices and fully enframed windows on the upper
floors cast deep picturesque shadows on the brick fronts.

In the spirit of the monumental streetscape popular at the time, the houses of The Triangle form
an impressive single composition rather than two rows of narrow houses on an awkwardly shaped lot.
The houses actually have different interior plans varying in width from sixteen to thirty-two feet and
in depth from sixteen to forty-eight feet, and the house at the point of The Triangle is cut off flat at
the end rather than following the lot lines to a sharp point. Recently planted trees along the street
curb soften the bold color and formal appearance of these houses.

The unusual street pattern near The Triangle came from the Stuyvesant family's holdings here
which stretched back to the seventeenth century and Peter Stuyvesant, the last Dutch governor of
New Amsterdam. The original Stuyvesant farm boundaries were present-day Third Street, Avenue C,
23rd Street, and the Bowery, once "Bouwerie," the Dutch word for farm. Peter Stuyvesant's mansion
stood near what became the intersection of Second Avenue and East Tenth Street, and today's
Stuyvesant Street was a road from the house to the Bouwerie Road. Several generations later, Petrus
Stuyvesant, the Dutch governor's great grandson, inherited the family farm and, as early as 1789,
mapped out the land into building lots on a grid street plan running exactly north to south and east
to west. Because the old road to the Peter Stuyvesant mansion ran exactly east and west, it was
incorporated within that street plan as Stuyvesant Street. Several years later, construction began in
the newly laid out area.

Two Federal style row houses survive from this construction activity around 1800—No. 21 Stuyvesant Street (1803–1804), the home of Petrus Stuyvesant's daughter Elizabeth and her husband Nicholas Fish, and No. 44 Stuyvesant Street (1795), the residence of Nicholas William Stuyvesant. No. 21 is one of the city's finest remaining Federal style dwellings. The original splayed brownstone lintels make for a pleasing contrast with the Flemish bond red-brick front, and two austerely handsome dormer windows in the pitched roof rise above a plain cornice. Although No. 21 Stuyvesant Street was an unusually wide and tall house at the time of its construction, it is dwarfed by the tall, narrow Anglo-Italianate row houses of The Triangle–a sign of rising land costs and changing row house plans in those sixty years.

By the time the city mapped out the present-day "grid" street plan in 1807–1811 to guide Manhattan's growth north of Houston Street, a number of Stuyvesant family houses had been built in accord with Petrus Stuyvesant's street plan, which ran due east and west. The streets of the city's grid map followed the axis of the island—a considerable discrepancy.

As the city laid out streets according to its 1807–1811 plan, all streets at variance with that grid normally were closed, the buildings torn down or moved, and the owners compensated for losses in houses or land. However, Stuyvesant Street became a part of the regular street plan, in the words of the Common Council in 1830, "both for Public convenience and for the accommodation of a large and respectable Congregation attending St. Mark's Church as well as the owners and occupants of several large and commodious dwelling houses . . . all of which would be destroyed, or rendered of little value, if that street were closed." In 1812 the city opened Third Avenue in this area, in 1816 Second Avenue, and in 1826 Eighth, Ninth, Tenth, Eleventh, and Twelfth streets.

In the following decades, the streets near lower Second Avenue largely were built up except for Tenth Street and Stuyvesant Street where the open land of the Stuyvesant family maintained the early-nineteenth-century rural feeling of the area. The site of The Triangle was then a garden for No. 21 Stuyvesant Street, the home of Elizabeth Stuyvesant Fish. With her death in the 1850s, the family sold off the land as row house building lots.

Despite the area's shabby and sometime frantic appearance today, Second Avenue and nearby streets formed one of the city's finest neighborhoods in the 1830s, 1840s, and 1850s. "The two great avenues for elegant residences are to be the Second and the Fifth," declared one newspaper in the mid-1840s. "Like the Fifth, the Second has it character established as a good neighborhood, by the number of elegant dwellings erected." The presence of notable families such as the Stuyvesants and their concern that the area be developed in an elegant manner contributed to its fashion. And, Second Avenue was just east of the elegant Bond Street area and Lafayette Place.

From the late 1820s to the late 1850s, elegant row houses and mansions were built along St. Mark's Place, the three blocks of Eighth Street east of Third Avenue. Although St. Mark's Place has the standard sixty foot width of a New York sidestreet, the row houses were built a uniform ten feet behind the front property line and gave the block an extraordinary spaciousness and dignity. The real estate advertisement for "A DESIRABLE RESIDENCE IN ST. MARK'S PLACE" in 1845 points out the street's one-time fashion and describes a New York mansion before the appearance of the Fifth Avenue palace around 1850.

The subscriber offers for sale the three story brick house No. 101 St. Mark's Place, his present residence, being 37 feet 6 inches front by 54 feet deep, the property extending through to Ninth street, and embracing three lots of land.

The under cellar is divided into pantries, wine vault, wood room and coal bin.

The basement contains a kitchen, laundry, breakfast room, store room and pantries.

The first floor is divided into two spacious drawing rooms, dining room, study and pantries.

The three upper floors contain each four large rooms, besides water closet, bath room, pantries, &c. and the Croton water is introduced as high as the third story.

The House is finished throughout in the most approved manner, without regard to cost and in perfect order.

The stable is 37 feet 6 inches by 30, including coach house, harness room and stalls for four horses, with court yard, well, cistern, &c.

Apply to JAS. B. MURRAY, 101 St. Mark's Pl. or 12 Old Slip.

St. Mark's Place between First and Second avenues has maintained a semblance of its original appearance, but drastic changes have overtaken the once patrician block between Second and Third avenues. Only a few pitched roof and dormer-window rooflines and original fanlight doorways, notably Nos. 4 and 20, remain in this hectic contemporary setting, renowned as the "hip" Main Street of America in the late 1960s. A walk down this crowded and littered block recalls Montgomery Schuyler's 1899 comments about the rapid disappearance of the city's early-nineteenth-century dwellings and, in particular, the "mansions that surround Washington Square, or the scattered reminders of old glories of St. John's Park and Second avenue, or of what little is left to recall what Bond street used to be, or the mild protest of faded gentility that is still entered by an occasional house front in East Broadway against the screeching vulgarity by which it is surrounded."

During the 1840s and 1850s, lower Second Avenue was one of the most fashionable thoroughfares in New York. Below 18th Street it was lined with palatial Greek Revival and brownstone-front Italianate dwellings, some of them among the first in both styles in the city. But, by the eve of the

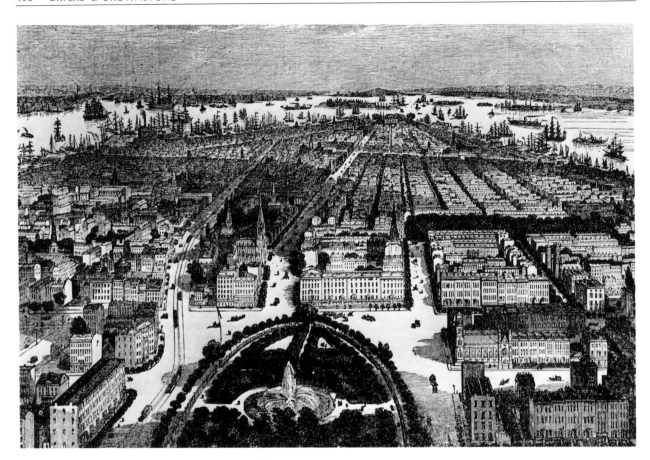

(top) A Bird's-Eye View of the City of New York, 1849, "Looking South From Union Square, Showing Both Rivers & Brooklyn & New Jersey Shores." By 1850, Manhattan was built up solidly with row houses and commercial buildings as far north as 14th Street.

(bottom) The Triangle (1860–1861), Stuyvesant Street, between Second and Third avenues. A fine range of Anglo-Italianate row houses in a beautiful and tranquil setting near the often-frantic lower Second Avenue area. St. Mark's Church in the Bouwerie (1799) stands in the distance at Second Avenue.

Civil War, lower Second Avenue had lost favor to "uptown" Madison Square and 34th Street, and real estate advertisements for the large houses in the declining area often noted: "Positively will not be rented for a boardinghouse." In the 1880s, one Englishman remarked that "early in the century it was what Fifth Avenue has become to-day, the fashionable residence avenue; and even yet some of the old Knickerbocker families cling to it, living in their roomy, old-fashioned houses, and maintaining an exclusive society, while they look down with disdain upon the parvenues of.Fifth avenue. Stuyvesant Square . . . is one of the quarters of the *ancient régime*."

In the late nineteenth century, lower Second Avenue did retain a sufficient aura of past elegance that it was not disturbed by any of the elevated train lines. The old Second Avenue "El" ran down Second Avenue to 23rd Street where it turned east to proceed south on First Avenue.

Today, the only unaltered dwelling on lower Second Avenue is the large Greek Revival row house at No. 110 Second Avenue (1839), between East Sixth and East Seventh streets. Now the Isaac T. Hopper Home, its well-maintained street front and intact doorway and parlor-window balcony lend an unexpected cheerful note to the otherwise grimy face of today's lower Second Avenue. However, a walk on the avenue from Houston to 14th Street reveals to the trained eye several dentiled Greek Revival style cornices or boldly protruding Italianate style cornices of old dwelling houses above storefronts on nearly every block!

Fifth Avenue.

Throughout the mid-nineteenth century, New Yorkers and visitors to the city marveled at the splendid brownstone-fronts and mansions along Fifth Avenue. In New York, the "avenues are springing up, lined, not with houses, but with palaces," declared one English magazine in 1859. "Neither London nor Paris, with all the accumulations of a thousand years, can show such a street as the Fifth Avenue."

Fifth Avenue's emergence as a "street of palaces" in the 1850s occurred with a much renowned "Aladdin-like splendor and celerity." Charles Dickens' *American Notes*, which described his tour of the United States in 1842, does not mention Fifth Avenue once. In the 1840s, the Bond Street area, St. John's Park, lower Second Avenue, and Washington Square were the city's most fashionable areas. Then, only a few, fine row houses and mansions had been built on Fifth Avenue, in the several blocks north of Washington Square. Row house construction swept into Fifth Avenue and the adjacent sidestreets north of 14th Street about 1850. The city directory for 1851 listed only twenty-eight of the one hundred and fifty street numbers between Washington Square and Madison Square as completed dwellings. One year later, in 1852, the number of finished dwellings on that stretch of Fifth Avenue had grown to forty-six—evidence that eighteen houses had been completed there in the year.

(top) Parlor, No. 61 University Place, about 1860. In the 1860s, *The New York Times* declared: "We must peep within the palaces if we would comprehend the full extent of their splendor. Their lavish adornment is a marvel even to traveled eyes."

(bottom) Moses Grinnell Residence (ca. 1846), Fifth Avenue and 14th Street, northeast corner, about 1860. This prominent merchant's mansion became Delmonico's restaurant after the Civil War. Demolished.

By the 1850s, Fifth Avenue was the axis of New York's finest residential area, a rectangular district bounded by Lexington Avenue on the east and Sixth Avenue on the west and always moving northward. On these favored streets, wrote one Englishman, "the edifices are entirely of brown sandstone, and of a richly decorated style of street architecture; all the windows are of plate-glass; and the door-handles, plates, and bellpulls silvered, so as to impart a chaste and light effect. The furnishings and interior ornaments of these dwellings . . . are of a superb kind; no expense being apparently spared as regards either comfort or elegance."

In the mid-nineteenth century, row house construction swept relentlessly northward up Manhattan Island—slowing only for depressions and the uncertainty of the Civil War years. The narrow width of the favored Lexington-to-Sixth Avenue rectangular strip, wrote one newspaper, forced status-conscious New Yorkers "to go further and further along it in order to secure fashionable homes." In its three-mile-long course from Washington Square to the shanty and rock-filled fields at the foot of Central Park, Fifth Avenue consisted of several patrician sections—the 14th Street, Madison Square, and Murray Hill areas. The changing architectural styles of the brownstone-fronts along Fifth Avenue pointed out these several areas and their development at different times. "Houses which were considered to be 'just the thing' ten years ago, are out of date today," declared one guidebook to New York in the early 1870s. "Observe the style of the houses about 14th Street, for instance; then 25th to 30th streets; and, again, those which are now being erected ten or twenty streets farther up."

Fifth Avenue epitomized the wealth, social whirl, and occasional vulgarity of mid-nineteenth-century New York. "Fifth Avenue has constantly represented the rage of lavish expenditure which characterize the uppermost stratum of society," observed one newspaper in 1867. After the Civil War, one magazine estimated that none of the 340 houses on Fifth Avenue cost less than a then handsome $20,000, and one newspaper reported that $100,000 and $200,000 mansions with $30,000 to $50,000 in furniture "are rapidly making their appearance" on Fifth Avenue. During the 1860s, house rents ranged from $4,000 a year—"never less"—to a "gentle and genial" $12,000. Fifth Avenue's residents, reported a guidebook, largely were "retired and active merchants and business men" who "live in a most princely style. They seem to float in an ocean of wealth, and their number is legion."

Fifth Avenue's wealth and world-renowned fashion did not awe all New Yorkers or visitors to the city. The showy brownstone-fronts, wrote one magazine, were "a paradise of marble, upholstery and cabinet-work . . . not much dignified, as yet, by works of high art . . . but in luxury and extravagance emulating the repudiated aristocracy of the old world."

A Fifth Avenue brownstone-front was the goal of many an ambitious businessman and his wife.

Architectural Desecration. This once-elegant range of brownstone-fronts shows the fearful devastation to the city streetscape of most row house façade modernizations. In the 1930s and 1940s the houses in the foreground had their stoops, doorway porches, and window enframements removed, and their shady brownstone was covered with a smooth coat of light-brown stucco. Lost forever are the patrician dignity, rich ornament, and dappled patterns of light and shade on brownstone façades enjoyed by the virtually unaltered houses in the distance. This startling contrast of architectural preservation and desecration is seen on Nos. 201–209 Washington Park in the Fort Greene area of Brooklyn.

"They are fighting hard for the grand, ugly house in the Fifth Avenue, for the gold and damask sofas and curtains that are ever shrouded in dingy coverings, save on the one night of every third year when they are unveiled to adorn the social martyrdom of five hundred perspiring friends," wrote George Templeton Strong in 1857. Other New Yorkers lampooned the rich, and often newly rich, residents of Fifth Avenue and nearby streets as "The Avenoodles" and "the shoddy aristocracy." "I know of no great man, no celebrated statesman, no philanthropist of note who has lived in Fifth Avenue," wrote a scornful Anthony Trollope in the early 1860s:

> That gentleman on the right made a million of dollars by inventing a shirt-collar; this one on the left electrified the world by a lotion; as to the gentleman at the corner there—there are rumors about him and the Cuban slave trade but my informant by no means knows that they are true. Such are the aristocracy of Fifth Avenue. I can only say that if I could make a million dollars by a lotion, I should certainly be right to live in such a house as one of these.

The fashion of Fifth Avenue and its haughty residents was not as solid as appearances indicated. Only several blocks east or west of its "unbroken line of brownstone palaces," one found overcrowded tenements, factories, stables, and littered and noisy streets. One British visitor reported the "incongruous sight" on Fifth Avenue of a "huge filthy hog devouring a putrid cabbage on a marble door-step."

The proud brownstone-fronts on the streets near Fifth Avenue were not always simply the residences of wealthy merchants or businessmen. In an era of soaring house rents and prices punctuated by occasional depressions, hard-pressed families on fashionable streets often took in boarders to make ends meet. "Many of the handsomest mansions in the upper part of the city were establishments of this nature," wrote one Englishman in the 1860s, "and I was not a little amused by the interviews I had with the pompous dames who received me in elegantly furnished drawing rooms, before showing me the dear and shabby apartments upstairs."

The glory of Fifth Avenue in the patrician 14th Street, Madison Square, and Murray Hill areas was fleeting. Throughout much of the nineteenth century, New York's population and commerce grew rapidly, and, as fine dwellings were built farther and farther uptown, once-fashionable downtown residential areas fell before a relentless tide of stores, warehouses, and tenements. The Bond Street area enjoyed only several decades of fashion before its wealthy families abandoned the elegant row houses to dentists, boardinghouse keepers, and sweatshop owners. One New Yorker in the 1860s foresaw that the wealthy merchants and businessmen building splendid brownstone-fronts in Murray Hill were only outfitting the fine boardinghouses of the next generation. In 1873 one magazine correctly foresaw that "rapidly advancing business" would displace New York's fashionable residential

(top) Parlor, No. 9 West 16th Street (1844–1845), about 1860. "The fashion of French furniture has come in lately, with a rush," wrote Nathaniel Parker Willis in the late 1840s, "and the nabobs are selling out from sideboard to broom, and furnishing a new *a la Francaise,* from skylight to basement." Architect Richard Upjohn reputedly designed much of the interior woodwork in the house.

(bottom left) Reception Room, No. 61 University Place.

(bottom right) Richard K. Haight Residence, in 1893, Fifth Avenue and 15th Street, southeast corner. In the 1870s, the Haight mansion was enlarged and turned into a fine apartment building. Demolished.

quarter from Murray Hill and Fifth Avenue in the Forties "ere long to the region about the Central Park where it will establish itself permanently."

The construction of several extravagant mansions along Fifth Avenue in the 14th Street area in the late 1840s and 1850s assured the street's already emerging fashion. The mansions of Richard K. Haight and Henry Benkard at 15th Street, Herman Thorne on 16th Street, and Henry Parish on 17th Street surpassed "anything I had hitherto witnessed in royal or ducal palaces at home," wrote one Englishwoman and introduced the Italianate style and brownstone front to New York dwelling houses.

Only a few families lived along Fifth Avenue itself. In the 14th Street area, attractive basement-and-four-story-tall, twenty-two, twenty-five, and thirty-foot-wide brick and brownstone-front row houses lined the quiet sidestreets from Sixth Avenue on the west to Second Avenue and, farther north, only to Lexington Avenue on the east. Particularly favored by fashion was 14th Street, described in the 1850s, as "a hundred feet in width, and containing residences of great beauty and truly splendid proportions." The same magazine pointed out West 21st Street, between Fifth and Sixth avenues, as a typical block of this splendid area, where "the quiet tone of color of these buildings, the inviting elegance of doorways and flights of steps, the absence of noise, the verdure of the shade trees against the brilliant sky, and some spire or tower picturesquely terminating the vista—all combine to produce an agreeable frame of mind in the passer-by."

Fifth Avenue's residential fashion in the 14th Street area lasted only into the mid-1860s—a scant fifteen or twenty years after the area's first development. "At one time a location is pleasant and even fashionable, and in a few years, presto! change—it has become degraded and almost uninhabitable by certain classes," wrote one newspaper in the late 1860s. The first store on Fifth Avenue opened in a house on the southeast corner of 17th Street, and in the years after the Civil War the area became known for its "pianoforte" showrooms. The Henry Parish and Henry Benkard mansions became elegant clubhouses, and the Richard K. Haight residence was enlarged and converted into one of the city's first apartment buildings. One by one, the handsome row houses of the pleasant sidestreets near Fifth Avenue became boardinghouses, and by 1875 one magazine observed that "in Fourteenth Street, today, the entire block between Fifth and Sixth Avenues, with the exception of the Van Buren mansion, is occupied by boarding-housekeepers."

New York's never ending growth and redevelopment have obliterated nearly all signs of onetime residential splendor in the 14th Street area. Shabby office buildings of the late nineteenth and early twentieth century line Fifth Avenue between 14th Street and Madison Square, and 14th Street is a raucous shopping street with discount department stores and street vendors. Decrepit six- and

West 21st Street, about 1870, View from Fifth Avenue Toward Sixth Avenue. This scene captures the onetime elegance and tranquility of the Madison Square area. The Union Club, at the corner, was "one of the greatest architectural attempts in this country," according to one magazine in 1855. "Magnificent and commodious edifices . . . are taking the places of tasteless, unornamented, and inconvenient structures." Office buildings, lofts, and warehouses have since replaced all the buildings in this photograph.

eight-story-tall lofts and warehouses now line the once handsome nearby sidestreets.

Only verdant Gramercy Park and Stuyvesant Square and the fine nearby row houses recall the nineteenth-century beauty and serenity of the area. A number of fine row houses surprisingly survive on West 16th Street, off Fifth Avenue—several basement-and-four-story-tall Italianate brownstone-fronts, a pair of charming Gothic Revival dwellings with unusual, protruding, wooden arched cornices, and several thirty-foot-wide, exceptionally well-preserved, late Greek Revival row houses with stunning cast-iron porches and the bow fronts usually associated with Boston's Beacon Street. The onetime Athenaeum (ca. 1859), with its early mansard roof, stands at No. 108 Fifth Avenue, the southwest corner of 16th Street. The banal Chelsea House apartment building at No. 16 West 16th Street stands on the site of the renowned Herman Thorne mansion.

In the prosperous late 1840s and early 1850s, row house construction swept into Madison Square and the East Twenties. "This part of the city is rapidly filling up with private dwellings, in many places entire blocks are going up, and in a few years this will be one of the most thickly settled parts of the city," wrote one newspaper in 1847. Madison Square, originally a potter's field, was opened as a park in 1847 and, together with nearby Fifth Avenue and 23rd Street, soon attracted the dwellings of the wealthy and fashionable.

In 1859 Leonard Jerome, a Wall Street speculator who made and lost several fortunes, completed his six-story-tall mansion on Madison Square at No. 32 East 26th Street. The extravagant mansion matched Jerome's flamboyant life style of fine race horses, costly carriages, tempestuous love affairs, and splendid parties. At the ball given to celebrate the mansion's completion, hundreds of New York's celebrated "Upper Ten Thousand" danced in the huge second-floor ballroom where one fountain spouted champagne and the other eau de cologne. The Jerome mansion was one of the first houses in the city to recall Second Empire Paris with a two-story-tall mansard roof, pierced with numerous dormer windows of varying sizes and shapes. Around the corner on 26th Street, the mansion had a fully-equipped private theater seating 600 persons, and beyond that were Jerome's stables appointed in black-walnut paneling, plate glass, and carpeting.

Leonard Jerome's daughter Jennie, who spent part of her childhood in the house, later married Randolph Churchill and was the mother of Winston Churchill. The Metropolitan Museum of Art was founded after an 1869 meeting at the Jerome mansion, and in later years, the fine dwelling was the University Club, the Union League Club, and the Manhattan Club.

Madison Square was the center of fashionable New York in the Civil War era. Around the edge of the park stood the Jerome mansion, one of the most extravagant in the city; the residence of Mrs. William Colford Schermerhorn, a social leader of the Upper Ten Thousand; the Fifth Avenue Hotel,

(top) A. T. Stewart Residence (completed in 1873), Fifth Avenue and 34th Street, northwest corner, about 1880. Stewart's mansion reportedly cost $3,000,000 to build and furnish. Demolished.

(bottom) Entrance Hall, A. T. Stewart Residence, about 1880. The full flowering of the extravagant mid-nineteenth-century Fifth Avenue mansion.

world-famous for its "vertical railroad" or elevator and then the finest hotel in the city; and "The Louvre," a lavish "concert saloon" famous for its opulent drawing rooms, mirrored bar with champagne fountain, and some of the prettiest "waiter girls" in town.

In a New York growing ever northward and abandoning fashionable neighborhoods to commerce, the residential splendor of Madison Square was sadly short-lived. Today, as on the blocks in the 14th Street area to the south, old office buildings and run-down loft buildings and warehouses have replaced the patrician brownstone-fronts of the Madison Square vicinity. The several high-rise office towers of the New York and Metropolitan life insurance companies now loom over the eastern side of Madison Square. With the demolition of the Jerome mansion in 1968, New York lost an irreplaceable part of its Civil War–era history, and Madison Square lost the last and grandest reminder of its gracious past.

In the 1860s, row house construction crossed 34th Street into Murray Hill, an area which took its name from the old country house of Robert Murray, at the present-day intersection of East 37th Street and Park Avenue. History recalls that during the Revolutionary War Robert Murray's wife served tea to the British General Howe and his staff, thereby delaying the British army while the American troops escaped to the north. During the 1860s, mansions and elegant brownstone-fronts were built along Fifth, Madison, and Park avenues and 34th Street, and fine row houses filled Lexington Avenue and the sidestreets from Sixth to Third avenues.

The grandest house in post-Civil War New York was the A. T. Stewart mansion at the northwest corner of Fifth Avenue and 34th Street. Stewart arrived in New York from Ireland as a child and, as a young man, ran a dry goods store which later became the nation's first department store.

With its marble façade, mansard roof, and lavish drawing rooms and galleries, the A. T. Stewart mansion epitomized the wealth and occasional vulgarity of the post-Civil War city. "This will unquestionably be, when completed, the most costly and luxurious private residence on the continent," declared one magazine in the late 1860s.

> Even in its present unfinished state, words are almost inadequate to describe the beauty and unique grandeur of some of the details of its construction. . . . Externally, the building must ever remain a monument of the splendor which, as far as opulence is concerned, places some of our merchants on a footing almost with royalty itself, and a glance at the interior will be a privilege eagerly sought by the visiting stranger.

On the other hand, the A. T. Stewart mansion did not impress architect Alexander Jackson Davis who described it as "the most vulgar house in ostentatious vain show, and unmeaning ornament."

The A. T. Stewart mansion and other splendid mid-nineteenth-century mansions have disappeared from Murray Hill, but fine brownstone-front row houses in the Italianate, Anglo-Italianate, and Second

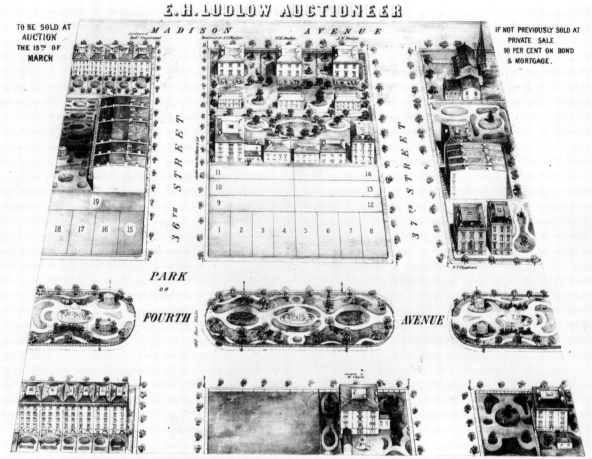

E. H. LUDLOW AUCTIONEER

TO BE SOLD AT
AUCTION
THE 13TH OF
MARCH

IF NOT PREVIOUSLY SOLD AT
PRIVATE SALE
90 PER CENT ON BOND
& MORTGAGE.

19 LOTS FOR SALE ON MURRAY HILL APPLY TO E.H. LUDLOW 3 PINE ST NEAR B'WAY.

SKETCH OF PARKS IN COURSE OF COMPLETION & SKETCH OF SHRUBBERY THAT MAY BE MADE.

(top) Property Map, Murray Hill *(ca.* 1865), E. H. Ludlow, Auctioneer.

(bottom left) Fifth Avenue, about 1894, View North from 35th Street. Fine shops invaded Fifth Avenue in the Murray Hill area in the 1890s.

(bottom right) Leonard Jerome Residence (1859), Madison Avenue and 26th Street, southwest corner, overlooking Madison Square, about 1877. In the 1850s and 1860s, palatial brownstone-front row houses and occasional mansions rose on the north, east, and south sides of Madison Square. The Fifth Avenue Hotel dominated the west side of the park. All the dwelling houses on Madison Square have given way to office buildings—the Leonard Jerome mansion disappearing in 1968.

Empire styles remain on many blocks between Madison and Third avenues. Although many of these dwellings have lost stoops and shadow-casting façade details in alterations of recent decades, their human four-story scale and largely residential occupancy offer a pleasant oasis in today's bustling midtown Manhattan.

Brooklyn.

In the mid-nineteenth century, Brooklyn, then a separate city, enjoyed rapid population growth and a frenzied building boom. Its population increased from 139,000 in 1850 to 279,000 in 1860 and reached 420,000 in 1870. Although a surprisingly large number of rich families lived in Brooklyn in palatial row houses or countrified mansions, the city was renowned for street after street of substantial middle-class dwellings. "*Our* architectural greatness," wrote Brooklyn resident Walt Whitman in the early 1860s, "consists in the hundreds and thousands of superb private dwellings, for the comfort and luxury of the great body of middle class people—a kind of architecture unknown until comparatively late times, and no where known to such an extent as in Brooklyn." For Walt Whitman, Brooklyn's advantages as a place of residence were many. "The topography of the City of Brooklyn is very fine. Indeed it is doubtful if there is a city in the world with a better situation for beauty. . . . As to its healthiness, it is well known. . . . There is the best quality and cheapest priced gas—the best water in the world—a prospect of moderate taxation—and, we will say, for our city authorities, elected year after year, that they will compare favorably with any of similar position in the United States."

Brooklyn was a thriving manufacturing city. "Few persons have any idea of the immense variety of manufactures, works, foundries, and other branches of useful art and trade carried on in the limits of our expansive and thriving city," Whitman declared. From the Manhattan side of the East River, the towers of the Havemeyer and Elder sugar refineries competed in the skyline with the city's noted church steeples.

Industry in Brooklyn, as in the rest of the nation, prospered in the Civil War and postwar years. Between 1860 and 1870, the value of its manufactured goods nearly doubled from $34,242,000 to $60,849,000, and between 1860 and 1880 the number of factories increased tenfold from 500 to 5,000. In 1880 Brooklyn was the third city in the nation in manufacturing output, fourth in capital investment in industry, fourth in the value of its manufactured goods, and second in total wages.

A bustling waterfront also contributed to Brooklyn's prosperity. From Greenpoint to the Gowanus Canal, grain elevators, docks, and warehouses lined the East River. In the 1840s, Brooklyn shipyards built Hudson River steamers and China clipper ships and, with the 1860s, many ironclad ships, including the "Monitor." However, Brooklyn's prosperous waterfront did not legally belong to the

(top) Pierrepont Place, Brooklyn Heights. The pair of brownstone mansions in the foreground are Nos. 2 and 3 Pierrepont Place (1856–1857) and still stand today. The Henry Pierrepont mansion (1856–1857), No. 1 Pierrepont Place, designed by Richard Upjohn, disappeared in 1946. The Penny Bridge, also now gone, spanned the continuation of Montague Street that once led down to the waterfront and the Wall Street ferry stop just below.

(bottom) Nos. 4–10 Montague Terrace *(ca.* 1870), Brooklyn Heights. These brownstone mansions enjoyed the view of lower Manhattan and New York Bay from their back windows. The two houses in the background survive today, but those in the foreground have given way to apartment buildings.

city, because the original Dutch charters of the seventeenth century, affirmed by the British after their seizure of New Amsterdam in 1664, gave the waterfront rights of western Long Island, i.e., Brooklyn, to Manhattan Island.

Despite its thriving economic and social life, Brooklyn was tied, practically and emotionally, to New York across the East River. Brooklyn residents, rich and middle class alike, usually worked in downtown Manhattan, and the city's omnibus lines and horse-drawn street railroads converged at the several ferries to Manhattan, particularly the original Fulton Street ferry. Well-to-do women preferred to shop on glamorous Broadway rather than in downtown Brooklyn, and, after the morning rush hour, ladies' carriages jammed the ferries for shopping or visiting in New York. Real estate advertisements in Brooklyn always stressed the property's proximity to Manhattan and the East River ferry stations. "One of the healthiest and pleasantest locations in the city for a gentleman doing business in New York." "Omnibuses pass by every few minutes." "Location good, and within ten minutes ride of either ferry."

Brooklyn Heights.

Throughout the nineteenth century, Brooklyn's most fashionable residential district was Brooklyn Heights. Men of "solid respectability and well-lined simplicity," often bankers and merchants who worked in nearby lower Manhattan, favored the area's quiet tree-lined streets and fine Greek Revival and Italianate style row houses. Brooklyn Heights residents, according to contemporary reports, looked down on the "vigorous, voluble, somewhat less respectable population" nearby and enjoyed the gracious life style of the city's well-to-do families in the mid-nineteenth century. The businessmen took the ferry at the foot of Fulton Street or Atlantic Avenue to Manhattan early in the morning and left work at 3:00 P.M. to be home for dinner at 4:00 P.M. In the evening, the family might go to one of Brooklyn's theaters or the old Academy of Music or, in good weather, for a carriage ride to Green-Wood Cemetery or the countryside around today's Prospect Park.

In the 1850s, boldly ornamented brownstone-front Italianate style row houses, a basement and four stories tall and twenty-two to twenty-five feet wide, introduced the splendor and monumental scale of the brownstone era to Brooklyn Heights' streets of modestly scaled Federal and Greek Revival dwelling houses. The finest Italianate and Second Empire brownstone-fronts were built along Columbia Heights, Montague Street, Montague Terrace, and Remsen Street. Although the Montague Street dwellings have been altered into shops, and many of the Montague Terrace and Remsen Street row houses have lost their stoops and ornamental façade details in remodelings of recent years, many Italianate style row houses along envied Columbia Heights have remained in largely original condition and continue to enjoy the spectacular view of New York Bay and the ever changing lower Manhattan skyline across the East River. There was not a "residence in all New York that approached in lavishness, size or luxurious appointments, the elegant mansions which covered the high bluff overlooking the river and the bay," one proud Brooklyn newspaper declared in 1870. "The situation on the Heights overlooking the bay can hardly be matched in any great city of Christendom," remarked George Templeton Strong, a resident of the fashionable Gramercy Park area in Manhattan, in 1865. "How often have I wished I could exchange this house for one of them, and that I could see from my library windows that noble prospect and that wide expanse of sky, and the going down of the sun every evening!"

South Brooklyn: Cobble Hill and Carroll Gardens.

Although row house construction in South Brooklyn commenced in the mid-1830s with the start of regular ferry service from the foot of Atlantic Avenue to South Ferry in lower Manhattan, it was not until the 1850s that large-scale construction began in those areas of South Brooklyn renamed Cobble Hill and Carroll Gardens within the past decade. The Greek Revival and Gothic Revival row houses of the 1840s are charmingly interspersed with mid-nineteenth-century Italianate and Second Empire dwellings.

In today's Cobble Hill, the large brownstone-front row houses, it has been noted, were built on Clinton and Henry streets, which run north to south, and modest row houses on east to west streets such as Warren, Baltic, and Kane and on the unusual one-block-long north to south streets such as Cheever, Strong, and Tompkins places. In Cobble Hill, as throughout the city, builders lowered land prices and the cost of construction by building houses that were narrower than the standard twenty-five-foot-wide lots. A common Cobble Hill construction pattern is three sixteen-foot, eight-inch-wide row houses, often in the Anglo-Italianate style, on two twenty-five-foot-wide lots.

A handsome instance of good site planning with narrow houses remains at the blockfront Nos. 206–224 Kane Street and around its corners at Nos. 10–12 Tompkins Place and Nos. 301–313 Clinton Street. Built in 1849–1854 by Gerard W. Morris, a New York lawyer, these eighteen row houses are fourteen and fifteen feet wide but, having been designed as a cohesive group, appear larger than their narrow width. Adjoining doorways appear paired in projecting sections which add an unusual spaciousness and rhythm to this group of houses.

Immediately to the south of Cobble Hill is Carroll Gardens, another handsome mid-nineteenth-century row house neighborhood presently enjoying a renaissance. Carroll Gardens takes its name from Carroll Park and the many blocks of row houses with deep and handsomely planted front yards. Just as today's Cobble Hill is an extension of Brooklyn Heights south of Atlantic Avenue, Carroll Gardens is an extension of Cobble Hill south of Degraw Street. Because of its somewhat later period of development, Carroll Gardens contains only a handful of Greek Revival and Gothic Revival row houses from the 1840s and consists primarily of Italianate brick-front and brownstone-front row houses. A surprising number of pitched-roof frame farmhouses and onetime country houses also remain throughout Carroll Gardens.

In the seventeenth and eighteenth centuries, South Brooklyn was productive farmland largely held under original Dutch land patents, but by the late eighteenth century oysters had become the mainstay of the local economy. These oysters were reputedly one foot long! The shells were burned for lime and the oysters exported to Europe.

With the start of scheduled ferry service between Brooklyn and Manhattan in 1820, South Brooklyn was reasonably accessible to downtown Manhattan, and well-to-do merchants and gentlemen farmers built country houses in the area on spacious grounds overlooking New York harbor. The last of these very comfortable country houses is No. 440 Clinton Street, one of the finest remaining mid-nineteenth-century country mansions in New York. Built in 1842 for John Rankin, president of the Humboldt Fire Insurance Company in downtown Manhattan, this freestanding house is a basement and three stories tall and has a Greek Revival front doorway with pilasters and entablature of gray granite. Although not among the mansions that once overlooked New York harbor, there are other onetime country houses in the Carroll Gardens area. One is a Downingesque Gothic Revival villa, with an overhanging roof supported on brackets, at the southeast corner of Sackett and Hoyt streets. Another is a picturesquely asymmetrical Italian villa, with a now roofless tower, at No. 98 First Place, at the corner of Court Street. Now part of a row of houses, No. 98 suffers the ignominy of peeling green paint and a Laundromat in the basement floor.

Large-scale commercial development in Red Hook, separated from today's Carroll Gardens by Hamilton Avenue, preceded the row house construction boom in Carroll Gardens. Starting in the late 1830s, a cotton-wadding factory, brick yard, distilleries, and warehouses were built in Red Hook. The Atlantic Docks, Atlantic Basin, and Erie Basin and Dry Docks were the major shipbuilding and dock facilities. In these decades, street after street of modest frame or brick houses were built for the ships' crews and workmen and their families. So dramatic was the growth of Red Hook in the 1860s that one newspaper stated: "In Brooklyn the work of building is increasing numerically more rapidly than in New York . . . particularly in the southerly portion of the city. On Court-street, below the line of Fourth-place, there are three-story and basement residences and stores in various stages of progress, covering in many places, entire blocks." Just south of Fourth Place and within the boundaries of

Carroll Gardens, the modest brick-front row houses on the oddly attractive one-block-long Dennett Place survive from the many streets built for workmen in Red Hook.

Large-scale row house construction began in Carroll Gardens around 1850. By then the streets to the north in today's Cobble Hill were filling up with row houses, and scheduled ferry service between Hamilton Avenue in Brooklyn and South Ferry in Manhattan brought the area within easy travel time of downtown jobs for commuters. Begun by Henry E. Pierrepont and Jacob A. Le Roy in 1846 to shorten the usual water journey from Manhattan to Brooklyn's fashionable Green-Wood Cemetery, the Hamilton Avenue ferry usually shipped goods from Red Hook factories and warehouses to Manhattan and carried thousands of commuters for a one-cent fare during rush hours.

Fine brownstone-fronts in Carroll Gardens were built near Carroll Park and at the high ground known as Bergen Hill near the intersection of Clinton Street and First Place. The June, 1872, listings from *Wyckoff and James Real Estate Bulletin* for Brooklyn shows that the row houses of today's Carroll Gardens area varied greatly in size and cost.

FIRST ST., bet. Bond st. and Canal, 2 story, 16 x 22, lot 63.6, stable on rear of lot, $1,000.

SACKETT ST., betw. Hoyt and Bond; 2 story brick, 20 x 34, 9 rooms, all modern improvements. Lot 100. $5,000.

SACKETT ST., bet. Henry and Hicks, 3 story marble, 19.3 x 43, extension 10 ft., lot 100. $7,500.

SACKETT ST., between Clinton and Court, 3 story brownstone 16 x 50, lot 100, $8,500

CARROLL ST., bet. Court and Clinton, 3 story brick 23 x 40, lot 100, $12,000.

UNION ST., betw. Smith and Hoyt; 3 story brown stone 20 x 45, 12 rooms, all modern improvements. Lot 115. $14,500.

THIRD PL., corner Court, 3 story marble front, 20.10 x 45. Lot 133, $16,000.

PRESIDENT ST., bet. Court and Smith, 3 story brown stone, 20 x 50, lot 100, $17,000.

CLINTON ST., bet. Sackett and Union, 4 story brown stone, 25 x 50, finished in hard wood throughout, billiard room, dome in fourth story, and all modern improvements, lot 90, $35,000.

In the last few decades, row house alterations and modernizations have despoiled many blocks in Carroll Gardens; few brownstone-fronts in the area retain all original and irreplaceable street-front features. But, in these same years, Carroll Gardens' many blocks with deep front yards have taken on additional charm and value to area residents. In an increasingly crowded city, these blocks are a pleasant oasis of sun, air, and quiet.

The Hill: Clinton Hill and Fort Greene.

By the 1840s, row house construction had spread eastward from the Brooklyn Heights vicinity to an elevated area known as "The Hill." Roughly bounded on the north by today's Willoughby Avenue, on the east by South Portland Avenue, on the south by Atlantic Avenue, and on the west by Franklin Avenue, The Hill was a pleasant residential district in the mid-nineteenth century, second in fashion only to patrician Brooklyn Heights. Although some wealthy families lived in the mansions along Clinton and Washington avenues or in the splendid brownstone-front row houses around the edges of today's Fort Greene Park, The Hill largely was the home of prosperous business and professional men. "To the rear of the boisterous city hall quarter was Brooklyn's other fine residential district, the Hill," wrote Harold C. Syrett in the 1890s.

> Located in the center of the city and surrounded by diverse elements, its position was not unlike that of the Heights; but its elegant residences were fewer in number and their owners slightly further re-moved from the traditions of genteel respectability. It abounded in churches and middle class houses, the majority of whose owners worked in New York, but took pride in living in Brooklyn.

Today, The Hill district consists of Fort Greene, Clinton Hill, and a small part of Bedford-Stuyvesant.

When row house development began in The Hill in the 1840s, suburban villas and frame row houses already dotted the rolling countryside. An advertisement for a country villa on Washington Avenue in the 1840s gives an idea of the area and its dwellings before transformation by large-scale row house construction:

> TO LET—The large double two-story and attic house, together with garden and stable situated on Washington-avenue, Brooklyn. The house contains four large rooms on the first floor, besides kitchen and washroom; six rooms on the second floor and five in the attic; cellar under the whole house. The garden covers nine lots of ground, contains a large number of grape vines in bearing order—has just been put in the best possible condition and planted with the usual variety of vegetables. To a desirable tenant the rent will be made very low. Stages pass the door. Fare to Fulton Ferry 6¼ cents.

Surprisingly, this countrified setting was no more than fifteen or twenty minutes by stage coach or omnibus from the Fulton Ferry station to Manhattan.

Clinton Avenue, at the highest point of the area, was the most fashionable street in The Hill and, according to some sources, in all Brooklyn. By the 1830s and 1840s, large frame country houses and occasional mansions on spacious grounds lined Clinton Avenue. From their houses, the fortunate residents enjoyed a view of the East River and Manhattan. Starting in the 1860s, palatial

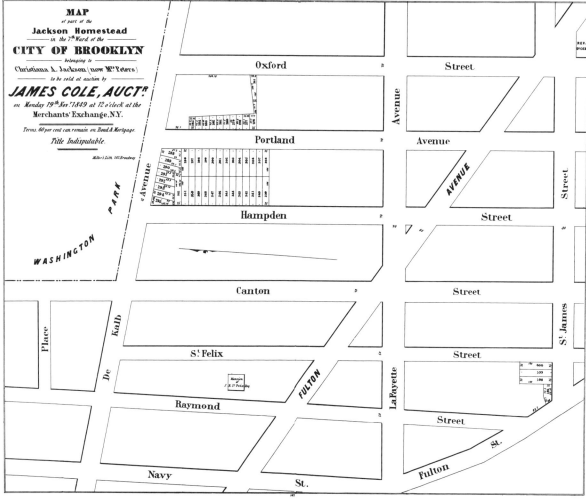

(top) Clinton Avenue, Brooklyn, in 1904. In the nineteenth and early twentieth century, elegant mansions on spacious grounds lined broad tree-shaded Clinton Avenue in The Hill district of Brooklyn —frame Gothic and Italian villas of the 1840s and 1850s, brownstone-front mansard mansions and row houses of the post-Civil War era, and the renowned Pratt family mansions from the turn of the century. Despite the construction of apartment buildings in the 1920s and 1950s, Clinton Avenue still retains many fine row houses.

(bottom) Map of the Jackson Homestead. Building lot auction of 1849 in Fort Greene, Brooklyn. Suburban villas and occasional frame and brick row houses rose in today's Fort Greene soon after this sale.

brownstone-front houses and detached mansions began to replace the earlier frame country villas and their spacious grounds.

An unusually detailed advertisement in 1871 for three fine brownstone-front row houses on Clinton Avenue recalls the splendor of these dwellings then rising on Clinton and Washington avenues and on the several streets around Fort Greene Park:

> FOR SALE IN BROOKLYN, On the northwest corner of Clinton and Lafayette avs., some of those elegant blocks of four-story high-stoop brown-stone front French-roof houses, 21, 22, and 23 x 48; lots 90 to 110 feet. . . . These houses have been built by day's work in the most thorough and substantial manner, under the supervision of the owner; all modern improvements replete; black-walnut front and vestibule doors; stairs and stair-casings of the most elegant design; black-walnut sash and polished plate glass; dining-room and hall wainscotted in black-walnut; independent laundry, two bath-rooms, three water-closets, eight wash-basins, butler's pantry, &c.; about eighteen rooms, twelve pantries, and any amount of drawers for table linen, &c. hot-air furnaces; 15 to 20 minutes by Green-av. cars from Fulton Ferry; five to seven blocks from Prospect Park grand entrance. Price $25,000, $30,000, and $35,000, about one-half cash. Must be seen to be appreciated. Immediate possession. Apply on the premises, to THOMAS FAGAN, Owner.

These three fine houses were similar to many then rising along Fifth Avenue and adjacent sidestreets in the Madison Square and Murray Hill areas.

Construction has continued to the present day in the area of The Hill now known as Clinton Hill. In the late nineteenth century, the Pratt family built several mansions with spacious grounds on Clinton Avenue, between De Kalb and Willoughby avenues. Charles Pratt, the elder, owned a profitable kerosene refinery in Greenpoint and, in 1874, joined John D. Rockefeller's Standard Oil Company. At the marriage of his sons, he gave each couple a mansion in the neighborhood of their choice as a wedding present. Three of these mansions still stand at Nos. 229, 241, and 245 Clinton Avenue across from their father's house at No. 232 Clinton Avenue. The last son, Harold, was married after World War I and, reflecting new residential fashions, built his mansion, also still standing, on Park Avenue at the southwest corner of 68th Street.

Since the turn of the century, many mansions on Clinton and Washington avenues have given way to apartment buildings and small parks. Since World War II, high-rise apartment projects and the expansion of Pratt Institute have altered the nineteenth-century streetscape of the Clinton Hill area further. Some of the mansions, however, still occupy their spacious grounds today, and the renascent area's largely unaltered row houses offer a nearly complete history of the city's row house architecture from the mid-nineteenth century to the early twentieth century.

Nos. 332–334 Clinton Avenue (1870–1871), northwest corner of Lafayette Avenue, Clinton Hill, Brooklyn. After the Civil War, sixteen- and eighteen-room brownstone-fronts—similar to those on Manhattan's Fifth Avenue—rose along the favored streets of The Hill district. In the past 100 years, a wave of modernizations and demolitions destroyed most of the similar houses of the era in Brooklyn Heights and the midtown Fifth Avenue area. The Fort Greene and Clinton Hill areas did not suffer this massive architectural depredation and, surprisingly, have some of the finest remaining Italianate and Second Empire mansions and row houses in New York.

Several blocks down The Hill toward downtown Brooklyn are the remarkably intact row houses of today's Fort Greene area clustered around the southern and eastern edges of historic Fort Greene Park. During the American Revolution, the park was the site of Fort Putnam, the main bastion in the fortifications designed to protect Brooklyn Heights and New York from British attack. From these ramparts, after the American defeat in the Battle of Long Island, George Washington on the night of August 29–30, 1776, withdrew his forces under the cover of darkness and fog in a brilliant retreat which saved the outnumbered American army from annihilation by the British.

With the War of 1812, New Yorkers, fearing a British attack and another occupation of their city, built new forts and repaired old ones, among them Fort Putnam, at that time renamed Fort Greene. When the "invading army was expected" in Brooklyn in 1814, "the enthusiasm of the people was raised to the highest point," recalled one Englishman. "The whole population of New York, rich and poor, all ranks and professions, without any exception, assisted with spades, wheelbarrows, and other implements; in one place, the lawyers; in another the merchants; there the different branches of mechanics; the ladies came in crowds to distribute refreshments; bands of music were playing at intervals, and it presented an animated scene." Even a seventy-two-year-old woman pushed a wheelbarrow in the rebuilding of the fort. Nevertheless, British forces never attacked New York in the War of 1812 and, in the following decades, the fort slowly decayed.

Much as on Clinton and Washington avenues several blocks to the east, country villas, frame row houses, and occasional brick row houses were built around the hilly old Fort Greene. This early growth spread out from the stage and later omnibus lines along Myrtle Avenue and Fulton Street. At that time, the blocks south of Myrtle Avenue and adjacent Atlantic Avenue largely were built up with frame dwellings. Among the small builders of row houses in the area at this time was Walt Whitman, better known as editor of the Brooklyn *Eagle* and a prolific poet.

Perhaps the Brooklyn city fathers foresaw the splendid future of this pleasant elevated land around the old fort, because the five principal north-to-south streets of the area proudly carry the names of renowned streets and terraces in early-nineteenth-century London: Portland, after the Adam Brothers' stately Portland Place of the 1780s; Oxford, after Oxford Street and Oxford Circus; Cumberland, after John Nash's breathtaking Cumberland Terrace at the edge of Regent's Park; Carlton, after the Carlton House palace of the Prince Regent and Carlton Terrace near Regent's Park; and Adelphi, after the Adam Brothers' magnificent Adelphi terrace along the Thames. The east-to-west streets of The Hill recall several generals of the American Revolution: Willoughby, De Kalb, Lafayette, Greene, and Gates.

During the 1850s and 1860s, substantial middle-class brick and brownstone-front row houses in

Architectural Contrast. In nineteenth-century New York, the poor lived in miserable shanties at the outskirts of the city as well as in decaying tenements and onetime family houses in the Lower East Side and waterfront streets. As the city marched relentlessly northward in the post-Civil War building room, fine row houses and mansions often reared their haughty brownstone fronts and fashionable Parisian mansard roofs above a rubbish dump or immigrant's shanty. The makeshift shacks, according to one newspaper, were "not generally fashioned after those in the Fifth av., though as *outre* in their architectural design."

the Italianate style began to fill in the numerous vacant lots in the area and replace some country villas. In the 1860s Frederick Law Olmsted and Calvert Vaux, landscape architects of Manhattan's Central Park and Brooklyn's Prospect Park, converted the site of old Fort Greene into the elegant thirty-acre Washington Park.

After the Civil War and the completion of the park, fashion favored the blocks at the southern and eastern edges of Washington Park. In the frantic building boom of the late 1860s and early 1870s, palatial brownstone-front row houses and occasional mansions—selling for $25,000, $30,000, and even $40,000—rose along South Portland Avenue, South Oxford Street, and Washington Park, that two-block-long stretch of Cumberland Street facing the park. Fine Italianate and Second Empire dwellings were built on nearby blocks in the area.

By the 1870s, row house construction in Fort Greene virtually had ended, and the area settled into several generations of pleasant living. On warm evenings and weekends, area residents strolled in Washington Park, later renamed Fort Greene Park, which in 1884 was described as "one of the most central, delightful and healthful places for recreation of which any city can boast." In 1908 President-elect William Howard Taft dedicated the park's Prison Ship Martyr's Monument, the world's largest Doric column and designed by Stanford White. Beneath the monument are the remains of some of the 12,000 American soldiers and civilians who died in the barbaric British prison ships anchored in the nearby Wallabout Bay during the American Revolution.

The Fort Greene area's precipitous decline in the 1940s and 1950s ironically preserved the boldly ornamented fronts of the area's row houses and, to a large degree, the interiors from modernizations that swept through affluent Manhattan and Brooklyn areas at a time when the city's mid-nineteenth-century dwellings were scorned as old-fashioned. In a troubled Fort Greene, few property owners spent the money to remove "ugly" Italianate style mantels from parlors or to strip carved stonework from the doorways and windows. Today, some of the largest and best preserved brownstone-front Italianate and Second Empire row houses in the city are found in the recently improving Fort Greene area.

South Portland Avenue, off Fort Greene Park, is one of the few blocks in the entire city almost solidly lined on both sides with Italianate and Second Empire style brownstone-fronts of virtually original appearance. With nearly all the cornices present, carved stonework on the fronts intact, and only a few of the chocolate-brown fronts painted an inappropriate light color, this 800-foot-long block presents the appearance of the hundreds of now destroyed mid-nineteenth-century streets in Manhattan and Brooklyn. In the spring and summer, the trees on each side of the street form a foliate archway thirty feet above the pavement and cast the dappled patterns of light and shade on the

ARCHITECTURAL CONTRAST.

Washington Park (ca. 1870), Fort Greene, Brooklyn. An impressive vista of brownstone-fronts along Washington Park, the two-block-long stretch of Cumberland Street overlooking Fort Greene Park. The uniform cornice line, elaborate doorway hoods, and prominent window lintels lead the eye down the street.

elaborate brownstone fronts that would have so delighted the nineteenth-century resident..

South Oxford Street, one block to the east, does not enjoy this unbroken sweep of trees and unaltered rows of brownstone-front dwellings. But on the block off Fort Greene Park, the street includes almost all architectural styles found on New York row houses from the 1840s to the turn of the century—the Greek Revival, Italianate, Second Empire, Neo-Grec, Romanesque, and Renaissance. The block of South Oxford Street between Hanson Place and Atlantic Avenue largely was demolished in 1970–1972 for an urban renewal project but once had the countrified appearance of row houses with deep front yards and detached mansions on grounds usually associated with nearby Clinton and Washington avenues.

The Decline of the Italianate and Second Empire Styles.

By the early 1870s, New Yorkers tired of the monumental streetscapes and showy ornament in the city's row houses. "When he has seen one house he has seen them all," complained one guidebook to the city—"the same everlasting high stoops and gloomy brown-stone fronts . . . the same huge cornices bristling with overpowering consoles and projections. . . ."

After twenty-five years of fashion, the monumental streetscape vistas and rich ornament which appeared so elegant in the late 1840s were merely commonplace and often vulgar to New Yorkers in the early 1870s. "The architecture" of Fifth Avenue, reported one New Yorker, "is not only impressive, it is oppressive. Its great defect is in its monotony, which soon grows tiresome. A variation, a contrast—something much less ornate or elaborate—would be a relief." One newspaper writing about the individual row house maintained that "what we lack in invention, we can cover over by 'ornamentation,' and hence we have miles of reiterated and unmeaning rope mouldings, filigreed jambs, and window-heads twisted into all sorts of conceivable contortions." The mansard roof also lost popularity for New York row houses after several years of frenzied fashion. "The very name is now more appropriately *the absurd roof,*" wrote Samuel Sloan. "Fashion begins to look coldly upon her recent favorite . . . and it is doomed." The Panic of 1873, a nationwide depression, curtailed building operations in New York for several years, and when full-scale construction resumed in 1878 and 1879 taste in architecture had changed, and the Italianate and Second Empire styles had disappeared from the city.

Colonial Revival Row House (1903), Charles Dana Gibson residence, No. 127 East 73rd Street, Upper East Side, McKim, Mead & White, architects.

Chapter Five
The New York Row House, 1875-1929

The Neo-Grec Style.

In the mid-1870s, the Neo-Grec style replaced the Italianate and Second Empire on New York row houses. "The tendency is now towards a purer and simpler style than has of late prevailed," observed one magazine. The Neo-Grec style first appeared in the 1840s at the École des Beaux Arts in Paris, and architect Henri Labrouste was the style's foremost advocate. Although American architect Richard Morris Hunt returned to New York from France in 1855 with a familiarity in the Neo-Grec style, he did not employ it here until after the Civil War—on No. 480 Broadway, the old Lenox Library on Fifth Avenue, and for the base of the Statue of Liberty. The Neo-Grec influence appeared on fine brownstone-fronts in the Fifth Avenue district around 1870 and, with resumption of construction in the late 1870s after the hiatus of the Panic of 1873, came to dominate row house architecture in New York.

The Neo-Grec row house, at first glance, appeared to be nearly identical to row houses in the preceding Italianate style, and, indeed, it did retain the smooth brownstone front, boldly protruding cornice, and heavy doorway and window details of earlier years. But, in a reaction to the round forms and foliate ornament of the longstanding Italianate style, the forms and details of the Neo-Grec row house took on a rectangularity and precision thought to be expressive of an increasingly mechanized and industrial society. "It is an established principle in the theory of design that decorative art is degraded when it passes into a direct imitation of natural objects," wrote English architect Charles L. Eastlake in his influential *Hints on Household Taste.* "Nature may be typified or symbolized, but not actually imitated."

On the Neo-Grec row house, the boldly protruding cornice rested on rectangular brackets rather than on the earlier rounded consoles faced with acanthus leaves. The massive door hood and full window enframements were rectangular in form and had squared-off edges. The stoop had immense newel posts and balustrade railings but with squared-off edges and ornamental knobs and strapwork.

An important feature of the style was incised ornamental detail cut into the smooth brownstone. The two most popular details were a stylized single-line flower or vine design known as the "Eastlake motif" and long, parallel, narrow channels known as "Neo-Grec fluting," although the lines were too far apart to be correctly called fluting. The incised "Eastlake motif" and "Neo-Grec fluting" usually appeared on door hoods and pilasters, window sills and lintels, stoop railings and fences, and brackets at the cornice.

Besides expressing the rising industrial society, the squared-off forms and incised detail of the Neo-Grec style were more economical than the round forms and naturalistic ornament of the Italianate style in view of rising workmen's wages after the Civil War. With the mechanical planers and *(top)* Row Houses in the Fields, about 1877. View of Nos. 53, 51, 49, vacant lots, 31, 29, 27, and 25 West 133rd Street, between Fifth and Lenox avenues, Harlem. A rare view of a nineteenth-century New York street only partly built-up with row houses.

(bottom) Fifth Avenue, West side, view North from 50th Street, in 1893. Notice first the immense scale of the Neo-Grec style row houses in the foreground in relation to the pedestrians, then the $3,000,000 William Henry Vanderbilt mansion, and then the William Kissam Vanderbilt turreted Loire Valley chateau which shattered the hegemony of the brownstone-front and Italian Renaissance mode on fine New York dwelling houses.

groove-cutting routers of the period, incised detail was cheaper to cut than consoles and acanthus leaves and, in the contemporary view, lent a feeling of modernity and individuality to a row house. Unlike the luxuriant and bold brownstone front of the Italianate style, the mixture of delicate single-line incised detail with the heavy, squared-off doorway, windows, and cornice on the Neo-Grec row house front sometimes presented a disturbing inconsistency in the scale and character of these parts.

Neo-Grec row houses maintained the monumental streetscape with smooth brownstone fronts, fairly similar doorway and window treatments, and uniform cornice lines. However, the popular incised Eastlake detail and Neo-Grec fluting and occasional bay windows on the street front reflected the rising taste for individuality in the row house. Around 1880 the Neo-Grec style lost favor to several styles which better expressed this newly popular architectural fashion.

Row House Plan and Interior Design in the 1870s and 1880s.

The floor plan and mechanical equipment of a New York row house in the 1870s and 1880s was little different from that of the 1860s. The first floor had a long, narrow front parlor and a back parlor, commonly used as a dining room, across the full width of the house. A handsomely appointed butler's pantry with a dumb waiter was often found near the stairway to the basement. In the basement, the front room still was an informal dining room and the back room, overlooking the garden, a kitchen and laundry. Family bedrooms, servants' rooms, and several bathrooms filled the two or three upper floors of the house.

In the 1870s and 1880s, the interior design of New York row houses was much different from that of the earlier Italianate brownstone-fronts. The elaborate white-marble mantels, gilt rococo-inspired mirrors, and lush ceiling plasterwork gave way in the 1870s to decorative ideals of relative simplicity and coherency in forms and materials.

Fine woods, polished to show the natural finish, dominated the front parlor and back dining room—in mantels, doorways, pier-mirror frames, built-in sideboards and china closets, and wainscoting or paneling. The fashionable black walnut and dark red mahogany of the Civil War era had given way to lighter woods, and more than one critic welcomed the demise of "the dark age of house decoration" and wondered "whether the goodness and cheapness of black walnut has not led us into making our rooms too sombre and heavy for cheerful life." The newly fashionable woods of the 1870s and 1880s were mahogany, quartered oak, bird's-eye and plain maple, cherry, tulip, sycamore, hazel, ash, birch, and poplar. Another handsome decorative innovation of the 1870s in New York row houses was parquet floors. The product of an ever advancing technology, parquet floors, partly covered

(top) Picturesque Asymetrically Massed Roofline (1880s), Montgomery Place, Park Slope, Brooklyn.

(bottom) East 116th Street, about 1895, north side, between Park and Lexington avenues, Harlem. Juxtaposition of row houses in the brick-front Italianate style, Neo-Grec mode, and gabled Queen Anne style. Demolished.

with rugs, better complemented the fine woodwork and the relative simplicity of parlors and dining rooms in the era than the earlier wall-to-wall carpet over wide, pine plank floors.

The Queen Anne Style.

During the 1880s and the life of the Queen Anne style, the architectural fashion that each row house have a measure of individuality and the streetscape a visually exciting appearance reached its culmination. The present "epoch of Queen Anne is a delightful insurrection against the monotonous era of rectangular building," declared one magazine in the early 1880s.

In America, the Queen Anne style combined the "Free Classic" work of the esteemed British architect Richard Norman Shaw and the colonial ornament coming from a renewed interest in America's long forgotten eighteenth-century buildings. Richard Norman Shaw's inspiration for the Free Classic mode was the early Georgian style brick city house of the eighteenth century. Besides the warm textured brick façade, Shaw's country houses in the Free Classic mode included a picturesquely irregular plan and silhouette, a pitched-gable roofline with large chimneys, large windows, and simple white trim.

The Queen Anne style emerged in the United States in the mid-1870s when architects added such colonial ornament as delicate pilasters, wreaths, and garlands to Shaw's robust and fairly simple Free Classic buildings. Strong American interest in our colonial past first emerged during the Exhibition in 1876 at Philadelphia which celebrated the 100th anniversary of our independence.

By the late 1870s, the Queen Anne style appeared in New York on residential and commercial buildings. The longstanding hegemony of the brownstone front for New York row houses ended, and some dwellings had red-brick fronts with light and dark color stone and wood trim. Architects admired the natural qualities of building materials and, on row houses, freely mixed brick and stone of different colors and textures or employed brick laid or cut in a decorative pattern.

The long-lived, monumental streetscape vista of flat row house fronts and uniform cornice line also lost favor with the emergence of the Queen Anne style. "In the erection of city houses," wrote one architect in the 1880s, "it has always been a mystery to us why those building them should persist in making the fronts all alike; in many cases they are so for whole streets, and look like a lot of bakers' loaves set on end; there is no sky outline, no visible appearance of any artistic conception in the makeup and the general perspective is about as bad as it is possible to conceive." In the 1880s, row houses abandoned the flat roofline and heavy cornice for a picturesque, large "A"-form gable and small dormer windows. A tile or slate roof and massive chimneys enhanced the picturesque asymmetry of the roofline.

The new style row houses often had recessed porches, set several feet into the house behind a half circle arch, to break the flat row house front dramatically with a mysterious dark volume. Normally, the porch appeared on the top floor of the house or as a sheltered entryway for the front doorway, but some city houses employed a stone half-circle arch on the flat front, known as a "blind arch," to recall the recessed porch.

A three-sided bay window at the first floor or running from the basement to the roof was another popular way to break the flat row house front, particularly those with the somewhat old-fashioned brownstone facing. Some new dwellings, especially those on a corner, had "oriels," a small one-story-tall bay window which sprang from the second or third floor wall on a bracket.

The windows often varied in size and shape and imaginatively employed different size glass panes for striking visual effect. Although New York row houses had employed plate glass windows for several decades by the 1880s, some windows on a Queen Anne style dwelling often included small panes, about four inches by four inches, which reflected the style's eighteenth-century early Georgian style antecedents. The diminutive wood panels on the front door recalled these small, quaint panes of glass. Decorative stained glass also appeared in first floor windows or the sidelights of the front doors.

For an even more picturesque appearance, the stoops of some New York row houses, beginning in the 1880s, abandoned the straight flight of stairs for a stairway with at least one landing and change in direction. "The staircase is no longer a railed ladder but has risen into a chief ornament of the house," observed one magazine in the mid-1880s.

This interest in the innate qualities of building materials and picturesque asymmetrical massing in the Queen Anne and contemporary Romanesque styles was a turning away from the tradition of historic revival styles and the reliance upon applied ornamental detail for a building's beauty and style. However, only a few Queen Anne style row houses actually adopted the daring brick front and asymmetrical massing. Most New York row houses still employed the respectable brownstone front and, in the tradition of the earlier revival styles, relied upon such applied ornament as garlands, sunburst forms, and foliate forms on the street front for stylistic identification.

Few New York row houses, whether brick or brownstone front, completely reflected the Queen Anne style. In American architectural history, the late nineteenth century saw the free mixing of different styles on a single building and a flexibility of forms and ornament within each style. The Queen Anne row house, therefore, often included forms and details of the passing Neo-Grec style and the contemporary Romanesque and Renaissance styles.

The Queen Anne style disappeared from New York row houses in the mid-1880s. It lacked any strong champions in the United States and, rather than becoming a relatively defined style, remained a loose collection of picturesque forms and ornament. "'Queen Anne' is a comprehensive name," wrote one magazine, "which has been made to cover a multitude of incongruities, including, indeed, the bulk of recent work which otherwise defies classification." And, by the late 1880s, one New Yorker wrote that "the extravagances of 'Queen Anne' have disappeared . . . that strange mode of building has spent its force."

The Romanesque Style.

The Romanesque style in the United States was the creation of the esteemed architect Henry Hobson Richardson, whose historical inspiration largely was the eleventh-century Romanesque buildings of southern France and Spain. However, the Romanesque mode of the 1880s and 1890s was not a revival style relying on historical forms and details for its elements. As with the concurrent Queen Anne style, a Romanesque building employed asymmetrical massing, building materials of varying colors and textures, and vigorously applied ornament for visual and architectural excitement.

Under Richardson's direction, the Romanesque style fulfilled the architectural taste of the era and, for nearly a decade, was the foremost architectural mode in America. With its easily adapted forms, ornament, and plan, the Romanesque style was suited for buildings as varied as city row houses and mansions, high-rise office buildings, warehouses, prisons, and railroad stations. Besides the heavy stonework and massive arches, the Romanesque building evoked a comforting sense of solidity and pastness. From the mid-1880s to the early 1890s, New York row houses employed the Romanesque style, occasionally as a pure style but more likely in a picturesque mixture with the Queen Anne or Renaissance styles. "One may find Romanesque features in countless houses that cannot be described as examples of Romanesque," wrote Montgomery Schuyler, and "there are comparatively few houses which an archaeologist would allow to have been designed in the Provençal Romanesque."

The chief form of the Romanesque style was the round arch at doorways and windows. Though best suited to large openings, the round arch often appeared in a modified form in handsome round-top windows on the second or third floor of a row house. To set off the doorway or window from the row house front, the arch itself was often a different color or texture material from the rest of the façade.

On most Romanesque row houses, picturesque combinations of limestone, brownstone, granite, and red, yellow, or brown brick replaced the smooth brownstone front. In many row houses, large rough-hewn blocks of stone appeared at the basement wall, as trim in round-arch openings, and for window lintels. Another common feature was a vigorous applied detail of spiky, intertwined leafwork

Byzantine Leafwork, a spiky intertwined luxuriant ornament found on Romanesque style buildings. No. 886 Carroll Street, Park Slope, Brooklyn.

known as "Byzantine leafwork." The rough-hewn stone and Byzantine leafwork, in theory, enhanced the structural elements of a building and were not applied ornamental detail in the tradition of earlier styles. A properly designed building's "decorative system," wrote one architect, "should be such as in no way conceals or masks the construction, but makes the construction features themselves ornamental."

In the 1880s and early 1890s, some architect-designed mansions and row houses in New York lacked such specifically Romanesque forms and details as large round arches and Byzantine leafwork but nonetheless were in the Romanesque style because of their materials, massive scale, and overall severity. The severe Romanesque design of No. 848 Fifth Avenue, wrote Montgomery Schuyler, "testifies to the architect's conviction, which is also that of a good many other people, that at present distinction in our domestic architecture can be attained in no other wise so surely as by extreme plainness." Although "the simple massing, the large unbroken wall spaces of rough granite, the severity of the treatment of the openings and the very sparing use of ornament give the house individuality and character," Schuyler wondered "whether this character is domestic."

By the early 1890s, the Romanesque style generally disappeared from New York row houses. With the death of Henry Hobson Richardson in 1886 and John Wellborn Root in 1891, the Romanesque style lost its two leading proponents. About the same time, New Yorkers tired of the style's massive scale and austere ornament which was somewhat inappropriate to a twenty-foot-wide row house. The Romanesque and Queen Anne styles quickly fell before the rising Renaissance style.

The Renaissance Style.

During the confusing architectural scene changes of the 1880s, such classically inspired motifs as wreaths, garlands, and pilasters appeared on otherwise Queen Anne and Romanesque style row houses and forecast the emergence of the Renaissance style on New York dwellings around 1890. "A change is rapidly taking place in the style of building and decorating," declared one magazine in the mid-1880s. The "Eastlake and the so-called Queen Anne have each had their day, and we are now turning to the Renaissance for fresh inspiration."

The first New York dwellings in the Renaissance style reportedly were the Villard Houses (1883–1886) on Madison Avenue between 50th and 51st streets, designed by McKim, Mead and White. The Villard Houses carried out the Renaissance style in the symmetrical plan, low roof, smooth-cut stone set off by quoins at the corners, and the Classical window treatment. The McKim, Mead and White design originally called for a light-color stone in the Classical tradition, but Henry Villard specified the traditional and distinctly unclassical brownstone for the façade. "The external treatment

Fifth Avenue and East 69th Street, Upper East Side, in 1924. Limestone-front Renaissance style row houses. Elegant mansions and row houses, built in the late nineteenth and early twentieth century, once lined Fifth Avenue opposite Central Park. After World War I, however, the town houses gradually gave way to high-rise apartment buildings.

is throughout very simple, after an Italian Renaissance fashion," one New Yorker nonetheless observed about the Villard Houses. "The effect is very quiet, a little cold, perhaps a little tame; but it is extremely refined."

The World's Columbian Exposition at Chicago in 1893 and its renowned white neoclassical buildings raised the emergent Renaissance style to national prominence. So great was the attraction of the Exposition's "White City" that, for the next few decades, public and commercial buildings throughout the United States adopted the white-marble or limestone façade, Classical columns and domes, and elaborate ornament of the Renaissance style. For many Americans, this extravagant mode was the only fitting style for the optimistic and prosperous America of the 1890s. The sixteenth-century "Renaissance was essentially optimistic, cheerful, gay in all its conceptions, and contrasted markedly with the ages preceding that were rustic and sombre, and full of weirdness and dim religious obscurities," wrote one architect in the 1880s. "Is not after all the Renaissance much more in keeping with our civilization of today which is sanguine and self-satisfied to an extraordinary degree, convinced of its own advance beyond achievement of any preceding age?"

In New York, architects and the public alike admired the showy buildings of the World's Columbian Exposition and had tired of the mixing of styles, asymmetrical massing, and dark brownstone or brick façades of earlier decades. By the mid-1890s, New York row houses adopted a Renaissance style which ranged from academically correct to wildly eclectic creations which recalled the architectural fantasies of the 1880s. Though grouped under the general label of the Renaissance style, these houses took inspiration and much form and ornament from many sources—the Roman, Beaux Arts, Italian Renaissance, French Renaissance, French Classic, and German Renaissance.

The Renaissance style row house usually abandoned the dark brownstone or red-brick front of the 1880s for a classically suitable façade of light-color limestone or limestone and yellow brick. Rather than relying on asymmetrical massing and qualities of building materials for architectural distinction, the row house had a symmetrical street front which formed part of uniform blockfronts in the classical tradition. The Renaissance style dwelling also relied upon applied detail for stylistic impact—the most popular motifs being wreaths, baskets of fruit, garlands of flowers and leaves tied with ribbons at the ends, and numerous foliate forms. The fluted pilaster was another common applied motif and often appeared in the front doorway enframement.

In the 1890s, some New York row houses were built without the longstanding high stoop and the floor plan in which rooms opened off a long stair hallway. Under the new "American front" plan, the doorway appeared in the center of the building one or two steps above the sidewalk level and opened into a large reception room, which occupied the full width of the house. A large stairway,

with several dramatic landings and turns in direction, led to the parlors on the next floor. In an American front row house, as in the Anglo-Italianate style dwelling, the stairway occupied the poorly lit and ventilated center of the house, and the parlors and bedrooms occupied the full eighteen-, twenty-, or twenty-two-foot width of the house. The reception room, sweeping stairway, and large parlors lent themselves to the extravagant life style of rich New York families at the turn of the century. "The high stoop house . . . is the survival of early and simpler habits, and should have been abandoned long ago for all city dwellings," wrote one architect. "Really, our wealthy New Yorkers ought to remember that their houses are not to live in only. They are to 'entertain' in too. . . . If, therefore, the thronged receptions and dancing-parties are to be made as agreeable as their nature allows, the houses must really be planned with some regard to their requirements."

With the American front floor plan, the basement floor contained the kitchen, laundry, and sometimes the furnace, the first floor included the reception room facing the street and dining room overlooking the back yard, the second floor the front and back parlors separated by the square stair hallway, and the third, fourth, and occasional fifth floors the family bedrooms and servants' quarters. On one side of the elaborate front doorway to the house at the street level, a small door, looking much like the window on the other side, was the service entrance to the basement kitchen and laundry. Only the finest New York dwellings required or could waste the space for the formal reception room and sweeping stairway in the American front plan, so most Renaissance row houses continued to employ the traditional high-stoop arrangement and plan.

The Colonial Revival Style.

In the 1890s, architects in New York looked to the Georgian and Federal styles of the eighteenth and early nineteenth century for the design of the city's row houses. However, Americans had not always admired the simple and small buildings of our colonial past. In the 1840s, Louisa Caroline Tuthill scorned New England's eighteenth-century farmhouses in her *History of Architecture*. "Happily they were all of such perishable materials that they will not much longer remain to annoy travelers in search of the picturesque through the villages of New England."

The Colonial Revival style first appeared on a popular level during the Centennial Exhibition of 1876 at Philadelphia, which focused national attention on all aspects of the nation's eighteenth-century past. After looking to distant times and places for architectural inspiration throughout the nineteenth century, American architects began to admire the restrained and thoroughly American city and country dwellings of our colonial past. The Colonial Revival, wrote one architect in 1876, is "no feeble-copy of foreign styles of questionable fitness and in little sympathy with our institutions, but something distinctly American."

In the late 1870s and 1880s, eighteenth-century architectural details such as garlands and pilasters enriched many a Queen Anne building, and architects—particularly in New England—occasionally designed a largely Colonial Revival city or country dwelling. This style, however, did not emerge full-fledged in the United States until the turn of the century. From then until the 1929 Depression, city and country houses, high-rise apartment buildings, and hotels in New York and throughout the nation employed this handsome style.

One of the first vaguely Colonial Revival row houses in New York was the Hugh J. Jewett residence (ca. 1879–1880) at No. 289 Madison Avenue, designed by G. E. Harney. The Jewett house included such distinctly colonial features as a red-brick front, a bow window such as those on New York's West 16th Street and Boston's Beacon Street, and the heavily molded Late Federal doorway once so prominent on Bond Street and St. Mark's Place. Despite these Federal details, the Jewett house revealed its ca. 1879–1880 origin in its plate glass windows and such rich details as inset Adamesque panels beneath the windows, heavy string courses, and marble rather than brownstone trim. Although some magazines described the Jewett house as "an exact reproduction" of the Federal style dwelling with a "most characteristic doorway of old New York," other architects in the eclectic 1880s believed that "the effect of the copy . . . is at best simply void of offense" and advised G. E. Harney to return to the creative designs fashionable at the time. By the turn of the century, architectural taste changed, and New York architects freely copied Federal doorways and entire dwellings of the 1820s for the city's fashionable new row houses.

The foremost features of a Colonial Revival row house were a red-brick front and marble or limestone doorway and window trim. The front doorway, whether in the high stoop or American front arrangement, had the fanlight and sidelight windows, with elaborate leaded patterns, that are found on fine Federal dwellings of the early nineteenth century. Although the earliest Colonial Revival dwellings had the then fashionable plate glass windows, most New York row houses in this style adopted the avowedly eighteenth-century small-sized panes and window blinds or shutters.

When turn-of-the-century architects directly looked to the city's original Federal style dwellings, they were unable to transplant the charm and character of the simple and small-scale, 100-year-old dwellings to large costly town houses. The Colonial Revival dwelling also employed the elaborate Federal fanlight doorway of the 1820s and generally ignored the simpler rectangular toplight doorways. And, characteristic of a revival style, the street-front forms and ornament in these row houses often were more elaborate or more intricate in composition than any early-nineteenth-century Federal dwelling.

Frame Row Houses (ca. 1866), Nos. 312 and 314 East 53rd Street, between Second and Third avenues, East Side. Unusual frame row houses—remaining from a once-countrified East Side of the 1860s.

The East Side.

During the 1850s and 1860s, the East Side of Manhattan was a far different setting from today's area of elegant apartment buildings, town houses, and shops. In 1867 George Templeton Strong described Madison Avenue in the Forties and Fifties as "a rough and ragged track . . . hardly a thoroughfare" but "rich in mudholes, goats, pigs, geese." Huge outcroppings of rocks, bare hills, occasional frame dwellings and villas, piles of trash, and decrepit shanties of the poor marked much of the East Side at the time of the Civil War.

Fifth and Madison avenues and the adjacent blocks already were becoming an elegant residential area like Murray Hill to the south, but on Park Avenue factories, saloons, and seedy tenements overlooked the ugly railroad tracks leading into Grand Central Station. Fashionable New Yorkers raced their fine horses up and down the gentle hills of muddy Third Avenue, then "the exercise and trial ground of all the fast trotters and pacers in the city," and frequented the taverns and blacksmiths' shops along the way. The foot of 42nd Street, at the East River, was Dutch Hill, "a droll-looking hamlet" of shanties teeming with garbage, dirty and poorly clothed children, dogs, and pigs. Further north, in the East Sixties, summer houses, vanishing patches of onetime forest, and beer gardens lined the East River.

In the post–Civil War building boom city growth crossed 42nd Street, and fine brownstone-fronts and modest brick-front row houses began to fill in the East Forties, Fifties, and Sixties. Palatial brownstone-front row houses and mansions soon lined Fifth Avenue from 42nd Street to the foot of Central Park and, above 59th Street, wrote one magazine in 1869, "the Avenue is so far very little built up; but the lots are held at extravagantly high prices, and it cannot be doubted that ere long all this portion of the street, overlooking Central Park, will be built up with a succession of elegant villas and mansions." Prosperous middle-class families soon settled in row houses along the sidestreets from Madison to Third Avenue. But few good one-family dwelling houses were built east of Third Avenue, and these streets soon were lined with tenements, factories, shops, and carriage houses. Some respectable row houses were built on the quiet sidestreets off the East River from the Forties to the Eighties. "Beekman Place, on the East River," wrote George Templeton Strong in 1871, "is unlike any other part of the city and dimly suggests Brooklyn Heights. Its brownstone houses look very reputable but are separated from civilization by a vast tract of tenement rookeries and whiskey mills, and streets that absolutely crawl with poor little slatternly pretty children."

With the Panic of 1873, the bubble of real estate speculation burst in New York and growth on the East Side and the entire city came to a halt. When the national economy revived in the late 1870s, real estate activity resumed in New York, and the East Side entered a several-year-long

Nos. 208–218 East 78th Street. Though in a charming but expensive enclave on today's densely built-up Upper East Side, these narrow brick-front row houses were built after the Civil War for middle class and prosperous working class families

construction boom. The opening of the Second Avenue elevated train in 1878 and the Third Avenue line in 1879 from downtown to Harlem encouraged this surge in building activity on the East Side. In the 1880s and 1890s, builders filled up the sidestreets with dwellings in the Seventies, Eighties, and Nineties—generally adhering to the social patterns to the south in the Forties and Fifties during the 1860s.

On Fifth Avenue and adjacent sidestreets, "our millionaires are vieing with each other in the erection of private dwellings," wrote one magazine in the 1880s. "These new palaces surpass in comfort and elegance anything we have yet seen in this city. Their massive and fortress-like foundations give token of buildings which will be not only ornaments to the finest part of the city but landmarks for the future." Between Madison and Third avenues, speculative builders erected rows of dwellings for prosperous middle-class families in the fashionable Neo-Grec, Queen Anne, and Romanesque styles. In contrast, by the 1880s the blocks from Third Avenue to the East River were "an almost unbroken series of tenements . . . for the full five miles above Fourteenth Street."

The West Side.

The growth of the West Forties and Fifties below Central Park generally began in the 1850s and 1860s. "The work of clearing the rocks from the Sixth avenue, above 44th street, is rapidly progressing," one magazine observed in the mid-1850s. "A large number of buildings are going up in the vicinity of 47th, 48th, 49th, 51st, and other streets. The selection of the site for the Central Park has given an impetus to the work." Fine row houses were built along most blocks in the West Forties and Fifties—the blocks generally more fashionable as one neared Fifth Avenue.

Unlike the East Side, row house construction on the West Side in the 1860s and 1870s did not go beyond 59th Street and into the blocks opposite Central Park. When building activity in New York resumed in the late 1870s after the Panic of 1873, the West Side was barren, open land marked with occasional shanties, vegetable gardens, menacing rock outgrowths, lowly taverns, and decrepit eighteenth- and early-nineteenth-century country mansions. The development of the West Side, opposite Central Park, was twenty years behind that of the corresponding blocks of the East Side. For one reason, the West Side was distant from the thrust of city growth northward along Fifth Avenue. In the 1860s and 1870s, row house construction logically marched into the Sixties and Seventies along Fifth Avenue and adjacent avenues rather than shift a mile to the west to proceed along Central Park West and Broadway. Noisome tenements and factories also had filled the blocks below 59th Street, west of Eighth Avenue and, to some New Yorkers, forecast more of the same for the adjacent West Side. A railroad, and not Riverside Park, also scarred the Hudson River shoreline.

(top) Madison Avenue and East 80th Street, about 1900, northwest corner, view toward Fifth Avenue.

(bottom) Frame Row Houses (1846–1847), about 1900, West 40th Street, north side, between Sixth Avenue and Broadway. These modest frame row houses were a strange sight among the fine theaters, hotels, and shops in the Times Square area at the turn of the century. The original real estate advertisement read: "A row of neat new two-story Cottage Houses, now finished, well-calculated for respectable families." The rent was $130 a year. By 1909, stores in the houses served the theatrical community—S. Capezio, Theatrical & Historical Shoemaker; A. Carillo, Custom Tailors; and V. Mingot. Demolished.

The foremost hindrance to the growth of the West Side was the virtual absence of public transportation to downtown Manhattan. Before 1870, the Eighth Avenue omnibus line only ran a single car from 59th Street to 84th Street at long intervals, which turned around and then returned south on the same track. Public transportation on the East Side, on the other hand, had included the Second and Third avenue omnibus lines since 1858.

The growth of the West Side got underway about 1880 with the completion of the elevated railway line along Ninth Avenue, now Columbus Avenue. The first developments of the early 1880s sprang up along Ninth Avenue at the elevated railway stops at 72nd, 81st, 93rd, and 104th streets and then along all of Ninth and Tenth avenues and 72nd Street. Row house construction on the West Side still was slow in the early 1880s. The streets in the area were in terrible condition or not yet open, and the city's large speculative builders were busy erecting rows of houses on the East Side and in Harlem. New Yorkers also were uncertain of the West Side's future social composition. Would it become an area of tenements, or workingmen's and middle-class row houses, or the dwellings of well-to-do and rich New Yorkers?

The only assured patterns of development seemed to be tenements just north of 59th Street and fine mansions along Central Park West and newly laid out Riverside Drive. Broadway was expected to become a residential boulevard, West End Avenue a street of small neighborhood shops, and Ninth and Tenth avenues largely to be lined with apartment buildings and tenements with shops at street level. The West Side, thought Montgomery Schuyler and many other New Yorkers, "offered an opportunity for a quarter of small houses" because "so much land was at once thrown open to settlement by the completion of the elevated railroad that its price was low enough to encourage speculative builders to provide for the wants of people of moderate means."

In the mid-1880s, New York's large row house builders generally left the heavily built up East Side for the more open and lower priced West Side, and the West Side entered a decade of frantic building. "The west side of the city presents just now a scene of building activity such as was never before witnessed in that section, and which gives promise of the speedy disappearance of all the shanties in the neighborhood and the rapid population of this long neglected part of New York," declared one newspaper in 1886. "The huge masses of rock which formerly met the eye, usually crowned by a rickety shanty and a browsing goat, are being blasted out of existence. Streets are being graded, and thousands of carpenters and masons are engaged in rearing substantial dwellings where a year ago nothing was to be seen but market gardens or barren rocky fields."

By the turn of the century, working-class families on the West Side only found shelter in modest row houses on sidestreets between Ninth and Tenth avenues or in four- and five-story-tall tenements

The March of Modern Improvement—Destruction of Old Buildings in Upper New York, 1871.

(top) Central Park West, View South from West 72nd Street, in 1887. The frame houses, shanty hamlets, open fields, and rubbish heaps were typical of the Upper West Side in the 1870s and 1880s. Although the West 60s off Central Park were vacant, the area around today's Lincoln Square area was built up heavily by the late 1880s. Notice the apartment buildings along Central Park South in the distance on the left side. View from the roof of the Dakota Apartments.

(bottom) West End Avenue and West 76th Street, northwest corner, about 1910. Demolished.

and apartment buildings along the two avenues. For these families, the better lit and ventilated buildings on the corners of the avenues were more desirable than those in the middle of the blockfront, and Tenth Avenue was a better place to live than noisy, El-shaded Ninth Avenue.

The West Side generally had become a well-to-do area of handsome town houses and mansions. "There can be no question that this section must become in time the most exclusive part of the city," declared one magazine in the 1880s. The wide avenues of the area and nearby Central and Riverside parks contributed to the fashion and sanguine forecasts for the West Side. "The conclusion is inevitable" that the West Side "has been held in reserve until the time when the progress of wealth and refinement shall have attained that period of development when our citizens can appreciate and are ready to take advantage of the situation," one New Yorker enthusiastically declared. "This entire region combines in its general aspect all that is magnificent in the leading capitals of Europe. In our Central Park we have the fine Prater of Vienna, in our grand boulevard [Broadway] the rival of the finest avenues of the gay capital of France, in our Riverside Avenue the equivalent of the Chiaja of Naples and the Corso of Rome, while the beautiful 'Unter den Linden,' of Berlin, and the finest portions of the West End of London are reproduced again and again."

Mansions on spacious grounds and palatial row houses rose along Central Park West and Riverside Drive, particularly after its completion in the 1890s. Riverside Drive, wrote one New Yorker at the turn of the century, "is universally acknowledged to be the most beautiful and picturesque [street] in the world. This dreamlike region [is] but little removed from the distracting noises of a busy section of the city." Contrary to earlier expectations, West End Avenue, north of 72nd Street, also became a fashionable residential avenue with "some of the most charming houses in New York." Broadway, which had been named the Boulevard or the Western Boulevard until 1899, had a handsome grass and shrubbery-planted mall in the center and soon was lined with fine shops and apartment buildings. In keeping with the fashionable tone of the West Side, humble Ninth Avenue, north of 59th Street, was renamed Columbus Avenue in 1890, and Tenth Avenue, for similar reasons, was renamed Amsterdam Avenue.

New Yorkers also admired the West Side for its showy and avant-garde row house architecture. "The houses that now characterize the West Side are without doubt the most interesting examples of domestic architecture that New York has to show," wrote Montgomery Schuyler in 1899. When the West Side's growth began in the early 1880s, the fashion for mixing several architectural styles on one building and for a house to be different from its neighbors were sweeping New York, and row houses in the well-to-do and socially competitive neighborhood reflected these ideals more thoroughly than the houses of any other area of New York. Outstanding streetscapes on the West Side which combined a measure of individuality for each house within the coherent row include the original twenty-seven Queen Anne row houses on the north side of West 73rd Street, between Central Park West and Columbus Avenue, built in 1883 and designed by Henry J. Hardenbergh of the Dakota apartments and Plaza Hotel fame and a number of blockfronts on West End Avenue, several of which remain in sadly altered condition. But the fashion for architectural individuality often led to excesses, and Montgomery Schuyler singled out several blocks on the West Side for "a clamoring restlessness all their own" which made the passerby "sea-sick."

When taste changed and row house "variety" lost favor, some outstanding monumental streetscapes of Renaissance style row houses were built on the West Side because of the availability of large tracts of open land and the financial and technical capabilities of the area's professional builders. These remaining streetscapes include the vaguely Georgian style row house mansions on the south side of West 74th Street off Central Park West designed by Percy Griffin and completed in 1904 and McKim, Mead and White's spectacular "King Model Houses," part of an enclave known as "Striver's Row" which incorporated 158 row houses in four blockfronts on West 138th and 139th streets, between Seventh and Eighth avenues, completed in 1903.

Brooklyn.

During the post–Civil War building boom, row house construction in Brooklyn entered today's Park Slope area, the handsome elevated land around Prospect Park and Grand Army Plaza. The name Park Slope came from the area's proximity to Prospect Park and the gentle slope from the park down toward low-lying Gowanus Canal and the harbor beyond.

As early as the 1830s, one New Yorker admired the "commanding situation" of the area and noted that "here is located a public house, a boarding school for boys, and 8 or 10 dwellings." During the 1850s, Edwin C. Litchfield, a lawyer who made his fortune in railroad development, purchased about one square mile of land here—now bounded by First Street, the Gowanus Canal, Ninth Street, and the projected line of Tenth Avenue. Litchfield's impressive mansion, designed by Alexander Jackson Davis in the Italian villa style, still stands in Prospect Park near Prospect Park West, between Fourth and Fifth streets.

The completion of Olmsted and Vaux's Prospect Park in the late 1860s undoubtedly focused attention on the Park Slope area, which was accessible to the Fulton Street ferry via an omnibus line on Flatbush Avenue. The area's rural setting and elevated situation also attracted well-to-do families to Park Slope. In 1871 George Templeton Strong visited Prospect Park and described the "outlook" from Grand Army Plaza as "panoramic and most striking. It takes in New York, Brooklyn with its numerous suburbs, the Jersey hills, the Bay, Staten Island, the Navesink Highlands, an expanse of ocean, Canarsie or Jamaica Bay, and the great belt of level ground that extends eastward from the Narrows to the latitude south of Jamaica."

In the prosperous late 1860s and early 1870s, Italianate and Second Empire brownstone-fronts rose along Sixth and Seventh avenues and the sidestreets just off Flatbush Avenue. With the Panic of 1873, building operations in the then outlying Park Slope area collapsed, and many builders lost their newly completed, but unsalable, houses in mortgage defaults. "The district about Prospect Park, where brown-stone houses sprang up like mushrooms a few years ago, is well marked already with bills of 'To Let' as well as 'For Sale'," observed one newspaper in the 1870s.

When building activity resumed in New York in the late 1870s, row house construction also began in Park Slope and lasted into the turn of the century. In Park Slope, growth generally marched up the slope from the Sixth Avenue area toward Prospect Park and from Flatbush Avenue and its omnibus line into the blocks to the south. The pleasant row houses of a prosperous middle class lined the sidestreets leading to the Park, and palatial row houses and mansions rose along Eighth Avenue and Ninth Avenue, which overlooks Prospect Park and is now Prospect Park West. Park Slope, observed one New Yorker in the 1880s, is "a location unexcelled for beauty of situation, orderliness and cleanliness" and, "on Eighth and Ninth avenues," declared one magazine in the 1890s, "are many houses of considerable showiness . . . revealing the varied individual taste of the owners."

Today, some of the finest late-nineteenth-century row house architecture in New York survives in the area. Although high-rise apartment buildings replaced many of the mansions and their grounds along Prospect Park West and Eighth Avenue in the 1920s and 1930s, generally unaltered row houses in the Italianate, Neo-Grec, Queen Anne, Romanesque, and Renaissance styles stand along Park Slope's quiet tree-lined streets. Sixth Avenue, for the seven or eight blocks off Flatbush Avenue, is the only street in New York which retains a semblance of the scale and character of the city's handsome mid-nineteenth-century avenues. Here, the basement- and three- or four-story-tall brownstone-fronts in the Italianate or a faintly Neo-Grec style enjoy the proper scale of a wide avenue not found on the usual sidestreet. On the 200-foot-long avenue blockfronts, the houses form impressive vistas occasionally set off by an additional floor or a mansard roof on corner houses. Several blocks away at Prospect Park, Montgomery Place was the development scheme of Harvey Murdock, and under architect C. P. H. Gilbert's design the one-block-long street displays all the architectural styles of New York row houses in the 1880s and 1890s.

During the late nineteenth and early twentieth century, Brooklyn was the home for thousands of middle-class families who lived in comfortable but architecturally undistinguished row houses along

No. 404 Stuyvesant Avenue, in
Bedford-Stuyvesant, Brooklyn. An
elegant Renaissance style limestone
dwelling house in the Fulton Park area.

ordinary streets. Several enclaves of rich families and their fine row houses and mansions in Brooklyn likely gave the handsome city a reputation of greater wealth and architectural distinction than actually existed there. In the late nineteenth century, Brooklyn Heights remained the city's most aristocratic neighborhood—although the invasion of shops along Montague Street and the construction of apartment buildings throughout the neighborhood in the late nineteenth century threatened its fashion. In "The Hill," the fine blocks of brownstone-fronts at the edges of Fort Greene Park saw little physical or social change, but several blocks away substantial mansions and handsomely planted gardens replaced the earlier frame country villas on Clinton and Washington avenues. Those two avenues, wrote one magazine in the 1890s, have "a fine array of frame and brick villas, set in spacious grounds, with carriage drives and trees, conservatories, flower beds, croquet and tennis grounds, and a combined effect of semi-rusticity."

In the 1880s and 1890s, the other newly building well-to-do neighborhood, besides Park Slope, was the area today known as Bedford-Stuyvesant. Costly row houses and occasional mansions rose on the streets north of Fulton Park and west of Brower Park. In the 1890s, one magazine praised the "beautiful part of town" near Brower Park "where New York, Brooklyn, and St. Mark's avenues pursue their ways between noble houses, decorating ample grounds. This is more modern, more beautiful, and is, perhaps, supported by greater wealth than the older beauty-spot of the town [Clinton Avenue]." Although much of Bedford-Stuyvesant today is badly deteriorated, the generally well-kept row houses of the 1880s and 1890s along the handsome streets of the Fulton Park and Brower Park areas sometimes rival those of the East Side, the West Side, and Park Slope in architectural distinction.

The Demise of the Row House in New York.

Row house construction in the traditional single-family mode continued in Brooklyn on a large scale until the 1920s and in a modest two-family pattern for working and middle-class families into the present day in New York's four outer boroughs. But after 1900, row house construction largely ended in Manhattan.

The row house as a single-family dwelling generally disappeared from Manhattan because of the growth of well-to-do suburbs linked to the city by reliable rail service, the much lamented "servant problem," and the new social order which valued the convenience of apartment living over the household obligations and implied roots of the town house. The foremost reason for the decline in town house construction in Manhattan was a rise in the cost of building lots in fashionable residential areas. In 1898 the popular seven-story-tall apartment building began to appear on the West Side and immediately drove up the price of land previously good only for four- and five-story-tall row houses.

(top) Sutton Place, in 1936, Anne Morgan residence, No. 1 Sutton Place, northeast corner of East 57th Street.

(bottom) East 62nd Street, between Second and Third avenues. A fashionable and lovely block on the Upper East Side. The one-time Italianate style brownstone-fronts of the 1860s and 1870s have been altered into vaguely New Orleans or London-inspired town houses.

The elevated train lines and IRT subway, which opened in 1904, made practical this high residential density.

The construction figures for row houses in Manhattan between 1881 and 1902 show the declining building activity and the sharply rising cost of new row houses at the turn of the century.

Year	Number Completed	Total Cost	Cost Per House
1889	759	12,733,000	16,700
1890	835	12,663,000	15,100
1891	661	11,225,500	16,900
1892	710	12,625,500	17,500
1893	511	9,516,750	19,000
1894	494	8,606,160	17,200
1895	515	8,799,750	17,000
1896	410	5,527,950	13,400
1897	492	7,492,100	15,200
1898	339	6,182,800	18,200
1899	338	8,329,700	24,600
1900	112	3,928,000	35,000
1901	99	5,927,000	59,800
1902 (Jan.–Sept.)	120	7,793,500	64,000

From about 1900 to the crash of 1929, the construction of one family town houses occurred only on the fashionable East Side from the mid-Thirties to the low Eighties. These Colonial Revival or pseudo-Georgian style town houses often were the complete remodeling of a Civil War era brownstone-front or rose on the site of an ordinary six- or seven-story-tall apartment building. Admiring the East Side about 1900, one New Yorker looked forward to the time "when the brownstone dwellings, if not entirely demolished, will at least cease to dominate that part of the city in which it once prevailed." As row house construction slowed to a halt in Manhattan in the early twentieth century, it is ironic that New York's rich and prominent families still willing to build looked to the Federal style "second-rate, genteel houses" of the 1820s for the inspiration and design of their sumptuous town houses.

At the turn of the century, many wealthy families began to leave their town houses for spacious homes in the countrified suburbs or for apartments in luxury buildings rising on fashionable East and

West Side avenues. Hundreds of brownstones were demolished for high-rise apartment or office buildings in the construction boom of the 1920s or turned into rooming houses and warrens of "studio" apartments.

Even as most people in the 1920s and 1930s scorned the city's once-proud brownstones as "old fashioned" or difficult to maintain, some well-to-do New Yorkers admired the pastness, quiet, and sun of the city's old row houses and streets and remodeled or restored hundreds of brownstones in Greenwich Village, Turtle Bay, Beekman Place, and Sutton Place.

Since World War II, faceless thirty- and forty-story-tall apartment buildings for the well-to-do and banal housing projects for the poor and middle class have risen throughout Manhattan over the graves of countless brownstones. Thousands of New Yorkers, nevertheless, readily moved into these supposedly stylish buildings which obliterated much of Manhattan's social variety, interesting neighborhoods, and visual richness. In the 1940s and 1950s, many middle-class families fled the city altogether, for the short-lived isolation and tranquility of the suburbs.

While some New Yorkers in these postwar years bemoaned the decline of the city and its loss of vitality, other residents quietly sought out and renovated the human-scale, four-story-tall brownstones along the often-charming streets of the East Side, east of Third Avenue, and Brooklyn Heights. In the 1960s, a "brownstone revival" blossomed in New York as more people than ever before recognized the pleasant living possible in the city's brownstones and found it sensible to own a house in an era of soaring apartment rents. Middle-class couples and families have now purchased hundreds of row houses in such previously run-down neighborhoods of Manhattan and Brooklyn as the Upper West Side, Chelsea, Boerum Hill, and Park Slope.

At a time when the death of the American city has been widely accepted, thousands of middle-class couples and families have remained in a sometimes trying New York and renovated houses, thereby restoring entire neighborhoods. Besides making for a healthier city, the brownstone revival also has saved thousands of fine nineteenth-century houses and several architecturally distinguished neighborhoods for the enjoyment of Americans as yet unborn.

Selected Bibliography

Primary Sources

Allen, Lewis F. *Rural Architecture.* New York, 1852.

Architectural Review and American Builder's Journal, articles in 1868 and 1869.

Arnot, David H. *Gothic Architecture Applied To Modern Residences.* New York, 1849.

Benjamin, Asher. *The Country Builder's Assistant.* Greenfield, Massachusetts, 1797.

———. *Practice of Architecture.* Boston, 1835.

———. *The Practical House Carpenter.* Boston, 1830.

Bentley's Miscellaney, Volume XXX, 1851, p. 5.

Biddle, Owen. *The Young Carpenter's Assistant.* Philadelphia, 1810.

[Blunt, Edmund T.] *The Picture of New-York, and Stranger's Guide.* New York, 1828.

Browne, Henri Junius. *The Great Metropolis: A Mirror of New York.* New York, 1869.

The Builder, articles in the 1850s, 1860s, and 1870s.

Cooper, James Fenimore. *Home As Found.* Philadelphia, 1838.

Croly, Herbert. "Renovation of the Brownstone District." *The Architectural Record,* Volume 13, Number 6, June, 1903.

Downing, Andrew Jackson. *The Architecture of Country Houses.* New York, 1850.

———. *Cottage Residences.* New York, 1842.

Fay, Theodore. *Views of New-York and Its Environs.* New York, 1831.

Field, M. *City Architecture.* New York, 1853.

History of Architecture and the Building Trades of Greater New York. 2 Vols. New York, 1899.

History of Real Estate, Building and Architecture in New York During the Last Quarter of a Century. New York, 1898.

[Hone, Philip] *The Diary of Philip Hone,* Allan Nevins, ed. 2 Vols. New York, 1927.

Hopkins, John Henry. *Essay on Gothic Architecture.* Burlington, Vermont, 1836.

Kennion, John W. *The Architects' and Builders' Guide.* New York, 1868.

The Knickerbocker, Volume I, July, 1833, [Lafayette Place] p. 71.

Lafever, Minard. *The Architectural Instructor.* New York, 1856.

———. *The Beauties of Modern Architecture.* New York, 1835.

———. *The Modern Builder's Guide.* New York, 1833.

———. *The Young Builder's General Instructor.* Newark, 1829.

Leslie's Illustrated Weekly Magazine, Volume IV, Number 90, August 22, 1857, "Dr. Burdell's House, 31 Bond Street," pp. 184–186.

New York Illustrated, New York, 1870.

New York Commercial Advertiser, real estate advertisements in the 1820s.

New-York Daily Tribune, real estate advertisements in the 1840s.

New-York Evening Post, real estate advertisements in the 1820s, 1830s, and 1840s.

New York Mirror, articles in the 1820s and 1830s.

New-York Daily Times (later *The New York Times*), articles and real estate advertisements in the 1850s, 1860s, and 1870s.

North American Review, articles in the 1830s and 1840s.

Philadelphia Monthly Magazine, Volume I, Number I, 1827, "The Art and Artists," p. 17.

Putnam's Monthly, Volume III, Number XV, March, 1854, "New-York Daguerreotyped Private Residences," p. 233–248.

[Ruggles, Edward] *A Picture of New-York in 1846.* New York, 1846.

Schuyler, Montgomery. *The American Architect and Building News,* Volume IX, Number 278, April 23, 1881, "Dwellings, Part III."

———. *The American Architect and Building News,* Volume IX, Number 279, April 30, 1881, "Dwellings, Part IV."

———. *The American Architect and Building News,* Volume XCVIII, October 10, 1910, December 2, 1910, March 1, 1911, and May 11, 1911, "The Old 'Greek Revival'," Parts I–IV.

———. *The Architectural Record,* Volume I, Number 1, July–September, 1891, "The Romanesque Revival in New York."

———. [Franz Winkler, pseudonym] *The Architectural Record,* Volume II, Number 2, October, 1901, "Architecture in the Billionaire District of New York City."

———. *The Architectural Record,* Volume 19, Number 2, February, 1906, "The New York House."

———. *The Architectural Record,* Volume VIII, Number 4, April–June, 1899, "The Small City House in New York."

Sloan, Samuel. *City and Suburban Architecture.* Philadelphia, 1859.

———. *The Model Architect.* Philadelphia, 1852.

[Strong, George Templeton] *The Diary of George Templeton Strong,* Allan Nevins and Milton Halsey Thomas, eds. 4 Vols. New York, 1952.

Sturgis, Russell, et. al. *The City House in the East and South—Homes in City and Country.* New York, 1893.

Tuthill, Louisa Caroline. *History of Architecture from the Earliest Times.* Philadelphia, 1848.

The United States Magazine, and Democratic Review. Volume XXI, No. CXIII, November, 1847, "Our New Houses," p. 392.

Van Rensselaer, Marianna G. *Century Magazine,* Volume 31, Number 4, February, 1886, "Recent Architecture in America; City Dwellings I."

———. *Century Magazine,* Volume 31, Number 5, March 1886, "Recent Architecture in America; City Dwellings II.

Vaux, Calvert. *Villas and Cottages.* New York, 1857.

Wheeler, Gervase. *Homes for the People in Suburb and Country.* New York, 1855.

———. *Rural Homes.* New York, 1851.

White, Richard. *Century Magazine,* Volume 26, Number 6, October, 1883, "Old New York and Its Houses."

[Whitman, Walt] *Walt Whitman's New York,* Henry M. Christman, ed. New York, 1963.

Travelers' Accounts

Ampère, Jean Jacques. *Promenade en Amerique.* 2 Vols. Paris, 1855.

Baxter, William Edward. *America and the Americans.* London, 1855.

Bishop, Isabella Lucy Bird. *The Englishwoman in America.* London, 1856.

[Bobo, William] *Glimpses of New York, By a South Carolinian, (Who Had Nothing Else To Do.)* Charleston, S.C. 1853.

Bremer, Fredrika. *The Homes of the New World; Impressions of the New World.* 2 Vols. New York, 1853.

Chambers, William. *Things As They Are in America.* Philadelphia, 1854.

[Cooper, James Fenimore] *Notions of the Americans: Picked Up by a Travelling Bachelor.* Philadelphia, 1828.

De Roos, Lieut. Frederick F. *Personal Narrative of Travels in the United States and Canada.* London, 1827.

Dickens, Charles. *American Notes for General Circulation.* London, 1892.

Duncan, John M. *Travels Through Part of the United States and Canada in 1818 and 1819.* 2 Vols. New York, 1823.

Fearon, Henry Bradshaw. *Sketches of America.* London, 1819.

Felton, Mrs. *American Life*. London, 1842.

Fowler, John. *Journal of a Tour in the State of New York, in the Year 1830*. London, 1831.

Glazier, Capt. Willard. *Peculiarities of American Cities*. Philadelphia, 1885.

Goodrich, C. A. *The Family Tourist: A Visit to the Principal Cities of the Western Continent*. Hartford, Connecticut, 1848.

Grund, Francis J. *The Americans in Their Moral, Social, and Political Relations*. London, 1837.

[Hall, Mrs. Basil] *The Aristocratic Journey, Being the Outspoken Letters of Mrs. Basil Hall, Written during a Fourteen Months Sojourn in America 1827–1828*. Una Pope-Hennessy, ed. New York, 1931.

Jouve, Eugene. *Voyage en Amérique*. Lyon, 1853.

Lambert, John. *Travels Through Canada, and the United States of North America in the Years 1806, 1807, & 1808*. 2 Vols. London, 1814.

Mackenzie, E. *An Historical, Topographical, and Descriptive View of the United States of America*. Newcastle upon Tyne, n.d.

Maury, Sarah M. *An Englishwoman in America*. London, 1848.

Pairpont, Alfred. *Uncle Sam and His Country; or Sketches of America in 1854–1856*. London, 1857.

Trollope, Anthony. *North America*. 2 Vols. London, 1862.

Secondary Sources

Abbott, Berenice, and Elizabeth McCausland. *Changing New York*, 1939.

American Institute of Architects, New York Chapter. *AIA Guide to New York City*. New York, 1967.

Andrews, Wayne. *Architecture, Ambition and Americans*. New York, 1964.

Brown, Henry Collins. *Fifth Avenue, Old and New, 1824–1924*. New York, 1924.

Burchard, John, and Albert Bush-Brown. *The Architecture of America: A Social and Cultural History*. Boston, 1961.

Burnham, Alan, ed. *New York Landmarks*. Middletown, Connecticut, 1963.

Early, James. *Romanticism and American Architecture*. New York, 1965.

Hamlin, Talbot. *Greek Revival Architecture in America*. New York, 1944.

Havens, Catherine. *Diary of a Little Girl in Old New York*. New York, 1920.

Hitchcock, Henry-Russell. *Architecture: Nineteenth and Twentieth Centuries*. Baltimore, 1958.

Huxtable, Ada Louise. *Classic New York: Georgian Gentility to Greek Elegance*. New York, 1964.

Kouwenhoven, John. *The Columbia Historical Portrait of New York*. Garden City, 1953.

Lancaster, Clay. *Old Brooklyn Heights, New York's First Suburb*. Rutland, Vermont, 1961.

Landmarks Preservation Commission. *Charlton-King-Van Dam Historic District Designation Report*. New York, 1966.

———. *Chelsea Historic District Designation Report*. New York, 1971.

———. *Cobble Hill Historic District Designation Report*. New York, 1969.

———. *Gramercy Park Historic District Designation Report*. New York, 1968.

———. *Greenwich Village Historic District Designation Report*. 2 Vols. New York, 1969.

———. *No. 804 Broadway* [Grace Church Rectory.] New York, 1966.

———. *No. 440 Clinton Street, Brooklyn*. New York, 1970.

———. *No. 47 Fifth Avenue* [Salmagundi Club.] New York, 1969.

———. *Nos. 428–434 Lafayette Street* [Colonnade Row.] New York, 1965.

————. *No. 21 Stuyvesant Street* [Stuyvesant-Fish House.] New York, 1965.

————. *No. 37 East Fourth Street.* New York, 1970.

————. *No. 28 East 20th Street.* New York, 1966.

————. *No. 32 East 26th Street* [Leonard Jerome mansion.] New York, 1965.

————. *No. 312 East 53rd Street.* New York, 1968.

————. *No. 313 East 58th Street.* New York, 1970.

————. *Nos. 157–165 East 78th Street.* New York, 1968.

————. *No. 120 East 92nd Street.* New York, 1969.

————. *No. 122 East 92nd Street.* New York, 1969.

Landy, Jacob. *The Architecture of Minard Lafever.* New York, 1970.

Lynes, Russell. *The Domesticated Americans.* New York, 1963.

————. *The Tastemakers.* New York, 1954.

Newton, Roger Hale. *Town & Davis, Architects.* New York, 1942.

Ostrander, Stephen M. *A History of the City of Brooklyn and Kings County.* 2 Vols. Brooklyn, 1894.

Pelletreau, William S. *Historic Homes and Institutions and Genealogical and Family History of New York.* 4 Vols. New York, 1907.

Roos, Frank J., Jr. *Writings on Early American Architecture.* Columbus, Ohio, 1943.

Stiles, Henry R. *History of the City of Brooklyn,* 3 Vols. Brooklyn, 1870.

————. *The . . . History . . . of the County of Kings and the City of Brooklyn, N.Y., from 1683 to 1884.* 2 Vols. New York, 1884.

Stokes, I. N. Phelps, ed. *Iconography of Manhattan Island.* 6 vols. New York, 1928.

Zeisloft, E. Idell. *The New Metropolis.* New York, 1899.

Index